T0301634

Markets, Planning and Democracy

NEW THINKING IN POLITICAL ECONOMY

Series Editor: Peter J. Boettke
George Mason University, USA

New Thinking in Political Economy aims to encourage scholarship in the intersection of the disciplines of politics, philosophy and economics. It has the ambitious purpose of reinvigorating political economy as a progressive force for understanding social and economic change.

The series is an important forum for the publication of new work analysing the social world from a multidisciplinary perspective. With increased specialization (and professionalization) within universities, interdisciplinary work has become increasingly uncommon. Indeed, during the 20th century, the process of disciplinary specialization reduced the intersection between economics, philosophy and politics and impoverished our understanding of society. Modern economics in particular has become increasingly mathematical and largely ignores the role of institutions and the contribution of moral philosophy and politics.

New Thinking in Political Economy will stimulate new work that combines technical knowledge provided by the 'dismal science' and the wisdom gleaned from the serious study of the 'worldly philosophy'. The series will reinvigorate our understanding of the social world by encouraging a multidisciplinary approach to the challenges confronting society in the new century.

Recent titles in the series include:

Explaining Constitutional Change
A Positive Economics Approach
Stefan Voigt

Ethics as Social Science
The Moral Philosophy of Social Cooperation
Leland B. Yeager

Markets, Planning and Democracy
Essays after the Collapse of Communism
David L. Prychitko

Markets, Planning and Democracy

Essays after the Collapse of Communism

David L. Prychitko

Department of Economics, Northern Michigan University
Program on Markets and Institutions, James M. Buchanan
Center for Political Economy, George Mason University

NEW THINKING IN POLITICAL ECONOMY

Edward Elgar
Cheltenham, UK • Northampton, MA, USA

Published by
Edward Elgar Publishing Limited
The Lypiatts
15 Lansdown Road
Cheltenham
Glos GL50 2JA
UK

Edward Elgar Publishing, Inc.
William Pratt House
9 Dewey Court
Northampton
Massachusetts 01060
USA

This book has been printed on demand to keep the title in print.

A catalogue record for this book
is available from the British Library

ISBN 978 1 84064 519 4

Contents

Acknowledgements

Over the past decade my research has been financially supported by the Earhart Foundation, the J.M. Kaplan fund, and the Atlas Foundation. I am indebted to them, for they have made it possible for this backwoods professor to enjoy scholarly pursuits, in addition to fish and game.

I thank my friend and colleague Pete Boettke for suggesting that I publish this particular collection of essays in his *New Thinking in Political Economy* series. Pete and I share the same vision of what an Austrian-inspired political economy ought to be, but we disagree on some of the details, such as the theoretical validity and normative value of self-managed enterprise. That he has supported my efforts all along speaks volumes for his kind-heartedness and intellectual generosity. I also wish to thank Alan Sturmer and Karen McCarthy at Edward Elgar Publishing for guidance in the production of this book, and Laura Kramer at Northern Michigan University for her secretarial support.

I wrote these essays over a twelve-year period, and have greatly benefited from the encouragement, comments, and support of several colleagues during that time. In particular, I wish to thank Jaroslav Vanek, who corrected a number of my illusions about workers' self-management, while I visited as a junior fellow in his Program on Participation and Labor-managed Systems at Cornell University in 1988, and for the decade that followed. I also gained a great deal from my experience as a Fulbright Grant recipient at the Philosophical Faculty at the University of Zagreb, during the Spring and Summer of 1989, and as a participant in several colloquia at the Inter-University Centre for Postgraduate Studies in Dubrovnik, particularly the sessions on 'Political Theory and Political Education – Anarchism: Community and Utopia'. I thank Duško Sekulić for sponsoring me during my research in the former Yugoslavia. I also thank Robert Hefner and Peter Berger, who organized the Second Annual Summer Faculty Seminar on Economy, Values, and Culture, at The Institute for the Study of Economic Culture at Boston University, 22 June–10 July 1992; my colleagues in the Economics Department at SUNY-Oswego, where I had been on the faculty from 1989–1997; and my present colleagues in the Economics Department at Northern Michigan University. My office door was often closed while I hammered away on this project, but it was still open for their warm conversation.

I appreciate the comments and criticisms provided by several people while I first circulated the essays in this book: Scott Beaulier (George Mason University), Pete Boettke (George Mason University), the late Kenneth Boulding (George Mason University), Ted Burczak (Denison University), Jeffrey Friedman (Barnard College), Steve Horwitz (St. Lawrence University), William Kern (Western Michigan University), John Kane (SUNY-Oswego), Israel M. Kirzner (New York University), the late Don Lavoie (George Mason University), Larry Moss (Babson College), Steve Pressman (Monmouth College), Mario Rizzo (New York University), Howard Swaine (Northern Michigan University), Karen I. Vaughn (George Mason University), and a host of anonymous referees.

My wife Julie, and our children Sonja Joanne, Emily Rose, and Anthony David, remain the unending fountain of love and joy in my life. I thank them for their patience while I worked on this project.

Finally, I dedicate this book to the memory of Don Lavoie, 'my' professor.

David L. Prychitko

Introduction: markets, planning and democracy in the age of post-communism

Contemporary society cannot flourish without markets, and therefore private or separate property rights in the means of production.

When Ludwig von Mises and F.A. Hayek advanced this argument in the 1920s and 1930s, they faced waves of criticism from defenders of market socialism, most notably Oskar Lange and Abba Lerner, but also from their Austrian colleague Joseph Schumpeter, in his magnificent but flawed book, *Capitalism, Socialism, and Democracy* (1950).

For the most part Mises and Hayek had geared their critique of socialism to central economic planning. In response, market socialists generally agreed that truly centralized economic planning had little basis in economic theory; instead they promoted a form of socialism that apparently allowed for markets and prices in consumer goods, and the imputation of consumer goods prices through the state-owned capital structure. Their theoretical solution earned the respect of the economics profession for years to come. Market socialism was considered at least consistent with neoclassical economic theory, and the Austrians were viewed as losers in the great socialist calculation debate, as it came to be called.

A renewed appreciation for the Austrian position would appear only by the late 1980s, as the problems of 'really existing socialism' came to a head. The collapse of the former Soviet Union and other socialist countries throughout Eastern Europe from the Fall of 1989 onward seemed finally to validate the Mises–Hayek case against central planning, and also cast serious doubt on the market–socialist hybrid.

It was during this time, a couple years before the Fall, that I began working in comparative political economy, using the Austrian theory of the market process. My first book, *Marxism and Workers' Self-Management: The Essential Tension* (1991), grew out of my George Mason University dissertation. There, I attempted to apply the Austrian argument to the theory of decentralized socialism, a theory championed especially by a group of Marxist academics in the former Yugoslavia, who disdained Soviet-style central planning and showed little appreciation for the neoclassical models of market socialism. I felt that the Austrians tended to focus almost exclusively on central economic planning – indeed, they seemed to equate socialism with central planning – and I hoped to extend the argument to self-managed socialism, represented in part by the efforts of Michael Albert and Robin Hahnel, but especially by the work of Branko Horvat (Yugoslavia's leading economist) and the Praxis Group (a group of Croatian and Serbian philosophers who attempted to resurrect the humanistic Marxian vision of radically democratic, decentralized planning).

I continued the common Austrian theme that contemporary society can flourish only with markets, and therefore private or separate property rights in the means of production. I argued that decentralized or self-managed socialism must fail because it, too, seeks to destroy the market process in capital goods. I also argued that central planning is one form of comprehensive economic planning; decentralized planning is the other. And so the problem should not be equated with central planning *per se*; the same epistemological difficulties appear with decentralized planning. *Comprehensive economic planning* – whether of the idealized Soviet-style, top-down variety or the idealized Yugoslav-style, bottom-up variety – cannot withstand the Austrian School test. Either approach to comprehensive planning, whether by command from above or radically democratic initiative from below, cannot demonstrate how dispersed and incomplete knowledge would be garnered to coordinate the capital structure.

THE FAILURE OF SELF-MANAGED SOCIALISM

I attempt to clarify further and extend my argument in this present book, particularly in Part One. Chapter 1 offers a general discussion of the Austrian theory of comparative economic systems, juxtaposed against Marxism. In Chapter 2 I examine the Albert–Hahnel model of decentralized socialism (among others), and in Chapter 3 I specifically address Horvat's alleged 'answers' to Hayek. I find that both models assume away what must be addressed by anyone seriously working in comparative political economy today: how, under a system of social ownership and non-market prices, would workers' councils and their elected representatives in the planning process tap the kinds of knowledge and information that are required for plan coordination?

A system of self-managed workers' councils, without the guidance of spontaneously-formed prices of consumer and especially capital goods, will fail to find an effective way to calculate the relative scarcities of those goods. They would face, as Mises argued back in 1920, a 'bewildering throng of possibilities'. It's not a matter of improving the vote, the talk, or the technology. Neither radical democracy, nor a more radically vocal Mihailo Marković, nor Cisco Systems can save socialism. Socialism as a system of comprehensive planning cannot be saved. Millions of often conflicting plans can only be coordinated through the institutions of a market process.

THE ESSENTIAL TENSION BETWEEN DECENTRALIZATION AND CENTRALIZATION, DEMOCRACY AND COMMAND

Even the purely theoretical vision of self-managed socialism betrays its own radically decentralized ideal by promoting centralized coordinating mechanisms. Although self-managed socialism holds radical democracy as the political ideal, the economic *logic* of comprehensive economic planning tends toward hierarchy and centralization, pulling away from the ideal of decentralized control over socially owned means of production. We witnessed this tension in Yugoslav practice (the subject of Chapter 3, and discussed in more historical detail in Chapter 4), but its roots are exposed even in the pure theory of self-managed socialism.

The roots of the tension between decentralization and centralization go back to Marx himself. Many readers see in Marx a case for the abolition of capitalism in favor of centralized economic planning. This was the typical Austrian view, too – Marx as command planner. The Yugoslav Praxis Group, however, offered an alternative reading of Marx, one that emphasized his praxis theory, his theory of alienation and exploitation, and the implied vision of socialism that is supposed to put an end to alienation and allow man 'to return to himself'.

In a review of my book, Steve Pejovich maintained that I gave 'too much credit to the so-called praxists and their interpretation of Marx' (1991). He views their interpretation of Marx as a ploy reflecting their self-interested attempt to market themselves to left-wing radicals in the West. While that may be partly true (indeed, it had taken a 180° turn for the worse: Mihailo Marković threw out all his earlier arguments and became the chief intellectual ideologist within Slobodan Milosević's Serb nationalist campaign in the 1990s!), the praxis-philosophy interpretation of Marx can be examined outside any peculiar motivations that might have been harbored by members of the Praxis Group. If we take their interpretation of Marx seriously, as I do, then surely the Stalin-style central planning board, even in theory, does not attempt to totally eliminate the kind of alienation that terrified Marx. Rather, the central planning board becomes, *de facto*, a universal capitalist controlling all the means of production.

But Marx himself struggled with the ideal of decentralization and workers' self-management on the one side, and the implicit logic of central-ization and coordination to make comprehensive economic planning effec-tive. This is the subject of Chapters 5 and 6. Of course, markets for the means of production cannot be reconciled with Marxian socialism. But central economic planning procedures, too, cannot be reconciled with a *self-managed* socialism worthy of the name. Marx struggled – and in my opinion, failed – to eliminate this tension. So, too, did the Praxis Group as a whole.

A HAYEKIAN SOCIALIST STANDING AMIDST PREOBRAZHENSKY AND STALIN?

We all know actions have unintended consequences. And I've learned the hard but humorous way that also includes scholarly debate.

My interest in the 'humanistic' interpretation of Marx, as critical as it is, spurred some rather incredible interpretations of my own work. Peter Abell, for example, has interpreted my efforts as trying to build a 'post-modern' case for self-managed socialism. Abell has gone so far as to say that I try to salvage a case for workers' self-management by focusing on Marx's praxis philosophy. (I rebut him in Chapter 6.) John Bellamy Foster interprets me as some kind of 'Hayekian Socialist' (mentioned in Chapter 8). And most glaring of all, I'm listed on some crazy website as one of the more important twentieth century Marxists, standing alphabetically (though not ideologically, to be sure) between Preobrazhensky and Stalin! (I'll let you track that one down yourself.) I plead not guilty to all of these ridiculous charges, and unlike Bukharin, who was purported to use Aesopian language at his tribunal, I have written as clearly and straightfor-wardly as I can in the essays in this book.

SELF-MANAGED FIRMS IN A MARKET PROCESS

Perhaps some of the confusion stems from my Austrian defense of self-managed *firms*. Both the attempts at central planning and self-managed socialism are failures. But, as I argue in Chapters 6, 7, and 8, (and later in Chapter 10), a case can be made for self-managed firms within the institu-tions of an open market process.

This is certainly not socialism. Nor, however, is it capitalism in the con-ventional sense of the term. I argue that a market economy comprised of self-managed enterprises is consistent with Austrian School theory. It retains private or separate property rights in the means of production, and the competitive bidding process and spontaneously-formed prices that reflect relative scarcities. It is fundamentally a *market system* (rather than 'socialist' *or* 'third way') that doesn't seem to face the epistemological hurdles (expressed by Mises and Hayek, or my contemporary colleagues Lavoie and Boettke) that prohibit rational economic calculation. Democracy appears at the level of individual enterprises, which is the essence of a self-managed firm. Democracy does not appear within some hypothetical comprehensive planning apparatus, for market processes are incompatible with a set of comprehensive plans.

Yes, planning does occur – and it occurs in *any* economic system, as Hayek found necessary to remind us. This issue is not 'planning versus no planning'. Instead, the issue is over *who* will be engaged in planning. It's a matter of appropriate institutions. A market system is a set of institutions that allows individuals, on their own or collaborating in organizations, to coordinate their plans. They are economically guided by relative prices and profit–loss accounting, and engage in the free exchange of property rights. The standard literature on workers' self-management has for too long remained content modeling self-management by reference to the firm's objective function, largely independent of its institutional context, whether those institutions are genuinely market-based, market-socialist, or social-ist. I argue that, at least as a theoretical exercise in comparative political economy, a market system composed of self-managed firms can be shown to work. And, depending upon one's normative positions, it might be pre-ferred to state or corporate capitalism.

In a way, I hope that my work begins to bridge the gap between Jaroslav Vanek, the leading defender of the principle of workers' self-management, and Steve Pejovich, the leading critic of its implementation in the former Yugoslavia. I am very pleased that Vanek (1996) has come to agree with my Austrian call for the necessity of market processes to coordinate the plans of self-managed firms, and that Steve Pejovich (in friendly conversation) has also come to agree (or at least disagree much less!) that my vision of self-managed firms operating within an open market process – without state intervention – is coherent in principle.

AUSTRIANS ON ANARCHO-CAPITALISM

My defense of self-managed firms represents a departure from the tradi-tional Austrian defense of the market system. In Part Two I take the oppor-tunity to challenge further some Austrian views of the market process, particularly the more utopian variants dressed up in the rhetoric of scien-tific certainty.

I have no doubt about the necessity of the market process. I must admit, however, that I have not been satisfied with the scientific assuredness of market outcomes in the Austrian theory of welfare economics, particularly with Murray Rothbard's praxeological approach. Rothbard claimed to offer a purely deductive, and apodictically true, case for total non-intervention in the market process. Although Rothbard also claimed to be engaging in a 'radically empirical' approach to studying economic systems, he failed to view market processes institutionally. I argue that his purely praxeological exercises are misleading and flawed, and his own case for the welfare-maximizing properties of free markets is theoretically and empirically unfounded. I examine Rothbard's approach, and Roy Cordato's more recent updating, in Chapter 9. Following Rothbard, Cordato implicitly argues for anarcho-capitalism, maintaining that the free market is the 'ideal institutional setting' for maximizing efficiency and social welfare. Both argue that any degree of state intervention cannot possibly improve efficiency and/or social welfare. This might be true. But neither Rothbard nor Cordato have demonstrated its validity.

My sentiments regarding the robust properties of the market process lie, of course, with Rothbard and Cordato. I even retain sentimental feelings for market-based anarchism. But sentiments aren't enough to make a clear scientific case – let alone some alleged praxeological proof – of the *maximizing* properties of market systems. I argue that both Rothbard and Cordato fail to meet *their own* scientific standards, and thereby fail to live up to their unqualified defense of the anarcho-capitalist ideal.

Rothbard, of course, was the twentieth century's leading defender of anarcho-capitalism. I further challenge Rothbard, and juxtapose his case for anarchism against Murray Bookchin's anarcho-communist variant, in Chapter 10 (Bookchin being the leading defender of anarcho-communism). I critically examine Rothbard's scientific case against self-managed firms, as well as Bookchin's moral case against markets and private or separate property rights. Bookchin's left-wing anarchist theory is flawed because it fails to recognize the insurmountable knowledge problems that arise when markets for the means of production are abolished. He demonstrates no understanding of economics. But Rothbard's corresponding call for the necessity of anarcho-capitalism does not persuade. Rothbard has shown us that anarchism – if it is to work conceptually at all – must be market-based, but his case against self-managed enterprise is weak. (Apparently, for Rothbard and many Austrians, self-managed firms have no part in a truly 'capitalist' economy, not even in principle.) In Chapter 10 I sketch the possibility of conceiving a market-based anarchist system with an expanded range of firms, from the traditional capitalist enterprises championed by the Right to the self-managed and cooperative enterprises championed by the Left.

DOES THE MARKET WIN BY DEFAULT?

The Fall of 1989 opened up new vistas for theorists in comparative political economy, and created quite a bit of excitement among classical liberals in general, including myself. But it is now over a dozen years later, and it still remains unclear just how much a genuine market process, and its potential for personal and political freedom, will emerge in its aftermath.

The remaining chapters in Part Two focus, therefore, on a variety of issues wedded to post-communism. In Chapter 11 I discuss the allure of the welfare state as the Left's next-best alternative to really existing socialism, with a focus on Claus Offe's argument about the irreversibility of the welfare state, and Schumpeter's theory of the potential collapse of the tax state. In Chapter 12 (a paper written specifically for this volume) I turn to Joseph Stiglitz's call for a 'new' model of market-based socialism, which doesn't appear to be much different from Schumpeter's old market socialism. I address the role of conservatism and radicalism in Hayekian social theory in Chapter 13, and in particular I defend his remarks on the role of tradition (tradition *without* a capital T). In Chapter 14 (a previously unpublished address of mine) I offer some reflections on the rise of nationalism and other transition problems in post-communism. I conclude the book in Chapter 15 with a brief essay that addresses my normative vision, and the motivation behind my criticisms of Austrian economic theory. Some readers might wish to read this chapter first.

Although it is mighty tempting to rewrite and improve upon some of my previously published articles, I have left them largely untouched, except for non-substantive changes that improve their stylistic consistency.

PART ONE

The possibility of economic democracy: self-managed socialism versus the self-managed firm

1.   Comparative economic systems*

Austrian economists are rather well known for their defense of capitalism and criticism of planning and intervention. Comparative economic systems – the comparative analysis of a society's fundamental organizational principles – has emerged as a popular, and powerful, field of study within contemporary Austrian economics. Here, many of the Austrian School's key theoretical concepts regarding prices and knowledge, profit and loss accounting, and rivalrous competition have been rigorously applied to examine the nature and logic of capitalism, socialism and interventionism. While the Austrians have developed a theory of comparative economic systems over the past several decades, only recently, since the collapse of 'really existing socialism' in the former Soviet Union and Eastern Europe, has their analysis – particularly of the problems of rational planning under socialism – become accepted by mainstream economists.

ROOTS OF COMPARATIVE SYSTEMS ANALYSIS

The field of comparative economic systems is neither an Austrian invention, nor unique to the school. Economists of all stripes have studied the theory and practice of capitalist and socialist systems. Its roots travel back to the nineteenth century. If, as contemporary economists commonly believe, Adam Smith's *An Inquiry into the Nature and Causes of the Wealth of Nations* offers the first attempt to study the economics of free market capitalism (which Smith dubbed the 'system of natural liberty'), then Karl Marx arguably provides the first major 'comparative' analysis: most notably, Marx's *Das Kapital* (1906) established both a critical (if not hostile and damning) analysis of capitalism, and also an implicit, general vision of socialist economic organization.

Marx's inquiry suggests that society may be founded upon three systemically distinct organizational principles: Tradition, Market or Plan. These categorical distinctions have, with some important exceptions to be discussed later, been generally accepted by contemporary comparative

* Originally published in Peter J. Boettke (ed.), *The Elgar Companion to Austrian Economics*, Aldershot: Edward Elgar Publishing, 1994.

systems economists from both the neoclassical school (Grossman, 1963, for example) and the Austrian school (Lavoie, 1985a, for example).

A Tradition-based society, such as primitive communal groups or hunter-gatherer tribes, tends to be organized along the following institutions: common ownership of (very simple) means of production; production for direct use; barter; little, if any, division of labor (at best, along gender lines without regard to rationality or efficiency); a consistent aversion to risk-taking behavior. Alternatively, a Market-based society (capitalism), affords a very different organizational logic. (According to Marx, in fact, the Market is the antithesis of Traditional society.) *De facto* private ownership of (technologically advanced) means of production replaces common ownership; commodity production and exchange wipe out production for direct use and face-to-face bartering; both a highly technical and hierarchical division of labor is created in the workplace, and a spontaneous, undesigned social division of labor emerges with the development of labor markets and specialized industrial production. The Market system requires a panoply of entrepreneurial risk-taking, in the form of discovering new avenues of investment, alertness to economic error, and technological and organizational innovation. Money – a universal medium of exchange – provides the basis for appraising the relative scarcities of consumer goods and the means of production (capital) in the form of competitive prices and profit–loss accounting.

For Marx, the Market system is ultimately 'anarchic', based upon an 'anarchy of production', in both a descriptive and pejorative sense. Marx argued that the Market system is an undesigned, uncontrollable series of commodity exchanges for the sake of personal gain and profit (here essentially agreeing with Smith's descriptive 'Invisible Hand' phrase). Consequently, for Marx, the Market would be plagued with ever-increasing bouts of recessions and depression, economic chaos and, ultimately, utter collapse (a pejorative sense of 'anarchy of production' which has no counterpart in Smith's Invisible Hand). Hence, Marx predicted that, just as sure as Market has abolished Tradition in the battle over organizational principles, so, too, would the Plan extinguish the Market and usher in a final type of economic system: socialism. (Employing the dialectic, Marx tried to demonstrate that socialism represented the inevitable synthesis between primitive communal society – Tradition, and industrial capitalism – Market.)

Socialism is a system based upon *de facto* public or social ownership of the means of production, the abolition of a hierarchical division of labor in the enterprise, a consciously organized social division of labor. Under socialism, money, competitive pricing, and profit–loss accounting would be destroyed. The 'anarchy of production' would be replaced outright with a scientifically settled, comprehensive economic plan. Tradition, Market and Plan thus emerge, with Marx, as three conceptual systems with unique organizational logics. This is not to say that people within a Market-based system, for example, fail to be influenced by certain customs and traditions, or fail to create and pursue plans. Rather (and this is the point of capitalizing each system), the *underlying economic principle* upon which the plans and purposes of people are coordinated within the Market – a competitive and spontaneous profit–loss system – is conceptually distinct from a society organized by a scientific, comprehensive Plan or by a pre-modern, cooperative pattern of face-to-face bartering, essential to a Tradition system.

AUSTRIAN CONTRIBUTIONS TO COMPARATIVE SYSTEMS ANALYSIS

Tradition-based economies have been interpreted by most economists, including Austrians, as having only historical–anthropological relevance (for understanding the emergence of civilization, for example), while offering little or nothing to the grand debate over economic organization under modernity. The Tradition-based economy, in other words, has generally been relegated to a conceptual organizational scheme with little contemporary empirical relevance. Economists who have worked within the field of comparative systems have, for the most part, directed their attention to the question of whether a Plan-based system (which we shall subsequently refer to as socialism) can achieve the same, if not higher, level of economic rationality or efficiency as a Market-based system (which will now be referred to as simply capitalism).

On this question, the conclusions drawn by Austrian economists have been notoriously consistent. Shortly following Eugen Boehm-Bawerk's (1896) relentless critique of the Marxian labor theory of value, the chief Austrian insight in comparative systems theory – that socialism will fail to calculate the relative scarcities of goods and resources rationally, and must therefore fail in practice – first surfaced in Friedrich von Wieser's 1914 work, *Theorie der Gesellschaftlichen Wirtschaft* (Wieser, 1967). Wieser had claimed that plans in a capitalist system can be coordinated

> far more effectively by thousands and millions of eyes, exerting as many wills; they will be balanced, one against the other, far more accurately than if all these actions, like some complex mechanism, had to be guided and directed by some superior control. A central prompter of this sort could never be informed of countless possibilities, to be met with in every case, as regards the utmost utility to be derived from given circumstances, or the best steps to be taken for future advancement and progress. (1967, pp. 396–7)

But the *locus classicus* of the Austrian criticism of socialism appears in Mises's 1920 essay, 'Die Wirtschaftsrechnung im sozialistischen Gemeinwesen' (translated as 'Economic Calculation in the Socialist Commonwealth'). The core of Mises's argument can be stated concisely: (1) socialism aspires to replace private ownership of the means of production with social ownership, and seeks to destroy spontaneous (anarchic) market exchange in favor of central economic planning; (2) therefore, the means of production (that is, higher-order capital goods) will not be produced for, and exchanged within, a competitive market process; (3) without this market process, competitively established prices – those that normally allow individuals to appraise the relative scarcities of the means of production – will be erased; (4) therefore, the primary economic goal of a socialist system – rational economic planning – will be impossible. The knowledge required for successful economic planning is dispersed among individuals within society, and cannot be effectively collected and used without competitive market pricing. As Hayek would later emphasize (1945), the relevant information is contextual, particular to time and place. More recently, younger Austrians (especially Lavoie, 1986) have argued that the type of knowledge supplied by rivalrous market pricing and profit–loss accounting is predominantly 'tacit' or inarticulate, and have thereby developed a phenomenological–hermeneutical analysis to defend their claim that this knowledge cannot be collected by even the most advanced computer systems.

Mises maintained that, at best, socialism 'is only conceptually possible' (1920, p. 109; also cf. Mises, 1927, pp. 70–5). Rational economic calculation may not pose a problem in the pure theory of a static socialist society (or in any theory that depends upon such extreme assumptions as, for instance, the end of scarcity, or full and complete information). Nevertheless, Austrian economists maintain that calculation is an eminently practical problem, one which must lead to the downfall of real-world socialist planning. (The Austrians were not, of course, free from criticism or misunderstanding. Soon Oskar Lange would attempt to answer Mises's claim by erecting a neoclassical model of 'market socialism' (Lange, 1964). Joseph Schumpeter, who should have been more aware of the intricacies of the Austrian position, would later follow Lange's lead (Schumpeter, 1976). The confused socialist calculation debate had emerged.)

The collapse of the Soviet Union and the Eastern Bloc after 1989 seems to suggest that there is empirical power to the Austrian analysis, and this has already rekindled some outside interest in the school's approach to comparative systems analysis (see Kornai, 1990, for example). But this collapse may also, perhaps ironically, suggest that the Austrian analysis will need to be clarified and critically re-evaluated as we move into the twenty-first century. Why is this so? The Austrians have claimed that socialism, as a Plan-based system, is only a conceptual possibility, void of empirical viability. Hence, although they have accepted the original Marxian systems schema of Tradition–Market–Plan, they have demonstrated that, for all practical purposes, the empirical status of a Plan-based system falls far short of that found even among Tradition-based systems. After all, Tradition-based economies *have* existed at one time or another, while a successfully functioning socialist system is, according to Austrian theory, a real-world impossibility. Here, the Austrian contribution to the comparative systems literature is nothing short of radical, and arguably represents a tremendous intellectual feat, one which distinguishes Austrian economists from Marxists and neoclassical comparative systems economists.

Moreover, the Austrians have consistently criticized the notion of a potential 'Third Way' – as proposed by models of market socialism, indicative planning, redistributive welfare states, corporatism, and the like. The Austrians have remained firm that Market and Plan are conceptually distinct economic systems, undergirded by different organizational logics. A notion of a 'third' system (barring Tradition), which purports to 'combine' Market and Plan, is grounded on a logical confusion, and either collapses into a system of central economic planning (as argued in Hayek, 1944 and Prychitko, 1991), or remains a Market-based system with mere state intervention (Mises, 1929; Littlechild, 1979; Lavoie, 1985a).

Yet, if their analysis is correct, then Austrians must ask themselves exactly what *did* collapse in the late 1980s and early 1990s. To be consistent, Austrian economists cannot claim that *socialism* finally collapsed, otherwise they face the embarrassing task of explaining how socialism – an economic system which they purport to be empirically impossible – lasted several decades, or indeed, how it lasted at all.

Here lay a potential weakness of applied Austrian systems theory, for Austrian economists, unfortunately, are traditionally prone to commit this intellectual mistake. Michael Polanyi's (1957, p. 36) criticism of Mises and Hayek is the most glaring:

> Of all the intellectual triumphs of the Communist regime – and they are vast – it seems to me the greatest is to have made these eminent and influential writers [Mises and Hayek] so completely lose their heads. Could anything please that regime better than to hear itself proclaimed by its leading opponents as an omnipotent, omniscient, omnipresent socialist planner? That is precisely the picture of itself which the regime was so desperately struggling to keep up. Such accusations supply the Soviet government with an incontestable 'testimony' of having achieved the impossible aspirations of socialism, when in fact it has simply set up a system of state capitalism – a goal which leaves the regime next door to where it started.

To claim today that the collapse of the Soviet economy represents a collapse of socialism (and a final vindication of the Austrian position) may simply prolong the above misunderstanding.

Fortunately, some younger Austrians (such as Boettke, 1990, 1993, and Lavoie, 1986–87) and others sympathetic to the Austrian position (Roberts, 1971, for example) have interpreted so-called socialist economies as Market systems with a tremendous degree of state intervention. In this manner, so-called socialist economies differ *in kind* from a comprehensively planned system because they crucially depend upon world market prices and a stupendous underground economy for scarce resources, which engenders *de facto* private property relations in spite of a *de jure* socialist constitutional framework.

But Austrians might now harbor a greater tendency to undermine the strength of their own analysis by interpreting the latest events in Eastern Europe as 'proof' of socialism's failure. Perhaps as the excitement over these economic reforms begins to wane, and new problems emerge, Austrian economists will be better prepared to understand more carefully the history of interventionism in the twentieth century, while avoiding unnecessary scholarly confusion.

2. Marxism and decentralized socialism*

A late 1980s discussion of the progress of perestroika reported that the pro-Gorbachevites 'claim they are the real socialists, advocating ways to reverse alienation of the workers and achieve a decent society. They base themselves on the works of "the young Marx, before the Communist Manifesto and the ideas on political economy," as one man put it' (Lewis, 1988, p. 31).

The works under review in this chapter (Albert and Hahnel, 1978; Bideleux, 1985; and Selucky, 1979) are among those which advance the notion that there are decentralist alternatives to the Soviet model of Marxist socialism, and that these alternatives are economically feasible. A discussion of them should properly begin with 'the young Marx', that is, most importantly, his Paris Manuscripts, though it is questionable whether the dichotomy of early against late Marx is as sharp as some Gorbachevites might wish.

MARX'S CRITIQUE OF MARKET ALIENATION

The worker under capitalism, according to Marx, is thrown into an objectified, alienated world. As the division of labor increases along with the extent of production for the market, the worker, being without land or capital, becomes more dependent upon his labor for mere survival. The worker sells his labor power to capitalists for a money wage: labor power, therefore, becomes a commodity, an object of purchase and sale in the marketplace. To be sure, the worker's productivity increases as capitalist production becomes more technical and is rendered more efficient within the firm. But the fruit of his labor, the final product, is not for the worker to enjoy – it is the property of the capitalist, who turns it over to the chaos of the market. In search of profit, it is sold to the highest bidder.

As a result, man confronts the object of his labor as something alien. It is exchanged in an anonymous market. Moreover, not only the object but the activity of production itself is alien to man, for it is no longer a creative

* Originally published in *Critical Review* 2(4), 1988, pp. 127–47.

activity *per se*. Instead, as Marx says, it is 'an activity which is turned against him, independent of him and not belonging to him' (Marx, 1964, pp. 111–2). Under capitalism, man also becomes alienated from nature, from other men, and, finally, from himself (which is to say, from the historical potential that lies before him).

Marx maintains that alienation is an empirical fact of capitalism, but his critique is not made for the sake of description alone. As Gajo Petrović (1983) recognized, '"self-alienation" is not merely a (descriptive) concept; it is also an appeal, or a call for a revolutionary change of the world'.[1]

This revolutionary change is to emerge under communism, which will transcend self-alienation and allow man to 'return to himself.' Alienation is not eliminated by simply abolishing private property, money, and competition, for these are only *expressions* of alienated labor, not its initial cause: 'though private property appears to be the source, the cause of alienated labor', says Marx, 'it is rather the consequence, just as the gods are *originally* not the cause but the effect of man's intellectual confusion' (1964, p. 117).

Consequently, alienation may appear even in societies that abolished private property, money, and market exchange. (What immediately comes to mind is the War Communism period that followed the Bolshevik Revolution.)[2] As Mihailo Marković (1974, pp. 71–2, 132) has pointed out, 'It does not make an essential difference to the worker whether the usurper is a capitalist or a bureaucrat', for 'this is just another form of appropriating the surplus value created by the working class'.[3]

Abolishing private property, money, competition – in short, abolishing the market and replacing it with conscious direction of economic activity – is nevertheless a *necessary* condition for de-alienation and emancipation. If alienation is finally to be extinguished under socialism, then the 'anarchy of production' that Marx and Engels so often railed at must be replaced by an *ex ante* coordination of economic activity. That is, just as activity within the capitalist firm is consciously unified and planned in advance, so must the activity *between* enterprises. Rivalrous competition and spontaneous economic order must give way to cooperation and human design.

WAS MARX A CENTRAL PLANNER?

That Marx calls for a conscious ordering of economic activity is incontestable.[4] He sees unified control in industry becoming an ever greater possibility as the vicissitudes of market competition leave in its wake only monopolies. With only a few competitors, decisions that were once made solely on the basis of market price signals will come under the direct control of the capitalist monopolists. Capitalist concentration of industry will, iron-ically, reduce the anarchy of production – as will post-capitalist socialism.

But must this *ex ante* socialist planning be *centralized*? Not necessarily, according to some Marxists. This position is held quite strongly by the Praxis group in Yugoslavia (Marković, Petrović, Stojanović and others). In fact, they are convinced that hierarchial central planning is inconsistent with Marx's humanistic vision. This vision, which runs throughout Marx's work, is said to yield a decentralized socialism based upon participatory economic planning and workers' self-management in industry.[5] The evi-dence for this view of Marx is to be found in his explicit critique of market alienation and of the division of labor.

It is worthwhile to distinguish between Marx's critiques of the division of labor within society and within the firm. The social division of labor is based upon a wide distribution of capital. It unfolds in a spontaneous, undesigned manner, through the rivalrous buying and selling of commod-ities that make up the market process. As such, it is inherently complex, emerging from the inevitable clashing of millions of independent plans among competing entrepreneurs and consumers. The division of labor within the firm, on the other hand, remains under the control of a single authority – the capitalist. It is based upon a concentration of capital. Commodities are produced not by any single worker, but by a group of workers subordinated to the capitalist's detailed plan. Marx sees the two differing not only in degree, but also in kind: the social division of labor is an unintended result, externally imposed by the competitive market process; the division of labor within the firm is determined well in advance and externally imposed by the authority of the capitalist. Thus Marx sees 'anarchy in the social division of labor and despotism in that of the work-shop' (Marx 1906 vol. 1, pp. 385–94) – two very different phenomena.

In *State and Revolution* Lenin remarked that, under socialism, 'the whole of society will have become one office and one factory', thus putting an end to the anarchy of production. Kautsky made a similar claim in *The Class Struggle*. No doubt this came from their reading of Marx. After all, Marx does argue in *The Poverty of Philosophy* that 'if one took as a model the division of labor in a modern workshop, in order to apply it to a whole society, the society best organised for the production of wealth would undoubtedly be that which had a single chief employer, distributing tasks to the different members of the community according to some previously fixed rule' (Marx, 1978, p. 125) This sounds like a central planning board. Furthermore, in his disquisition on the division of labor in *Capital*, Marx offers the following remark, 'It is very characteristic that the enthusiastic apologists of the factory system have nothing more damning to urge against general organization of the labor of society, than that it would turn

all society into one immense factory' (1906 vol. 1, p. 391). Many commen-
tators see this as Marx's call for hierarchical planning. For instance, in
Marxism, Socialism, Freedom Radoslav Selucky argues that 'it follows from
Marx's statement [in the *Poverty of Philosophy*] that this arrangement
would be only welcome' (1979, p. 13). Selucky then uses the 'one immense
factory' statement from *Capital* to bolster this argument.

But these quotations from Marx actually do not clearly support the 'one
nation, one factory' view of socialist planning. First, it takes little reflection
to conclude that Marx is no admirer of the division of labor in the factory.
In the *Poverty of Philosophy* he is criticizing Proudhon for actually grant-
ing too much to the division of labor; for simply juxtaposing its pros and
cons ('He should have shown us the drawbacks of the division of labor in
general, of the division of labor as a category'); and for confusing the division of labor within the factory with the social division of labor in general.
Marx is simply pointing out that, according to Proudhon's modeling of the
division of labor after that of the modern workshop, one would expect to
see a 'single chief employer' despotically organizing the social division of
labor within *capitalist* society as a whole. 'But this is by no means the case',
argues Marx, for 'modern society has no other rule, no other authority for
the distribution of labor than free competition' (1978, pp. 122, 125).

Nor does Marx's statement in *Capital* seem to be a recommendation that
a socialist society be turned into an immense, centralized factory. On the
contrary, Marx is now criticizing what he considers mere 'bourgeois ideology' – an ideology which celebrates the division of labor within the factory
and the iron hand of capitalist organization, but at the same time ridicules
any notion of a centralized authority which treats the whole of society as
a single factory. He is pointing out what he considers to be an inconsistency
in bourgeois thought, but this does not entail embracing either side of the
antinomy. For *conscious* planning need not necessarily be *centralized*.

Rather than calling for central planning, Marx argues that self-alienation
can end only after workers gain conscious control over the coordination
process within society and, equally important, after they gain control over
the labor process within the enterprise. He can be seen, then, as a proponent of decentralized socialism and workers' self-management.

Marx sees little revolutionary potential for labor unions *per se*, for they
are given a false sense of control within despotically organized enterprises,
just as citizens are given a false sense of control over the democratic voting
process. Man will 'return to himself' only after both the anarchy of commodity production and the despotic control of the capitalist are abolished
through revolution. Marx thinks this is an ever greater possibility as capitalism progresses, for that which supports the social division of labor – the
wide distribution of capital – is undermined by monopoly capitalism; and

that which supports the division of labor within the enterprise – the concentration of capital – is eroded by joint stock companies, banking and credit. These economic conditions set the stage for the final overthrow of capitalism.

Marx believes that 'the life-process of society, which is based on the process of material production, does not strip off its mystical veil until it is treated as production by freely associated men, and is consciously regulated by them in accordance with a settled plan'. Here alienation comes to an end, and man becomes free. Marx concludes:

> The freedom in this field cannot consist of anything else but of the fact that socialized man, the associated producers, regulate their interchange with nature rationally, bring it under their common control, instead of being ruled by it as by some blind power; that they accomplish their task with the least expenditure of energy and under conditions most adequate to their human nature and most worthy of it. (1906 vol. 1, p. 92; cf. vol. 3, p. 954)

Rather than a strict division of labor within enterprises, and a hierarchical organization stemming from the authority of a central planning board, these ideas lend support to autonomous workers' self-management in industry, and participatory democracy in society. In short, Marx may well have been open to decentralized socialism.

A MODEL OF DECENTRALIZED SOCIALISM

What would decentralized socialism look like? How would planning and coordination occur?

Michael Albert and Robin Hahnel (1987) make the rare claim that they have provided a 'detailed description' of decentralized socialism in their book *Unorthodox Marxism* (1978) which purports to be a 'clear vision of what socialism will be like'.[6] Do they support this claim adequately?

Albert and Hahnel recognize the totalitarian nature of 'centrally planned' economies. They also admit that central planners lack adequate information and motivational incentives to muster a socially efficient allocation of scarce resources. Thus their 'radical' alternative. Simply democratizing the central planning process offers nothing for 'true' socialism: 'Although it would be possible to elect the central planning board to accord with the fullest of known democratic principles', they warn the reader, 'to conclude that this would resolve the problem is to miss the point. Self-management does not mean electing some person or agency to make our decisions for us' (1978, p. 267). They propose, instead, a 'revolutionary councilist view' – democratic, participatory planning by relatively autonomous workers' and consumers' councils which coordinate their activities by an iterative checking procedure. Planning takes place from the 'bottom up' rather than the 'top down'. Furthermore, markets have no place in their model – a conclusion consistent with Marx's call for the abolition of market forms of alienation.

Albert and Hahnel focus on dialogue – something which few economists do. Certainly the neoclassical mainstream, with its exclusive focus on equilibrium market prices, has no concern for dialogical processes: the standard models are completely devoid of dialogue and any notion of interpersonal relationships among market participants. All economic activities are coordinated on the basis of prices alone, prices which, in perfectly competitive conditions, contain all the relevant information necessary for individual optimizing behavior and Pareto-optimality. Albert and Hahnel's concern for reconciling dialogical processes with economic systems is an interesting exercise which warrants careful consideration.

Albert and Hahnel go to great pains to impress upon the reader the interconnectedness of human systems. Following the Marxian notion of causality, they maintain that no human event, economic or otherwise, can be reduced to a single cause, or even a finite number of causes. Each event is both a cause and an effect. Everything depends on everything else. 'To abstract from the whole', therefore, 'is to ignore important aspects of each act' (1978, p. 139). Because they often abstract from a system's complexity, neoclassical economists consequently view markets as 'informational miracles'. Empowered with Marxian notions of causation and over-determination, Albert and Hahnel pierce the veil to expose markets as 'cybernetic disasters'. Time and time again they tell us that markets 'delete all the information about different groups' activities that would allow those groups to coordinate their activities in a way promoting social well-being' (1978, p. 140). Rather than utilizing information in an efficient way, we learn that markets suppress the flow of information:

> [The market] price leaves us in ignorance concerning what went into a commodity's production, what needs were met or left unsatisfied, and what human characteristics were simultaneously produced. Prices someone will pay for goods we are producing don't let us know what pleasures and character development they will promote. Market institutions hide all this information about the concrete relations that are necessary for morale and empathy, and thereby preclude the development of solidarity based on each unit's concern with the well-being of others. (1978, p. 142)

Their critique of the market is perhaps best expressed in a single phrase: 'Markets make it almost impossible to think relationally and historically about one's involvements with other productive processes' (1978, p. 142).

How right they are! In a complex economy it is undeniably impossible to know in detail how one's own actions affect all others.

Now participatory planning, planning without a market, will replace imperfect market prices with dialogue between all concerned parties. First, a council must democratically agree (probably by majority vote) upon its own production (or consumption) activity; then it must ensure that its plan fits with the plans of all other relevant councils. Of course, to expect an initial convergence of plans would be fantastic. Perhaps one discovers that the demands of one council exceed the character development of another; that the plans agreed to by one group of councils would economically harm another; that technology would be better utilized in one sector of the economy than another, and so on. These possibilities, for Albert and Hahnel, are not *problems* to be faced by decentralized socialism; rather, they demonstrate how socialism is an *information-enhancing procedure*. Thus, confronted with the disjuncture of their original plans, council members would go back to their collective drawing boards with this new information in mind, and sit down for a new round of proposals and debate. Because 'there is no reason to suppose that the initial proposals will provide an immediate mesh or economic plan', one can only conceive 'the planning procedure as a potentially continuous process' (1978, pp. 270, 271).

This iterative procedure of proposing/denying/re-proposing requires a hierarchy of democratic bodies. If a disagreement persists between two or more councils, or if, having reached a mutually satisfying agreement, the new plan disrupts the plans of other councils, a vertical structure of councils must be developed to smooth over the conflicts created by horizontal decision making. 'Federations would be necessary. Every "industry" would have regional councils with representatives from all the work-place councils, and national councils made up of representatives from all the regions. Neighborhood councils would federate similarly' (1978, p. 271).

But here, just when we need a clear vision of what socialism will be like, we receive only ambiguity and contradiction.

Decision making can be bumped up the hierarchy of councils for only so long. If production and consumption are ever to start, someone (or some supreme council) must make a decision which binds all relevant parties. After judiciously weighing the social costs and benefits of various courses of action, the supreme council must decide upon the best course of social action. It must judge the merits of one plan over another. It must force inferior councils to accept a feasible plan. It will thus become, *de facto*, a central planning board. In Albert and Hahnel's words, a 'forcing mechanism' will be necessary to guarantee plan convergence.

Moreover, because even the authors don't expect everyone in society to absorb, understand, or take a genuine interest in the plethora of technical and local details which must be discussed in order for the final council to rationally construct a feasible course of action, the relevant producers and consumers must be represented by a council of elected *delegates* (subject to rotation and strictly recallable, of course). This no longer rings the radical bell of meaningful self-management. Instead, one hears the drone of reformist representation.

Only if conflicts of interest do not continuously arise – only if, at some level, groups of councils could reach agreements without the intervention of a 'forcing mechanism' – would central planning be unnecessary. But why should we believe this to be a real possibility? A world of scarcity is a world with conflicts of interest.

Moreover, while Albert and Hahnel strongly condemn others for not thinking 'relationally', thereby failing to take into account the universal interdependence of all events, their own model goes no further in explaining how every individual's actions affect everyone else. It merely analyzes conflicts between a few councils at a time. To the extent that they remain content with this partial view of the system, their criticism of other analysts loses its force. On the other hand, to the extent that they adopt a mathematical model which accounts for interconnectedness by way of general equilibrium shadow prices (which is, by the way, the goal of the same authors' (1991) work), their emphasis on genuine dialogue must give way to the standard economist's interest in equilibrium. In this case dialogue must be 'forced' into the neoclassical model – not a promising prospect.

If the intricacies of Albert and Hahnel's ideal decentralized system are too complex to be developed in theory, what should we expect in practice? How, for instance, would the actual final arbiter determine the relative importance of the conflicting demands made by the rivalrous councils?

Finally, Albert and Hahnel's model ignores the fact that the market is, as Don Lavoie (1986; cf. 1985a, ch. 3) puts it, a 'procedure for the discovery and conveyance of inarticulate knowledge'. If knowledge is significantly tacit, as contemporary philosophers of knowledge argue, then Albert and Hahnel, by abolishing the market, will be left with no means of using the bulk of this knowledge in discovering new and better ways to allocate scarce resources. Subjective valuations of resources cannot be determined by discussion and debate alone; nor can they be imposed by central edict or by votes. A single mind or council of minds will not have all the knowledge necessary to design a complex economy rationally. This is the essence of what has come to be called the 'knowledge problem' posed by the Austrian-school economists, the problem Ludwig von Mises described in his classic 1920 essay which ignited the socialist calculation debate within the economics profession.[7]

Contrary to the Albert and Hahnel view of prices, Austrians argue that freely established market prices act as 'aids to the mind' under the anarchic organization of capitalist industry. Though imperfect from an ideal standpoint, monetary calculation allows for the practical coordination of a set of intricately connected, complex production processes. Rational economic calculation becomes impossible outside simple face-to-face communities if market-generated prices and thus monetary calculation are abolished.

Albert and Hahnel condemn market institutions for concealing detailed information about the millions of unique events which make up the market process. But they ignore the fact that this complexity arises precisely as the orderly *result* of anarchic exchange. It is simply absurd to condemn market prices for not exposing all the intricate details of interconnected economic activities, when in fact those activities owe their *raison d'être* to market prices, and could not be preserved if anarchic organization were replaced by a unified plan.

Albert and Hahnel's model cannot deliver the goods. They fail to see that the necessary scarcity-indicating valuations, valuations which assist in rational economic calculation, are determined within the social context of individuals pursuing changing courses of action. Valuations emerge in the form of market prices which capture, though imperfectly, the relative scarcities of economic goods to those individuals. Prices become meaningless if they are not determined through rivalrous production and consumption among actually exchanging individuals.

Thus, a system of councils – with no guidance from spontaneously formed prices of consumer and capital goods – cannot rationally calculate the relative scarcities of those goods. No single mind or council of minds possesses the knowledge to think 'relationally' about the present, let alone the future. To take even the simplest example: a consumer who declares at a council meeting that she values five pounds of potatoes as much as a gallon of milk, or that she prefers apples to pears, adds nothing to rational economic calculation. Tallying up her requests, along with all others, and comparing them to the current and anticipated supplies gets us no further, even if the plans converge. For valuation takes place at the moment of decision, when she actually goes out to collect her groceries; it is affected by tastes, expectations, fleeting moods, the weather, and so on. Some days she may wish to have more potatoes, other days no potatoes at all. Called to justify this unpredictable behavior at the next council meeting, she could do nothing but admit that her previously submitted 'valuations' were wrong. In short, there is no reason to believe that, even in the case of the simplest decisions, individuals will be able to think 'relationally' about future circumstances.

This problem is compounded when we move from consumer goods allocation to the roundaboutness of the production process itself, and the allocation of capital goods within that process. In this case it is not only a question of matching the demands of consumers with the final supplies of commodities. Instead, the entire capital structure itself must be intertemporally coordinated. Here the dynamic issues of saving, investment, and resource depletion (to name the most obvious) come to the fore.

If it is impossible for people to think relationally in real-world markets, as the authors claim, then how will they be able to do so without prices? The standard economist's concern with price alone, it is true, leads to an unrealistic model of the way the world works. Albert and Hahnel's concern for dialogical processes within economic systems provides a critical turn away from the mainstream which those within the Austrian School would do well to follow. To be sure, Mises (1983, p. 13) recognized that 'language opens up the way for a person of exchanging thoughts with all those who use it' in such a way that its influence on 'thinking and the expression of thought, for social relations, and for all activities of life' are immensely significant. But in particular, spontaneously formed market institutions are *not* the result of atomistic individuals responding to a given array of prices, but the result of individuals already involved in truly dialogical relationships. Trade journals, industry studies, marketing agreements, business lunches, conference calls, higgling and haggling, the interpretation of accounts and so on are all part of the grand conversation we call the market process.

Albert and Hahnel's problem is that they go much too far: their exclusive focus on conventional dialogue leads them to neglect the more subtle dialogical role of market-generated prices and monetary calculation. They see market prices as *getting in the way* of dialogue rather than being the *consequence* of dialogue. Prices, in reality, allow for a much *greater* degree of diversity and complexity in dialogue.

Albert and Hahnel do not account for the complexities of contemporary economic systems, and by thus excluding the knowledge-generating role of market prices, they build an equally unrealistic model of the way the world *should* work. Jürgen Habermas, who has done some of the most important and interesting work on dialogical processes, admits that the complexity of modern systems would have to be sacrificed if we were to institute a completely democratic, conventionally dialogical model of socialism: 'all modern economies are so complex that a complete shift to participatory decision-making processes, that is to say, a democratic restructuring at *every* level, would inevitably do damage to some of the sensitive requirements of contemporary organizations.' Hence, Habermas questions whether socialists 'should not preserve part of today's complexity within the economic system, limiting discursive formation of the collective will precisely to the decisive and central structures of political power; that is, apart from the labour process as such, to the few but continuously made fundamental decisions which will determine the overall structure of social production and, naturally, of distribution' (Habermas 1986, pp. 45, 67).

Why should a *restricted* dialogue, one that is not allowed the full play to yield market prices, be thought of as the more rational mechanism with which to conduct economic activity? Conversely, isn't a true conversation itself 'irrational' in the sense of being somewhat unpredictable? I have in mind Gadamer's (1985, p. 345) point: 'We say that we "conduct" a conversation, but the more fundamental a conversation is, the less its conduct lies within the will of either partner. Rather, it is generally more correct to say that we fall into a conversation, or even that we become involved in it.' An unplanned order emerges during the course of a free dialogue: 'The way in which one word follows another, with the conversation taking its own turnings and reaching its own conclusion, may well be conducted in some way, but the people conversing are far less the leaders of it than the led.' Like the anarchic market process in general, 'no one knows what will "come out" in a conversation. Understanding or its failure is like a process which happens to us.'[8] This I take to be the essence of dialogue. Rationality is not synonymous with predictability.

To deny the spontaneous outcomes of voluntary dialogue – to abolish the market institutions of price and monetary calculation – seems to me to deny dialogue's epistemological relevance in a complex social setting.

MERGING MARX WITH MARKETS

Robert Bideleux offers an alternative Marxist defense of decentralized socialism in *Communism and Development* (1985), an alternative which allegedly solves the knowledge problem.[9] Bideleux argues that the market is indeed a necessary feature of decentralized socialism precisely because it has knowledge-enhancing properties. Radoslav Selucky also expresses this argument in his *Marxism, Socialism, Freedom* (1979), which had much influence on Alec Nove's (1983) work. Selucky recognizes the Austrian School theme that 'if the market is wholly eliminated and replaced in all its functions by a central plan, there is scarcely a *practical* possibility of rational economic calculation' (1979, p. 48). But combining Marx and the 'alienating' market seems puzzling, if not contradictory.

Primarily a book which reappraises various communist development strategies, Bideleux's work advocates a system of decentralized socialism based upon market exchange and village-based development. It provides a wealth of statistical data (which may prove valuable to the specialist in economic development) while seeking to provide a Marxist justification for Bideleux's village-based market socialism.

Bideleux maintains that while Marx could be interpreted as a political centralist, as Lenin had done, this interpretation neglects Marx, the admirer of the Paris Commune, and Marx, the supporter of autonomous village communes. Bideleux, concerned with developing the latter Marx, translates and extensively quotes three drafts of the *Sochineniya* manuscript Marx tried to finish before his death, one which positively discusses the development potential of the village commune in peasant Russia.

We find Marx most candid in the third draft of the manuscript: 'All depends on the historical context . . . Communal property in land offers Russia a natural base for communal appropriation, and its historical context – coexistence with capitalist production – grants it ready-made the material conditions for co-operative labor, organized on a broad scale . . . Once placed on normal footing in its present form, it can become the *direct point of departure* for the economic system towards which modern society is moving' (Bideleux, 1985, p. 10). From this reading of Marx, Bideleux concludes that 'a peasant society' could be led '*directly* to a village based communism', without initial heavy industrialization strategies.

The author combines his commune-ism with a defense of market socialism. 'In principle', writes Bideleux,

> Collective ownership and control of the means of production ought to go hand in hand with some form of 'producers' democracy' and a market economy in which prices are allowed to broadly reflect relative costs and scarcities and so enable spontaneous market forces to promote an increasingly efficient use of resources to produce goods and services which consumers really want. (1985, p. 176)

Indeed, Bideleux stresses that 'village communism must . . . maintain a *market system* and hence a reasonably disciplined and confidence-inspiring *monetary system*' (1985, p. 70).

Yet Bideleux does not attempt to place his pages of Marx quotations within the context of Marx's overall work – a fundamental hermeneutical error. He never attempts to reconcile Marx's supposed market socialism with Marx's critique of market alienation. It is highly dubious simply to assume, as Bideleux does, that the *Sochineniya* manuscript implies a retreat from Marx's earlier, well-known condemnation of the market (Bideleux, 1985, p. 10), or to link Marx with the Oskar Lange's defense of commodity production under socialism (Bideleux, 1985, p. 70), without making any effort to square this new 'late' Marx with the old 'late' and 'early' ones, let alone with the unified Marx one finds in the work of such interpreters as Walicki (1988); all of these 'Marxes' unequivocally condemn market exchange.

Radoslav Selucky, on the other hand, squarely confronts the issue, but from another direction. His *Marxism, Socialism, Freedom* (1979) represents a scholarly commitment to Marxist interpretation and revisionism, and promises to be a classic in the ongoing debate over decentralized socialism and the Marxist tradition.

Selucky begins with a question: 'Can socialism be democratic in the sense of guaranteeing individual freedom?' He attempts to answer the totalitarian problem of contemporary 'centrally planned' economies, and the socialist 'knowledge problem' as well. He believes solutions exist only under a decentralized system characterized by social property, labor self-management, and market exchange.

Selucky does not hesitate to link totalitarian socialism to Marx. The author argues that its origins are found in a 'theoretical mistake' in Marx's critique of the market, a 'cleavage' between his interpretation of the economic and political emancipation of man:

> While Marx's economic concept of socialism consists of a single social-wide factory based on vertical (hierarchical) relations of superiority and subordination, his political concept of socialism consists of a free association of self-managed work and social communities based on horizontal relations of equality. Whoever accepts in full Marx's first concept has to give up the latter, and vice versa; they are mutually exclusive. (1979, xi)

Lenin accepted the first concept, and failed. In a world still characterized by imperfect knowledge and scarcity – characteristics which Selucky sees little hope of transcending – abolishing the market will destroy any hope of achieving equality and freedom. 'Here lies the main problem of the Marxist approach: the abolition of the market is, at the same time, the abolition of the economic base for equality and freedom' (1979, p. 21). For he concludes that, without first overthrowing scarcity, 'centralism [and thus inequality and tyranny] is an inevitable price which must be paid for the abolition of the market' (1979, p. 34). (Hence the inevitability of central planning in Albert and Hahnel's model.) Selucky maintains that in calling for the abolition of market exchange relations, Marx was nothing less than utopian, for he assumed that the social division of labor and scarcity could be extinguished immediately after the revolution (a point which Bideleux never discusses). Selucky sees this as a 'very appealing' humanistic goal for man's distant future, but simple unrealistic for the period following the socialist revolution and, at least, for the early stages of communist development (1979, p. 24).

I don't find the 'cleavage' between economic centralism and political decentralism as apparent in Marx's writings as Selucky does. As I have shown above, it is not all that clear that Marx calls for 'one immense factory', as Kautsky and Lenin would have us believe. But in the end this may be of largely academic interest, since Selucky agrees that in conditions of economic scarcity a non-market model of workers' self-management must ultimately collapse into a model of central command planning, whether this was Marx's intention or not.

Selucky the economist recognizes the necessity of the market as a knowledge-enhancing institution; ironically, Selucky the socialist also sees the market as the only hope for the economic and political liberation of man. He wants a viable self-managed socialism which does not collapse into command planning. In fact, he builds his model of socialism upon Milton Friedman's (1962) discussion of the relationship between economic and political freedom.

Selucky recognizes that economic freedom (the market) is a necessary, though not sufficient, condition for political freedom (defined in the negative sense as the absence of coercion by other people). He sees that the '*definitive* resolution' of alienation is 'unrealistic in political and utopian in economic terms' (1979, pp. 148–9). Consequently, a more realistic goal of socialism, in Selucky's view, is to maximize positive freedom – individual self-mastery and a share in the controlling authority – which implies the participation, autonomy, and creativity of the associated producers. A central plan, though it may free man from the blind forces of the market, is itself a source of alienation because the worker produces not for direct consumption, but according to the dictates of the plan. It forces the individual to choose between his interests as a producer and those as a consumer, which under the incentives that arise under actual attempts at central planning, are contradictory. As Selucky keenly observes:

> The situation is totally absurd: Man works, fulfils the plan targets, gets his wages, but is unable to use a part of his earned income to get what he needs. Owing to the logic of the non-market system, he is forced to behave as a schizophrenic: his material interest as a producer is tied to the plan targets. His interest as a consumer can be spelled out only through effective demand. If, as a producer, he meets the effective demand expressed by himself as a consumer, he would behave against his interest as a producer. If, as a producer, he does not meet the effective demand expressed by himself as a consumer, he would behave against his interest as a consumer and live in permanent frustration. Under the circumstances there is no way out. The market alienation of his labor not only has not been overcome or even lessened but, on the contrary, it has been augmented by another specific alienation created by the non-market system, *the alienation of man from his wages.* (1979, p. 39)

Central planning would (if it worked) free man from economic necessity, but it would do so only through coercion by the state. This violation of negative liberty, in turn, blocks the development of the positive political liberties socialism should enhance, because it can only be implemented hierarchically.

Thus the necessity of the market to guarantee political freedom. Meaningful self-management needs the market, as the market allows for true autonomy between enterprises. Which is to say, a decentralized and voluntarily coordinated economic base is necessary for a decentralized and voluntarily coordinated political superstructure.

Rather than state ownership of the means of production, then, Selucky calls for social ownership; rather than command planning, indicative planning will tame the anarchic forces of the market. Social ownership means that, though society formally owns the means of production, management is vested in those who participate in production. To quote the 1974 constitution of Yugoslavia, social ownership implies the following: 'Nobody has any legal right to appropriate products of common work, to manage them, and to dispose of public means of production on the ownership basis.' Veljko Rus, a prominent Yugoslav sociologist, points out that this existential notion of a 'nobody' is operationalized as a legal entity, the work organization (see Rus, 1986). Responsibility becomes collective, or 'anonymous' (to use Rus's term), resting with the work organization, rather than among individual social actors.

The idea of social ownership is vague at best. Who will be responsible for allocating capital goods? How will their values be calculated? What procedures will be implemented to reward the efficient use of resources and punish inefficiency? And who will do the punishing?

Under social ownership, relatively free markets would exist for consumer goods. Yet social ownership can mean that capital goods, though 'owned' by 'society', are 'rented' by the workers' management councils', or it can mean that the state actually allows workers' councils to sell capital goods while paying a depreciation charge to the state. (In the economic sense, this is the difference between a *usus fructus* right and a *right of use.*) Neither Bideleux nor Selucky make this distinction. I can only imagine that they would opt for the former alternative, since this is more consistent with Marxian exploitation theory.[10] If so, however, the only information the market would provide to the owner of capital goods – the state – would consist of consumer preferences as revealed by consumer goods prices. Since market prices would not be spontaneously determined for capital goods, there would be no procedure by which to assess their relative scarcity. The state, working with various councils, would have to allocate capital goods between competing enterprises on an arbitrary basis. How many machines to devote to specific agricultural concerns, and how many to devote to industry? Indeed, how could it even be determined what specific types of capital equipment need to be produced? In a world of scarcity, how will limited resources be allocated among competing means of production? The knowledge problem articulated by Mises in 1920 appears once again, and would endanger the political liberation sought by decentralized socialism.

If we suppose that, instead of *usus fructus*, the *right of use* is granted, so that enterprises buy and sell capital goods in a market setting (as in contemporary Yugoslavia), then for all practical purposes, property has become privatized. Judgments concerning the best use of scarce resources become radically decentralized, as each enterprise is free to allocate them to the highest bidder. The primary coordinating vehicle, then, is market exchange. Planning becomes a series of interventions in this dialogical process, attempting to steer the conversation and its results in one direction or another. Here Plan and Market are not reconciled. On the contrary, each sets off a series of unintended and mutually antagonistic consequences. A market-based, decentralized socialism which allows for the purchase and sale of capital goods among competing organs of self-management (such as the Yugoslav system) is fundamentally a market system with a great degree of state intervention. The difference between capitalism and decentralized socialism becomes, therefore, a difference in degree, not a difference in kind: a question of how far a society is willing to allow for genuinely dialogical relationships and their unplanned results.

MARXISM IN CRISIS?

Those decentralist Marxists with little awareness of the socialist calculation debate which occurred among economists during the 1930s and 1940s (including the Praxis philosophers, and, apparently, Albert and Hahnel) call for the complete elimination of market alienation through the democratic, discursively dialogical development of a unified economic plan. They consider this to be a consistent Marxist position. But they do not offer a persuasive account of knowledge transmission and utilization in a complex economy, and therefore the danger of their model falling into a hierarchical 'command' economy is great.

Those with a somewhat better understanding of economics recognize the need for anarchic exchange relationships in order to achieve political liberation (Selucky) or to assist in calculating the economic value of scarce resources (Bideleux, Selucky). This allowance for markets by ostensible Marxists, although at first glance striking, may be understandable given that Marxism also recognizes the state to be an alienating force. Conflicts of interest, if *not* settled under institutions of voluntary discourse, can be 'settled' only by a totalitarian state, which Marx vehemently opposed. However, it is not very clear how far market institutions, the unintended outcomes of economic dialogue, can be allowed to operate by the new

Marxists. If markets merely allocate consumer goods, Bideleux and Selucky cannot explain how the requisite knowledge for rational capital goods production will be transmitted and utilized – certainly the values of capital goods are not simply imputed, as Schumpeter erroneously believed, from the equilibrium prices of consumer goods. This is crucial because in reality the totalitarian consequences of eliminating the market stem from abolishing capital goods markets, not those for consumer goods. On the other hand, if Bideleux, Selucky or any other market socialist grants this point and is willing to allow capital goods markets tempered by indicative planning, then he ends up with a market-based, non-socialist, non-Marxist (albeit interventionist) system.

The problem of unorthodox Marxist economics is one of coming to terms with both market alienation and state alienation, of reconciling Market and Plan. On those points agreement has become the exception rather than the rule. Rather than a sign of crisis, however, I believe these new debates are a healthy alternative to the monolithic position held by the orthodox Marxist earlier in the twentieth century. I will leave it up to the Marxists themselves to decide which position is more consistent with what Marx himself 'really meant'. The more important issue is what Marxism – as a living body of ideas – means today, given the knowledge we have gained over the past century, and the critical economic scrutiny to which socialism is too rarely subjected.

NOTES

1. This is not an isolated interpretation. Don Lavoie (1985b, p. 29) has argued that 'Marx's scientific socialism was not merely an excuse for avoiding any examination of socialist society. It was a recommendation of a particular method for the conduct of such an examination – that is, that socialism be described through a systematic critique of capitalism.' Similarly, Mihailo Marković (1974, p. 60) states that 'Marx's key concepts invariably refer either to structures which *are, but could be abolished*, or to those which *are not yet, but which could be created*' (original emphasis).
2. In addition to Roberts' (1971) classic work, see Boettke (1988) and Lavoie (1986–87).
3. Moreover, Pedrag Vranicki (1965, pp. 305–6) comes close to Hayek's (1944) position on the logic of planning when he states: 'Man as a producer finds himself again in the alienated position of hired labor if he has been wholly deprived of participation in the management of production and in the distribution of the resultant product under such a system, which consists not only of total state planning but also of the disposal of surplus value by the state. *The only difference in this instance is that capitalist monopoly has been supplanted by the universal monopoly of the state*' (emphasis added).
4. This is implicit in Marx's radical critique of market alienation and his call for the abolition of private property, money, and commodity production. In volumes one and three of *Capital*, Marx calls for production regulated by 'freely associated men' according to 'a settled plan'; men who 'regulate their interchange with nature rationally', bringing it 'under their common control'. Moreover, in *The Civil War in France* Marx explicitly recognizes the need for a unified plan if the anarchy of capitalist production

34 *The possibility of economic democracy*

is to be abolished: 'If unified co-operative societies are to regulate national production upon a common plan, thus taking it under their own control, and putting an end to the constant anarchy and periodical convulsions which are the fatality of Capitalist production – what else, gentlemen, would it be but Communism, "possible" Communism?' (Marx and Engels, 1969, p. 224).

5. Many have divided Marx into an 'early', philosophical Marx (The Paris Manuscripts), and a later, 'mature' Marx (the Marx beginning with *The German Ideology*): the early Marx is said to be humanistic, focusing primarily upon alienation, while the later abandons humanism for materialism, philosophy for economics. This division is somewhat suspect. The theme of alienation runs throughout the entire corpus. It simply takes on new labels such as abstract labor, reification, and commodity fetishism. See, for instance, Marković (1974). For a classic account of the unity in Marx's work, see Avineri (1968).

6. Their other book, Albert and Hahnel (1981), adds little, if anything, to their original decentralized socialist model.

7. These ideas are further developed in Mises (1981). The Austrian contribution has grown tremendously since Mises's original writings. See, for example, Hayek (1948a, 1975), Hoff (1949), Kirzner (1984), Lavoie (1985a, 1985b, 1986), Polanyi (1951), Vaughn (1980b).

8. For the libertarian consequences of Gadamer's hermeneutics in general, see Palmer (1987). (I should add, today, that Palmer's position, and perhaps my own on the dialogical properties of markets, are subject to the criticisms advanced by diZerega (1989) and especially Quinn and Green (1998). I address the issue of dialogue and communicative rationality much more carefully in Prychitko (2000).)

9. See Bideleux's (1986) review of Lavoie (1985b).

10. Vanek (1971, p. 10) points to the *usus fructus* right as a fundamental characteristic of any market-based decentralized socialist system.

3. Did Horvat answer Hayek? The crisis of Yugoslav self-management*

At a time when one Communist regime after another is toppling in Eastern Europe, Yugoslavia gets remarkably little press. We watched with excitement the collapse of the Berlin Wall, the rise of poet-statesman Vaclav Havel in Prague, the fall of the Party in Budapest, and the bloody fate of Nicolae Ceausescu in Bucharest. We haven't heard much about Yugoslavia. The sweeping changes in the rest of Eastern Europe seem to be passing Yugoslavia by. But don't let that fool you. The peoples of Yugoslavia, like those of the neighboring East European countries, are calling for, and slowly attaining, an end to the monolithic Communist Party, and the introduction of private property rights and a full market economy.

Yugoslav-style socialism, with its ideological emphasis on decentralization and workers' self-management of socially owned resources, was once touted as a fundamental, more humane alternative to the command planning of the Soviet Union. Indeed, Yugoslavia was the first country to break away from Stalin's yoke of power back in 1948 to create a perestroika of its own. Under Tito's leadership, Yugoslavia attempted a massive decentralization toward workers' self-managed socialism, which began in 1950 with the adoption of the Basic Law on Movement of State Economic Enterprises and Larger Economic Associations by their Working Collectives. The central planning bureaucracy would be dismantled. State property would be erased. In Tito's words,

> The takeover of the means of production by the state has not made accomplished fact of the fighting slogan of the workers' movement, 'Factories to the Workers,' because the slogan 'Factories to the Workers, Land to the Peasants' is more than just an abstract propagandistic battle cry. It contains deep and weightly [sic] meaning. It sums up the entire program of socialist relations in production; it speaks of social ownership, it speaks of the rights and duties of workers and – therefore – can and must be accomplished in practice if we want indeed to construct socialism. (quoted in Kardelj, 1980, pp. 51–2)

* Originally published in *The Freeman*, February 1991, pp. 64–70.

Enlightened workers' councils would be in charge of planning society from the bottom up, rather than the top down. 'Social' ownership would replace state ownership. No longer the legal privilege of private capitalists or state bureaucrats, the means of production would officially be the property of society at large. State enterprises were to be freed from the hands of an oppressive bureaucracy and handed over to workers' councils; a market for consumers' goods would emerge, reducing the shortages and long queues that plagued other East European countries. Socialism would no longer restrict and destroy democracy. It would embrace it in the workshop, factory, and planning bureau.

The heyday of 'market socialism' had arrived.

CLAIMS OF RATIONALITY

The Austrian economists apparently suffered an intellectual beating. Seventy years ago Ludwig von Mises argued that socialism was impossible. By abolishing unhampered market exchange of the means of production – and thus market prices that reflect underlying economic scarcities – the central economic planners, Mises argued, would lack the knowledge necessary to coordinate the economic system rationally. They would stand confounded in the face of a 'bewildering throng of economic possibilities', as Mises (1981, p. 101) so eloquently put it. F.A. Hayek agreed with Mises, and would later add that comprehensive economic planning, even if it begins with the most democratic and humane aspirations imaginable, must lead to a totalitarian dictatorship, 'because dictatorship is the most effective instrument of coercion and the enforcement of ideals and, as such, essential if central planning on a large scale is to be possible' (1944, p. 70).

The Austrians wielded a double-edged sword. One side chopped to pieces the belief that central economic planning was possible in the complex, modern world. The other side cut through the veil of socialist democracy, and exposed the fact that any democratic ambitions must ultimately be abandoned in the utopian struggle to overthrow the market system. Or so the Austrians thought.

It seemed that, by the 1960s, Yugoslavia had finally proved that sword powerless. The Yugoslav model of decentralized socialism, which allowed markets for consumer goods as well as limited resource markets, along with its emphasis on democratic planning and management by workers, was considered by many comparative systems economists to be the final answer to Mises and, even more so, to Hayek.

At that time Yugoslavia enjoyed a relatively higher degree of economic growth compared with its neighbors behind the Iron Curtain. Queues for consumer goods dwindled. Workers were officially in charge of their work-places and enterprise planning decisions. Yugoslavia's borders were open to Western tourists.

Economists tended to consider Yugoslavia the closest practical application of the theoretical model of market socialism devised by Oskar Lange. Morris Bornstein (1965, p. 78), for example, claimed that 'a number of the problems identified by Hayek have been met in the Yugoslav variant of market socialism'. Thomas Marschak (1968, p. 569) wrote that 'the classic idea (of Hayek for example) that the burden of assembling managers' intimate technical information at one center is a major obstacle to any sort of central planning seems to lose weight in the Yugoslav context'.

Statements like these were not unusual among comparative systems economists in the 1960s and 1970s. But the most forceful challenge to the Austrians was published less than ten years ago. Branko Horvat, Yugoslavia's leading economist, made it loud and clear in his magnum opus, *The Political Economy of Socialism*:

> Hayek framed his argument so as to prove the superiority of the free market over central planning. In the context of this book, it may be of some historical interest to note the following claim made by Hayek in 1945: 'nobody has yet succeeded in designing an alternative system in which certain features of the existing one can be preserved which are dear even to those who most violently assail it – such as particularly the extent to which the individual can choose his pursuits and consequently freely use his own knowledge and skills.' . . . I shall not leave this challenge unanswered. (1982, p. 577 n. 56)

Horvat believes the blueprint of self-managed socialism answers Hayek:

> *Social control* is maximally effective – and the possibility of managerial abuses drastically reduced – because management operates before the watchful eyes of the workers' council and the entire working collective. It is both impossible and illegal to keep socially important decisions secret. Contrary to *monopolistic* tendencies elsewhere, the concentration of capital is discouraged. The working collective in a labor-managed firm is not inclined to overexpand the firm by mergers because it then loses control over the firm's affairs. On the other hand, because of the different social organization, financial power is no longer so important. A competitive firm can be neither bought nor owned. Thus, a labor-managed economy is likely to operate much closer to the textbook model of the competitive market. Social ownership *implies planning, but does not eliminate the market*. Consequently, the labor-managed economy achieves what Hayek considered to be impossible: an alternative form of organization in which genuine autonomy on the part of the firm is rendered compatible with *ex ante* coordination of economic activities and full use is made of the existing knowledge while losses due to market failures are avoided. Planning and social property render financial speculation almost impossible and substantially reduce the scope of wasteful advertising. *Interventions by the state* are minimized since decisions are

automatically controlled at every stage, and taxation is simple because of egali-tarian income distribution. (1982, p. 208; original emphasis)

Horvat maintained that 'The Yugoslav solution should not be regarded as the end of a process, but rather as a promising beginning in the develop-ment of a genuinely self-governing society' (1982, p. 165). But the Yugoslav experience with self-managed socialism – which has now entered its fifth decade – illustrates anything but Horvat's claims. Let us therefore consider those claims in light of the reality of Yugoslav socialism.

WORKER CONTROL VERSUS PARTY POWER

We begin with the most important point: the democratic, self-managed enterprise as revolutionary vehicle of social control. Supported by Tito's call for 'Factories to the Workers' in 1950, Yugoslavia is considered to be grounded in workers' democratic control of enterprise. The self-managed enterprise is composed of various workers' councils. Communist ideology in Yugoslavia claims that, through democratic processes, workers elect a managing board that oversees and assists in coordinating the enterprise's operation. Workers, in their respective councils, officially manage the 'socially' owned means of production (it is as if they rent capital resources from the state, instead of holding full legal ownership claims). Not forced by the dictates of Stalinist command planning, the Yugoslav constitution allows workers to distribute any enterprise profits as they see fit, whether it be in the form of personal income (over and above the workers' standard wages) or in the form of reinvestment into the enter-prise itself.

The self-managed socialist enterprise is thought to be a relatively auton-omous planning entity, an enterprise of the workers, by the workers, and for the workers. Furthermore, because the worker is also a citizen, because self-managed enterprises follow general planning procedures, such as enter-ing into planning agreements with other enterprises, social councils, and government bureaux, and because this overall process is supposed to rep-resent the best interests of society as a whole, the socialist system of self-managed enterprises is also thought to be a system of society, by society, and for society. The distinction between individual and society becomes, in such a Marxist Utopia, blurred if not outright abandoned.

Hence, Horvat can say that social control is 'maximally effective' and managers have little opportunity to abuse their positions. In actual prac-tice, however, workers have enjoyed far less autonomy and power over deci-sion making than Horvat's theory would have us believe.

The Communist Party in Yugoslavia has managed to maintain a great degree of power within the enterprise. One avenue of power is found in the *aktiv*, which is a crucial link between the enterprise and other socio-political organizations. Organized by Party members who generally hold important positions in those outside organizations, the *aktiv* has a tremendous degree of influence over internal enterprise policy.

The *aktiv* 'assists' the enterprise in helping persuade officials within the local commune, the republic, or within the Party itself to secure bank loans, to attain higher prices for their output, receive construction permits, and so on. But, because it enjoys such a strong position of power, managers within the enterprise have little incentive to resist Party pressure. Enterprise autonomy is thus sacrificed for new permits, loans and licenses, lower prices on scarce inputs, higher output prices, and enhanced foreign exchange allocation, any of which may be necessary for the success of the enterprise (see Lydall, 1986, pp. 115–22).

The typical enterprise in Yugoslavia is riddled both with conflicts of interest and worker apathy. Workers tend to lack real interest in managing the enterprise. In fact, as Egon Neuberger and Estelle James (1973) have argued, the workers would rather not take responsibility for decision making, because decision making is too risky. Good decisions may bring about higher incomes, but they may also bring about greater expectations by the Party and thus greater responsibilities in the future. Moreover, bad decisions hurt immediately. Workers therefore tend to fall into routine. They attend council meetings, but lack initiative to introduce significant dialogue concerning most enterprise matters. The general apathy among enterprise workers further allows the Party, directly or indirectly, to assume control over the elected managerial board. Rather than the ideal of democratic self-management, a technocratic elite has emerged to control enterprise operations.

This is not to say that workers don't become vocal, and fail to bargain or fight for certain issues within the enterprise. Apathetic as they may otherwise be, workers nevertheless have a huge personal interest in the distribution of enterprise profit. Bitter conflicts of interest appear over the issue of how much profit should be handed over to the workers for personal consumption and how much should be ploughed back into the enterprise for investment.

Though the Party would like to see investment increased, workers have little, if any, incentive to invest voluntarily in the socialist enterprise. Eirik Furubotn and Svetozar Pejovich have demonstrated this problem in a number of theoretical and empirical studies (Furubotn and Pejovich, 1970; Pejovich, 1973). Because the Yugoslav worker does not enjoy full ownership rights to the means of production, only the right of use, he is not free to recover any money invested into the enterprise if he leaves the firm or is fired. From the worker's point of view, it is more rational to 'invest' one's personal income in durable goods such as refrigerators, automobiles and furniture – things that are treated as private property under the owner's full control – rather than throw his money into a collectively owned pool that is not at his full disposal.

As a response, the Yugoslav state imposes huge taxes on gross enterprise income and engages in a policy of forced investment. Workers must then strike for higher wages. Strikes for increased wages are not unusual in Yugoslavia. In fact, thousands have occurred in the past few years. This is a source of tremendous embarrassment to Yugoslavia's Communist Party with its self-management rhetoric. If Yugoslavian enterprise really were a 'true' self-managed system as the Party would have us believe, the workers would appear to be striking against themselves!

MARKET SOCIALISM, MONOPOLY AND PRIVILEGE

Horvat claims that the 'labor-managed economy is likely to operate much closer to the textbook model of the competitive market'. This is far from true, nay, it is outright ludicrous in light of the actual Yugoslav experience. The Yugoslav 'market' historically has been plagued by a horrendous lack of entry. Citizens have the legal right to form their own self-managed enterprises, but the compulsory screening of 'Competition Committees' has, in practice, eliminated this form of entry. Instead of new rivals forcing existing firms to lower their costs of production and/or make products of better quality, incumbent firms (generally established by the state) have tended to expand by creating new plants. Curiously, though newly established plants have the right to secede from their founder, they have rarely exercised it and in many cases instead form what amounts to a cartel arrangement with the founding enterprise (Sacks, 1973, ch. 1; Prybyla, 1980, pp. 103–4).

The lack of entry has also brought about, without surprise, a lack of exit. Inefficient, costly enterprises, enterprises that would surely go bankrupt in a true profit-and-loss economy, have typically been supported, like most socialist firms throughout Eastern Europe, through enormous state subsidies. In Yugoslavia, as elsewhere under socialism, enterprise survival depends mostly on political entrepreneurship – the ability to cooperate effectively with the Party – as opposed to the type of managerial adeptness necessary to survive truly competitive markets. Though political entrepreneurship of this sort helps to preserve jobs, it does so at significant cost, including poor quality products, lack of innovation, and an overall decline in economic growth.

PLANNED CHAOS

Horvat stresses that 'social ownership' combines both market and planning; it does not eliminate the market in favor of centralized command planning. I agree with Horvat at least in that, for Yugoslavia, the market has yet to be eliminated. There has been a market for consumer goods that has, in fact, been more open than in other East European countries. But the full benefits of the market process in the means of production and higher order goods are severely restricted by state intervention.

The role of the Party *aktiv* that I mentioned above is one way the state intervenes in the exchange of scarce resources. The bureaucratic obstacle to entry is another. And the fact that the state has engaged in a policy of administrative pricing of scarce resources since 1965 – by fixing the prices of 90 per cent of industrial products – is a third example. Centralized state banking in Yugoslavia, which resorted to printing money in order to subsidize terribly inefficient enterprises, is responsible for Yugoslavia's incredible rate of inflation – which grew from roughly 40 per cent per year in 1981 to over 2000 per cent by 1990 (the money supply grew by more than 9.5 times between 1985 and 1988 alone). Yugoslavia's foreign debt has surpassed $20 billion.

As in the USSR, Yugoslavia's extreme economic hardship has rekindled the fires of nationalism. Slovenia, Yugoslavia's most Western-oriented republic, has threatened to secede. Croatia may soon follow. Ethnic tensions in Kosovo, the troubled province in southern Serbia, are currently pushing Yugoslavia closer to an outright civil war.

Yugoslavia, once hailed as a watershed in market socialism, now stands at the brink of catastrophe. President Stipe Šuvar's (1988) keynote address to the Presidency of the League of Communists in Yugoslavia (LCY) during the 17th Session of the Central Committee meeting in October 1988 is telling:

> The past thirty years, since the adoption of the LCY Program, have been marked by our efforts to emerge from the stage of state socialism. All our efforts, in which milestones have been the LCY Program, the 1965 economic reform, the constitutional reform of 1971–1974, the model for the political system provided at the 11th Congress in Edvard Kardelj's work, *Democracy and Socialism*, the Long-Term Program of Economic Stabilization, and the decisions of the 13th LCY Congress and stands taken at the LCY Conference held in May [1988], have aimed at further elaborating this original model of our revolution and at channeling the organized social energies of our society to realize them. The past three or four decades have seen a life-and-death struggle between state socialism and the forces of self-management waged over the character of production relations and the lines along which they should change. Society developed rapidly, but today all the postponed crises and earlier mistakes have caught up with us,

and society is in the throes of a profound structural crisis. In other words, today's crisis is the culmination of all the social contradictions that have been building up over all these years. In the meantime, considerable confusion has been created in people's minds; there are many ideological misconceptions and illusions, and attempts to cover up the real situation. (1988, pp. 7–8)

The argument put forward by Mises and Hayek – that the attempt to build socialism, even decentralized, democratic market socialism, will be plagued by gross inefficiency, waste, struggles for power and domination, blinding propaganda, and must eventually fail – that very argument applies with profound force to the Yugoslav system. As Šuvar (1988) continues:

> Today's serious crisis in our society is the product of all the crises of yesterday, and for this reason it is all the more severe and disruptive. If there was nationalism in the past, today's nationalism is its consummate expression; if there was bureaucracy in the past, today's bureaucracy is totally hidebound and unproductive; if there was demagoguery and attempts to pull the wool over people's eyes by false promises of homogeneous communities, the examples we see today far exceed anything from the past. In effect, the position of the creative strata of society which have been pushed into the background, and the status of workers, peasants and the vast majority of the intelligentsia are the best gauge of how much power has been concentrated in the hands of bureaucratic and technocratic forces in the past few decades. (1988, p. 8)

THEORY AND PRACTICE

Branko Horvat may have criticism similar to, if not stronger than, that of Stipe Šuvar concerning the way the Yugoslav system of self-managed socialism has worked in practice, especially now that the crisis has become all-consuming. Something, indeed, 'went wrong'. He would argue, I suppose, that in reality the Yugoslav economy needs more market exchange, a certain freeing up of prices, fewer technocrats and less Party pressure in the workplace, and more enterprise control in the hands of the workers.

This is just what the Yugoslavs are desperately trying to achieve in the midst of their present political and economic chaos. They are going even further than that: within the last year they have begun introducing other forms of ownership – private, cooperative, joint, and so on – to compete with socially owned, self-managed firms. They are taking some of the biggest steps in Eastern Europe to promote joint ventures with the West, and are preparing the framework for a unified, open stock market in Yugoslavia. With the traditional ideology of socialist self-management now illegitimate in the minds (and budgets) of the typical Yugoslav citizen, the potential for radical market reform and political pluralism indeed exists.

Without question, Yugoslav reality has failed, terribly, to live up to the theoretical blueprint of self-managed socialism.

This poses a dilemma both to the socialist theoritician and to the statesman. Who was at fault? What went wrong? If it were truly a worker-managed system then the workers are the most likely candidates. But, of course, the crisis is not the workers' responsibility. They are the victims. The ideologue must now consider whether the theory can still be salvaged, in light of its obvious practical failure. This question is reflected in Šuvar's statement at the 17th Session: 'it is high time that we resolve the dilemma of whether this is the result of a crisis of theory and an imperfect system, or whether it is the result of poor implementation and incompetent people'. This, I am sure, will be debated for quite some time among the Yugoslav economists, philosophers, Party members, workers, and citizens.

It also brings up an important point with regard to Horvat's alleged 'solution' to Hayek's analysis. Does the Yugoslav blueprint refute the claim that socialism breeds both statism and inefficiency, and will eventually end in failure? Surely the fundamental problems in the Yugoslav experience were predictable from the Mises–Hayek position. But what of the ideal model itself?

The Austrian economists granted that socialism might 'work' in theory. But that isn't much of a concession, if a concession at all. After all, we can distinguish between good theory and bad theory. Given the appropriate assumptions, perhaps anything might work in theory. It is neither intellectually impossible nor logically contradictory to design an abstract theory which argues that, for instance, a cat could swim the Atlantic Ocean. The important thing is what is likely to happen when the cat is thrown in the water. That's the test. A theory that cannot be tied to successful practice, though perhaps appealing in a purely intellectual or spiritual way, may not only qualify as a bad theory. It may be outright dangerous and inhumane.

Horvat did not answer Hayek. He responded to criticisms with bad theory, with an abstract model that had no potential for being realized through the actions of living men and women. In the meantime, Yugoslavia, once thought to be the epitome of socialist self-management, drowns in what is probably the most disturbing socio-political crisis it has ever faced.

4. Perestroika in Yugoslavia: lessons from four decades of self-management*

We in the West tend to equate perestroika with the whirlwind of economic reforms in the USSR and the Eastern Bloc. But perestroika, as an attempt to fundamentally restructure socialist society, goes back much further. Yugoslavia launched a significant series of reforms beginning in the 1950s. Hungary followed in the late 1960s. The questions were the same then as now: how to decentralize a rigid, bureaucratic, planning apparatus? How to transform state-owned enterprises into efficient, profitable businesses? How to increase worker morale and improve productivity? In short, how could a market-governed economy be introduced without abandoning every aspect of socialism?

The Yugoslavian experience with workers' self-management and market socialism once appealed to its Eastern European neighbors. Western intellectuals called it socialism with a human face. Growth rates were respectable during the 1960s and 1970s, queues for consumer goods were virtually non-existent, particularly in Slovenia and Croatia, the most Western (geographically and culturally) republics of Yugoslavia. Workers were said to enjoy much greater control over enterprise decision making. In other socialist states, workers were herded like cattle by Communist Party authorities in a rigid, command planning structure. Yugoslavia officially recognized the right of self-determination in the socialist enterprise and in most other aspects of life, cultural and scientific. Moreover, Yugoslavia, outside the Iron Curtain, became a symbol and leader of the non-aligned movement.

But the economy came to a halt by 1980. The yearly rate of growth of the gross material product averaged 5.7 per cent from 1970–1980. From 1980–1984 it fell to 0.7 per cent. Labor productivity, which grew at a yearly average of 2.1 per cent from 1970–1980, toppled to –1.7 per cent per annum during the 1980–1984 period (Lydall, 1986, p. 190). Yugoslavia's foreign indebtedness climbed from nearly $12 billion in 1978 to over $20 billion in 1984.[1] Retail price inflation, 13.4 per cent in 1978, surpassed 30

* Originally published in *Global Economic Policy*, **2**(2), 1990, pp. 25–37.

per cent in 1980. By 1987 retail prices were increasing at an annual rate of over 218 per cent.[2]

The thrill was gone.

Yugoslavia's version of privatization, which transformed state-owned enterprises into 'socially' owned firms, managed by workers' councils, which engaged in some degree of market exchange, had failed. Were the workers to blame for the present crisis? If it really were a worker-managed economy, who else should be responsible for the chaos? On the contrary, the problem lay more in the institutional framework of Yugoslav society, specifically the 'market', 'ownership' as defined by the constitution, and the role of the Communist Party:

- The state intervened in markets and set prices. Markets were dominated by monopolies created by a lack of free entry and exit.
- Workers had little, if any, incentive to invest in their enterprises. Social ownership meant their investment could not be recovered nor their shares sold when they left the enterprise.
- A technocratic elite backed indirectly, if not directly, by the Communist Party, typically controlled the enterprise.

Yugoslavia's experience illuminates problems that other socialist economies will face as they attempt to decentralize bureaucratic and managerial decision making. Like Yugoslavia, these countries may also be reluctant to accept the market as a fundamental organizing principle, a constitution founded on a rule of law, and private ownership.

THE TURNING POINT: ORIGINS OF THE YUGOSLAV MODEL

In his widely read book, *Conversations with Stalin*, Milovan Djilas (1962) traced the conflict-ridden relationship between Tito and Stalin, a relationship which began with Tito and his inner circle enraptured by Stalin and ended in a complete, philosophical split. This break would fundamentally influence the course of socialism in Yugoslavia. In the late 1940s Marshal Tito, party leader and government head, and Josef Stalin struggled over the creation of a Communist Party information bureau, the Cominform. Their power struggle was also a bitter personality clash. Stalin was not pleased at Tito's desire to be considered a true leader of the socialist revolution, and grew increasingly reluctant to aid Yugoslavia in its five-year plan. Tito and the party leadership felt that Stalin was attempting to impose his will on Yugoslavia.

Something had to give. Tito's Yugoslavia successfully broke from Soviet authority and the fledgling Cominform in 1948. Tito's new communism was an anti-Stalin, anti-Soviet ideology, which still preserved the Party's role as vanguard of the socialist revolution. This was the dawn of 'workers' self-management', a turn toward worker control and decentralized planning. The Yugoslav Communist Party now maintained that Soviet-style central planning, while perhaps necessary in the past, had become too technocratic and inhumane. Soviet workers were cogs in the bureaucratic machine, tools of party apparatchiks and planning ministries. Soviet workers and citizens saw no sign of the withering away of the Soviet state. In Marxist parlance, the people of the Soviet Union were alienated, no longer by capitalists, but by an all powerful socialist state. Workers were promised a different fate in Yugoslavia.

Yugoslavia's push toward workers' self-management was to mark a new stage in socialist thought and practice. It was, with respect to the USSR and other East European countries, the first attempt to restructure the political and economic relations of a socialist country.[3] Tito and his inner circle argued that the workers, rather than party apparatchiks or state bureaucrats, should manage the socially owned means of production. The Yugoslav ideal was to turn Stalinism on its head by coordinating the socialist society from the bottom up, as opposed to the top down. The Yugoslav Communist Party, later renamed the League of Communists of Yugoslavia, largely to distinguish itself from the Communist Party of its Eastern European and Soviet neighbors, was still responsible for organizing and carrying out the revolution and retained its encompassing power and influence.

Workers were to be organized in democratic councils. According to this blueprint, the councils would base their production on a general plan, itself democratically determined by councils of workers and higher-order councils formed by elected representatives. The internal affairs of the worker-managed enterprise would, ideally, retain a great degree of autonomy from the state. Additionally, though far from being determined in genuinely free markets, prices would still play some role in coordinating the activities among worker-managed enterprises and in measuring the value of outputs. But these are not prices as we know them in capitalist countries. Prices would be used to assess the 'social' value of output, and, hence, could not be determined in a typical free-market setting, but rather through 'agreements' reached between enterprises and higher-level planning bureaux. This typically meant that the Federal Office for Prices and similar planning agencies would either freeze prices at levels consistent with overall macroeconomic goals, or prices would float within a strict range determined by the planning authorities.

Ideally, worker-managers would ultimately decide the best way to produce their products, determine hiring and firing policies, and distribute enterprise 'income' (total enterprise revenue over and above total operating cost, what we call profit). Workers could spend their share of enterprise profit on consumer goods or reinvest it in the enterprise in the hope of receiving higher incomes in the future. This was the general principle of socialist self-management.

This attempt to restructure a rigid, clumsy system of Stalinist central planning took years to complete. And, in many ways, the actual restructuring went both too far and not far enough. Yugoslavia has been caught between extreme economic decentralization and a great degree of political centralization. This tension largely explains the present crisis.

THE EARLY YEARS OF REFORM: 1950–1965

Self-management and economic decentralization were introduced in enterprises in 1950, following the Basic Law on the Management of Economic Enterprises and Higher-Level Economic Associations. Within two years 4600 organizations, most of them state-owned enterprises, had introduced workers' councils. About 90 per cent of those were organizations in which the functions of the workers' council were discharged by all workers. By 1956 almost 6000 organizations were managed by workers' councils.[4]

During this initial stage, the state, not the workers, controlled investment funds. In an effort to direct investment, the state allowed interest rates to vary according to an enterprise's capital needs (capital-intensive firms enjoyed lower rates of interest compared to labor-intensive firms). The interest rates themselves were determined by the centralized state banking system in conjunction with the investment planning bureau. In short, the majority of investments were implemented by state decrees in five-year plans.

THE 1965 REFORMS: MIXED RESULTS OF MARKET SOCIALISM

Self-managed socialism means that workers should control the profits of the enterprise, especially the investment of such profits. The Communist Party officially recognized that right in 1965. These reforms replaced explicit state investment with a self-managed investment policy. Moreover, general, comprehensive planning of all goods and services gave way to relatively free markets for consumer goods. Consumer prices could respond to market pressures within a range set at the republic level.

But the prices of 90 per cent of industrial products were frozen in 1965. The Communist Party argued that this was a necessary, temporary measure to ease the economy toward the market and to ward off possible inflation (Prout, 1985, pp. 164–5). This argument has been made in the past and is currently being made in the USSR, Eastern Europe and China. There is good reason to expect, in a planned economy characterized by shortages, that a sudden leap into free markets would create a substantial rise in prices. But one should also expect, given repeated experiences of this type, that the day rarely comes when the time is politically 'right' to finally free up prices. In Yugoslavia, the state continued to administer prices. Price reform and legitimate markets for resources and intermediate industrial products never really appeared because of the continued threat of inflation.

Moreover, though self-managed investment was now the official policy in Yugoslavia, workers rarely practiced it. The 1965 reform called for 66 per cent of gross revenue to be controlled by workers (for wages and investment), with the remaining 34 per cent to be taxed by the state for public services, health care, housing, and other forms of collective consumption. But this ratio was rarely reached. As much as 45 per cent of gross revenue remained outside the control of workers (through state taxes). Of the 55 per cent in workers' control, 85 to 90 per cent, a strikingly large portion, was allocated to wages alone. Little investment actually took place through the autonomous decisions of worker-managers. Instead, self-managed enterprises developed a form of quasi-external finance where enterprises established banks, and these banks would bail out their own enterprises.[5]

Furthermore, the Yugoslav economy came to be dominated by large, monopolistic firms. A series of laws restricted the ability of citizen groups to create their own self-managed enterprises. Although citizens groups had, on paper, the right to establish new enterprises, they had little actual potential. A maze of bureaucratic red tape, the discretionary authority of local government 'competition committees', and prohibitions on the creation of new enterprises in wholesale trade and intermediate service industries, created a huge and effective barrier. Instead, established firms tended to expand their scale and scope of operation by establishing new plants within the existing enterprise. A 1965 law allowed new plants formally to secede from the founder, on approval of the workers' council of the founding enterprise. However, this rarely happened. Rather than try to survive on their own, new plants would often retain formal ties with the founder while enjoying a degree of practical independence. The relationship between these plants and the founding enterprise had more the character of a cartel (Sacks, 1973). Markets in Yugoslavia were thus rarely, if ever, open and competitive.

A 1968 constitutional amendment called for further decentralization and gave workers' councils the right to decide all forms of intra- and inter-enterprise relations by direct vote. In an attempt to encourage managerial initiative and enterprise autonomy, enterprises were given greater flexibility in determining their internal organization and managing boards. While the amendment appeared promising on paper, and accorded well with humanistic Marxist rhetoric, it actually took power from the workers. In practice, existing influential groups were able to become a technocratic managerial elite and power shifted all the more toward the top of the enterprise and the managing boards. Instead of decentralized, democratic firms managed by workers, Yugoslavia's experiment in self-management had led to a *de facto* ruling elite, a Yugoslav nomenklatura, and Communist Party control.[6]

THE 1974 YUGOSLAV CONSTITUTION: UTOPIAN BUT FLAWED

Left-wing critics of the 1968 reform called for true self-management in the enterprise and regulation of existing markets even though the markets were anything but competitive. Their longing for the ideal of a truly cooperative, democratically organized and comprehensively planned society seems to have played right into the hands of the League of Communists of Yugoslavia. The Party sought to retain, if not increase, its political power, but needed the legitimacy to do so.

That legitimacy appeared in the 1974 Constitution of Yugoslavia, a tome of 406 articles. It was to be the blueprint of 'integrated' self-management not only for business but education, the sciences, culture and the arts too. Yugoslavia was to be organized around democratically formed workers' councils and citizens' councils concerned with the social and cultural programs. Social and economic planning was to take place from the bottom up through the interaction of autonomous councils, a reverse of Soviet-style command planning. Remnants of a bureaucratic state were to wither away. Politics and economics would then, as Marx had anticipated, merge into one activity.

The 1974 Constitution and the 1976 Act of Associated Labor are truly utopian in nature. The legislation would establish an 'agreement economy', where all economic decision making would be at once democratic, decentralized, and comprehensively coordinated. Both the 'anarchy' of markets and 'technocracy' of actual enterprise management were, at long last, to be replaced by true worker participation.

But the Communist Party would not yet allow itself to disappear. The Constitution empowered the Party to intervene in any conflicts of interest during the difficult transition to a fully implemented agreement economy. Just how it was to do this was unclear.

REAFFIRMATION OF SOCIAL OWNERSHIP AND SOCIAL PLANNING

The 1974 Constitution maintains that private ownership of the means of production is 'alienating' to workers, as is state ownership in Stalin-type command planning. 'Social' ownership replaced both. It is a legal category thought to be most consistent with comprehensive, democratic planning. But social ownership has proven to be a vague, if not meaningless, constitutional category. If everybody in society owns the means of production, then nobody owns the means of production. If nobody owns the means of production, then apparently, there can be no ground for exploitation and alienation. But can the rule of non-ownership bring about a prosperous, orderly society?

Today the Yugoslavs themselves, from academicians to Party officials to worker-managers, admit that they never really understood the meaning of 'social ownership'.

With such a strange notion of ownership, the 1974 Constitution had to redefine the political–economic unit in Yugoslav society and create the Basic Organization of Associated Labor (BOAL). The notion and role of the BOAL is articulated at tremendous length in the 1976 Act of Associated Labor, itself some 500 articles. The basic idea of the BOAL is rather simple. The BOAL is an association of workers who share common tasks within a given self-managed firm. Members of a BOAL would decide upon their specific tasks in a democratic manner; the various BOALs within the enterprise must then coordinate their activities and responsibilities by democratically forming compacts.

The enterprise itself would be radically decentralized and democratically planned from the bottom up. Each self-managed enterprise would then enter into contractual agreements with other self-managed enterprises and self-management 'communities of interest'. Each BOAL within a given enterprise would elect a delegation, based on the size of its workforce. Each BOAL delegation, in turn, would elect enterprise representatives to a larger commune, the Council of Associated Labor, which was the formal link between the self-managed enterprises and the state.

In short, the economy was to be organized with the BOAL as its most basic planning unit. All economic decisions, from the securing of scarce resources to the delivery of final outputs, would be determined democratically by direct votes of the workers or agreements established by elected representatives of workers and workers' councils. On a political level, self-managed communities of interest would be formed through contracts among work organizations and other organizations to ensure that production activities fit the 'best interest of society'.

The 1974 Constitution was nothing less than a utopian blueprint of decentralized socialism. On paper, it created a democratic and integrated, planned society. Decision making would be delegated from the lower units upward – from workers' councils up to delegates from the seven republics.

This political and economic federalism would be the mirror image of Stalin's centralized, command planning. Did it work? No.

LIMITS OF THE REFORMS

The 1974 Constitution fragmented the Yugoslav economy by establishing a meaningless notion of property and by creating arbitrary, excessively decentralized units. Conflicts arose frequently even in enterprises that had been subdivided into only a few BOALs.

Ellen Comisso's (1979, chs 7–9) brilliant study of a machine tool plant in Zagreb is a case in point. The enterprise employed 528 workers divided into three BOALs. BOAL I encompassed the production division, consisting of workers in the main plant, technicians, and their respective supervisors, totaling 282 people. The production/service division formed BOAL II and consisted of 135 people who serviced and repaired plant equipment. The collective services division, involved with finance, sales, personnel, research and development, and legal and general services, formed BOAL III, and included 110 people. Each BOAL had its own council. But the responsibilities and jurisdiction of these councils were poorly defined and led to many conflicts. Should BOAL II, for example, be held at least partly responsible if its members could not repair plant equipment, because the state failed to deliver parts? How should this affect workers' wages? This last question leads to the major source of conflict in existing self-managed firms: the distribution of income. Decisions on allocation of wages, profits, and collective funds often resulted in heated discussions, conflicts of interest, and deterioration in worker morale.

The problem was compounded in large industrial enterprises, which could have dozens of BOALs. These organizational complexities, coupled with a lack of interest in market mechanisms, made it virtually impossible for BOALs to reach agreements that fostered economic growth and efficiency.

Within four years of the 1974 reforms, there were over 19000 BOALs, over 4100 work communities of organizations of associated labor, and over 6800 self-management communities of interest. By 1984, more than 122000 organizations and communities were struggling to manage the economy.[7]

As more and more enterprises were carved up into arbitrary units, the present crisis of Yugoslavia became all too apparent.

In Yugoslavia's case, economic decentralization brought in its wake only economic chaos. The present constitution is a vague, incomprehensible, irrational design for society, a blueprint which, while striving to promote harmony, solidarity, and economic prosperity, has unintentionally created factionalism, apathy and disorder.

In summary, there are at least three fundamental problems endemic to the Yugoslav economy.

Lack of Market Knowledge

Worker-managers were expected to operate enterprises efficiently without a genuine, competitive market for capital goods and scarce resources. Without free markets and prices, enterprises could not determine the true cost of goods. A democratic, decentralized socialist society may be in principle and on paper more appealing than a dictatorship of central planning bureaux. But without prices that reflect underlying economic scarcities, economic chaos is always imminent. Both theory and the Yugoslav experience bear this out.

Lack of Investment Incentives

Workers have little, if any, incentive to invest in the enterprises they manage, because they do not have the right to recover their investment when they leave the firm. They retain property rights in net income, but not in net worth, and therefore are only allowed to enjoy their share of enterprise revenues as long as they continue to work in that enterprise. Any personal income that a worker reinvests in the firm will be forfeited if the worker retires, quits, or is fired. Moreover, expecting workers to reinvest significant portions of their income in the same managed investment is not an attractive financial decision from the worker's point of view.

State-guided investment through various taxation schemes, monetary expansion and subsidies has become the rule. Such investment seems to contradict the ideal of workers' self-management and encourages political lobbying for scarce financial capital. This political process wastes resources and rarely encourages economic efficiency.[8]

Decision Making Retained by Party

Decision making was, on paper, decentralized within the enterprise as well as from the federal to the republican level. But arbitrary and excessive economic decentralization within the enterprise allowed the League of Communists in Yugoslavia to retain, if not strengthen, its power over the enterprise. Party members formed the activist core within the enterprise BOALs.[9] Splitting enterprises into arbitrary councils and forcing them to plan according to self-managing agreements did not improve the lot of the typical worker. Rather, workers tended to fight amongst themselves over income distribution. Party members retained a great deal of influence, if not outright control, over most other matters related to enterprise control.

These three problems stem, at least in part, from the vague notion of 'social ownership,' where society, and thus nobody in particular, enjoys full ownership of scarce resources and capital goods. Yugoslavia's experiment shows that neither incentives, nor morale, nor productivity are likely to be enhanced by giving workers a stake in the production process. This is particularly true when the means of production are owned by 'society' at large, not by individual workers or private entrepreneurs who cooperate and compete in a genuine market process.

WHAT'S NEXT?

By the late 1980s it became apparent that Yugoslav self-management was a failed Utopia. Yugoslavia's rate of inflation approached 2000 per cent by December of 1989. From January to December 1989, the currency collapsed from 3000 dinars to the dollar to over 120000 dinars to the dollar. This extreme economic instability has rekindled the fires of nationalism, which, in turn, has created greater strains within the Party. Last fall the Slovenes voiced their constitutional right to secede. Though they haven't done so yet, they did manage to break from the League of Communists of Yugoslavia and introduce political pluralism in the republic. By 22 January 1990, prompted largely by the fate of Nicolae Ceausescu, the deposed and executed president of Romania, the Party voted to give up its own 45-year monopoly on power and introduce political pluralism throughout the federal level of Yugoslavia.

Yugoslavia has engaged in nearly continuous reform since the 1950s. Can we expect much from the next wave of constitutional reform? Although a new constitution is in the works, Yugoslavs are still grappling with basic social units. The 1974 Constitution, which created the Basic Organization of Associated Labor as the primary unit in Yugoslav society, unintentionally created disastrous results. The typical citizen-worker, who initially supported socialist self-management, no longer does. In an attempt to pull the country out of its growing crisis, the Party adopted an amendment to the 1974 constitution, effective 1 January 1989, which defines the enterprise as the new relevant unit in society. This move, which holds little promise in itself, calls for private, cooperative, joint, and state ownership, in addition to social ownership. Just how enterprises will be transformed on this basis is still unclear. In addition, plans have been introduced for the creation of a stock market.

A November 1988 amendment officially recognized the workers' right to strike: thousands of strikes have taken place before and after this amendment. This raises an embarrassing question for self-managed firms. Whom are the workers striking against? Themselves? The enterprise? The state?

This spells the 'end' of self-management in Yugoslavia. Indeed, I question the extent to which there ever was self-management. Much of the rhetoric and ideology of self-management did, however, serve the interests of the Party through four decades. Now this is changing. The grip of the Party is loosening. The Yugoslav peoples have realized that an overhaul of the system is necessary to pull them out of their crisis.

Ante Marković, Yugoslavia's prime minister, has managed to curb inflation through a tight monetary policy, a comprehensive freeze on wages and the pegging of the Yugoslav dinar to the West German mark. Consumer prices, which rose 60 per cent during December 1989 alone, rose only 4 per cent in the month of April. Foreign exchange reserves have also been increased to $8.5 billion by the end of May and are expected to total $10 billion by the end of 1990. A decree on 1 January 1989 has opened the door for foreign investment and joint ownership, which allows foreign investors and their domestic partners to contract for an unlimited period. Moreover, foreign investors have the right to manage or participate in managing enterprises based on the value of their invested funds. Shares are transferable. Foreign capital has yet, however, to race into Yugoslavia. It appears that potential investors are taking a 'wait-and-see' approach. Yugoslavia, much like the USSR, has been riddled with increasing ethnic tension in the past several months, tension that has pushed the country to the brink of civil war.

The Yugoslav reform experience over the past four decades should humble proponents of market-socialism. Economic decentralization is not enough. At the risk of stating the obvious, fundamental political and economic reforms are inseparable. A political and economic system must ground itself in the rule of law and recognize the individual as the fundamental unit in society. As they embark upon their own individual experiments with decentralization, it would be wise for the USSR and the other highly centralized Eastern European countries, particularly Bulgaria, Romania, and Czechoslovakia, to heed Yugoslavia's past experience with socialist reform. That would surely reduce the likelihood of yet another perestroika gone sour.

NOTES

1. *Statistical Pocket-Book of Yugoslavia*, Belgrade: Federal Statistical Office, 1989, p. 69.
2. *Jugoslavija 1918–1988: Statistički Godišnjak*, Belgrade: Federal Statistical Office, 1989, p. 158.
3. It was not until two decades later, in 1968, that another East European country, Hungary, would embark upon significant economic reform, with the introduction of its 'New Economic Mechanism'. Though it did not go so far as to implement workers' control, Hungary's New Economic Mechanism tried to foster fundamental economic decentralization and increased autonomy of state-owned enterprises by eliminating most directives on what firms should produce, by sharing investment decisions among planners, banks, and the enterprises, and by officially allowing markets to coordinate enterprise activities on the basis of profit–loss accounting. The reform, on paper, appeared promising. The results have been poor, as is true of the Yugoslav experience. The market was never allowed to work. For an overview of the Hungarian experience, see Prybyla (1980) and Kornai (1980).
4. According to official statistics as given in *Yugoslavia 1945–1985: Statistical Review*, Belgrade: Federal Statistical Office, 1986, p. 32.
5. These statistics were presented by Ivo Bičanić (1989). The incentives of workers to allocate enterprise income in the form of personal wages, rather than reinvest it in the enterprise, have been well documented in a number of theoretical and empirical studies by Eirik Furubotn and Svetozar Pejovich. See, for example, Furubotn and Pejovich (1970).
6. The following empirical studies, among others, helped pierce the veil of self-management rhetoric and expose the contradiction between the ideology of decentralization and worker control and the practice of technocratic hierarchy and Party control of enterprise: Županov (1978a, 1978b), Rus (1978).
7. *Yugoslavia 1945–1985: Statistical Overview*, pp. 29–30.
8. The federal regional development fund is a case in point. It is a compulsory method of transferring a portion of the gross revenue of relatively successful enterprises in one republic to develop enterprises in another republic (allocated as preferential credits with low interest and/or longer periods of repayment). Slovenia and Croatia, the two republics which have historically permitted a greater use of the market than their Eastern and Southern neighbors, have enjoyed the highest rates of per capita income. But much of the gross revenue of these Western-style enterprises is taxed away to support the preferential credits given to Montenegro and Serbia's autonomous province of Kosovo.
9. As Laura Tyson (1980, p. 8) remarks, the 1974 Constitution restored power to the Party so that it would become 'the final authority over all decision makers'. For the specific role of the Party in the BOALs and work organizations, see the empirical study by V. Goati, et al. (1985).

5. Marxisms and market processes*

Critics of the Austrian School appeared in many forms, from Schmollerian historicists and Veblenian institutionalists to Keynesian interventionists. Compared to their traditional rivals, Austrians seem furthest removed from Marxism on almost any level we wish to compare. For instance, Austrian methodology is deductive, Marxism's is dialectical. The Austrians developed a radically subjective theory of value, while Marxians, with their own unique twists, followed Ricardo's labor theory of value. Austrians champion the capitalist market system and claim the impossibility of socialist planning. Marxians championed socialist planning, and claimed the death of capitalism.

The differences between Marxians and Austrians are almost too obvious to list. This chapter has a different task: it will explore some of the contemporary Austrian (and non-Austrian) interpretations of Marxian socialism to suggest to younger Austrians that something might be gained by picking through the rubble that characterizes the crisis in contemporary Marxism.

MARX AND THE UTOPIANS

Socialism is by no means a homogeneous movement (see Wright, 1986). There are as many visions of socialism as there are socialists, maybe even more. Marx, in his criticism of Saint-Simon, Fourier, Owen, and their disciples, ushered in a self-proclaimed 'scientific' (as opposed to 'utopian') socialism. Rather than design a detailed blueprint of some imaginary socialist community, and try to convince well-meaning bourgeois types that socialism can be the best of all possible worlds (a practice the utopians were inclined to do – and fail at), Marx would instead thrust forward a radical criticism of capitalism, and from it demonstrate socialism's inevitability.

Marx focused on the organizational principles that structure capitalist and pre-capitalist societies; in this way he may be interpreted as an originator of comparative economic systems analysis. Marx conceived of three

* Originally published in Peter J. Boettke (ed.), *The Elgar Companion to Austrian Economics*, Aldershot: Edward Elgar Publishing, 1994

categorically distinct ways to organize society (either through Tradition, Market or Plan), and claimed that conflicts of interest and structural contradictions of the modern Market system (capitalism) must eventually lead to its demise. An entirely different system – socialist planning – would unfold, ending the class struggle and alienation.

Perhaps the key difference between Marx and the earlier utopian socialists was this: Marx tried to ground his criticism of capitalism in an exhausting analysis of its 'base' – the commodity mode of production and the circulation of capital. Hence, while the utopians attacked the morality of capitalism, and offered intricately detailed blueprints of some future socialist alternative, Marx focused on capitalism as an organizational system first, and argued that the moral/legal/religious dimension (what he called the 'superstructure') cannot be understood separately from capitalism's economic base. Thus, Marx believed the utopians were wasting their time (and stunting the revolution) by ululating over the immorality of capitalist institutions such as profit seeking, wage labor and private property. Without an adequate (indeed, for Marx, 'scientific') analysis of the structure of capitalist economic organization, the utopians failed to pierce capitalism's ideological veil; rather than exposing the alleged 'Laws of History' (such as the necessity of the class struggle and the revolutionary potential of the proletariat), the utopians dreamed of phalansteries, New Harmonies, and oceans brimming with lemonade.

Marx resisted the utopian temptation to write 'recipes for the cookshops of the future'. He meant this literally. After all, Fourier *did* provide details on food preparation and kitchen table management for the future socialist society. Marx also meant it metaphorically. He would rather focus on the contradictions of capitalism and let the implications for socialism speak for themselves.

But followers of Marx, and critics alike, have disagreed on just what, or how much, Marx has to say about socialism. We can identify at least three interpretations that may be of interest to Austrian economists: an orthodox interpretation, an organizational–economistic interpretation of Marx (as an advocate of centralized, command planning), and a philosophical–humanistic interpretation of Marx (as an advocate of decentralized, self-managed socialism).

THE ORTHODOX INTERPRETATION OF MARX

The orthodox interpretation suggests that Marx – a furious critic of utopian socialism – was necessarily silent on the topic of socialist economic organization. He instead left it up to his followers to decide all the difficult details. In this view, Marx offered a radical criticism of capitalism, but no vision of fully evolved socialism. For instance, the leading soviet economic historian, Alec Nove, supports the orthodox interpretation when he writes that 'Marx had little to say about the economics of socialism, and . . . the little he did say was either irrelevant or directly misleading' (1983, p. 10). Nove applied the orthodox view to interpret the early Soviet experiment with socialism (during the so-called 'War Communism' period from 1918–1921) as 'forced reaction to an emergency situation' (Nove, 1969), rather than a revolutionary attempt to plan inspired by Marx's vision of socialism. Contemporary Austrians in general have not subscribed to the orthodox view.

MARX AS AN ORGANIZATION THEORIST

A second interpretation of Marx, which claims Marx is an organization theorist who necessarily advocates central planning, stems from a criticism of the orthodox view. Economists Paul Craig Roberts and Matthew Stephenson, and Austrians Don Lavoie and Peter Boettke, argue that Marx's assault on the organizational 'anarchy' of the market process suggests definite, consistent implications for the socialist economy, and thus Marx's overall research program and revolutionary agenda cannot be understood without this organizational interpretation. Boettke claims, for example, that

> Viewing Marx as an organization theorist enables the student of Marx to see a tremendous unity in Marx's life-work that is denied by those who wish to split Marx into a young Marx and a mature Marx. The young Marx, just as the mature Marx, was concerned with transcending the organizational form of alienation, that is, the commodity production of capitalist social relations. (1990, p. 44, n. 29)

Lavoie claims that 'Marx's scientific socialism was not merely an excuse for avoiding any examination of socialist society. It was a recommendation of a particular method for the conduct of such an examination – that is, that socialism be described through a systematic critique of capitalism' (1985b, p. 29). He further contends that 'there is implicit throughout Marx's writings a single, coherent, and remarkably consistent view of socialism' (1985b, p. 30) – namely, economic planning – which 'Marx consistently foresaw . . . as centralized and comprehensive' (1985a, p. 19). Roberts and Stephenson contend that, indeed, central planning constitutes the 'defining characteristic of Marxian socialism' (1973, p. 94).

This theme – that Marxism ultimately strives for centralized economic planning – is common in the Austrian comparative systems literature. Their well known argument that central planning must fail due to a severe lack of knowledge confronting the central planners need not be repeated here (see Lavoie, 1985b). More recently, viewing Marxism as promoting central, command planning has prompted a revisionist account of the War Communism era immediately following the Bolshevik Revolution. Contrary to Nove and other Soviet historians, Roberts (1971) and Boettke (1990) have demonstrated that Lenin and the Bolsheviks tried to plan the fledgling Soviet economy centrally in order to revolutionize Russia and create socialism, and thus the failure of War Communism in 1921 was, in effect, a failure of Marxian socialism.

MARX AS A PRAXIS PHILOSOPHER

A third interpretation of Marx emphasizes his philosophical–humanistic dimension, as opposed to the dialectical materialism of the orthodoxy, or the organizational interpretation of the Austrians. Here, the focus is upon Marx's praxis philosophy and his corresponding notion of alienation. Writers in this tradition – most notably the Yugoslav Praxis Group (see Marković and Petrović, 1979), fellow travelers Karel Kosik (1976) and Erich Fromm (1961), and contemporary economists such as Branko Horvat (1982) – do agree that Marx's critique of capitalism offers a vision of socialism. But they disagree that his vision must be one of centralized command planning. Contrary to the organization-theory interpretation, they argue that central planning does not abolish alienation, but in fact may intensify it.

This is curious because both the organizational interpreters of Marx and the praxis interpreters claim to draw their conclusions from Marx's concept of alienation. Boettke claims, for instance, that 'The transcendence of alienation means to Marx the transcendence of market relations' (1990, p. 44, n. 29); Roberts emphasizes this point: 'in the Marxian scheme, central economic planning eliminates *Marxian* alienation by eliminating the exchange relationships of commodity production' (1971, p. 10). The praxis interpretation claims that abolishing the market system constitutes a necessary, but not sufficient, condition for de-alienation.

In other words, the organization-theory interpretation tends to limit alienation to its economic dimension, while the praxis philosophy interpretation focuses on Marx's concept of praxis as a totality: as Kosik writes, 'In the concept of praxis, socio-human reality is discovered as the opposite of giveness, i.e. at once as the process of forming human *being* and as its specific form. *Praxis* is the *sphere of human being*' (1976, p. 136). To say that a human is a praxis-being is to say that he or she has the potential to be a free, creative being – to participate democratically with others and rationally design, create, and control society. To be alienated, then, means that, for whatever reason, our praxis potential is blocked. By definition, alienation is the gap between human essence and human existence (Horvat, 1982, p. 84). For Marx people are alienated under the 'anarchy' of the market system. (This is clear in his *The Economic and Philosophic Manuscript of 1844* (1964).) But Marx also attacks political alienation that results from bureaucratic hierarchy and control. He writes in the *Critique of Hegel's 'Philisophy of Right'* (1970), for example, that 'in true democracy the *political state disappears*' (1970, p. 118). As long as the modern bureaucratic state exists, it is separated from civil society with a hierarchy of knowledge and control. Under the state 'Man's content is not taken to be his true actuality' (1970, p. 82).

According to the praxis philosophy interpretation, the implications for socialism are clear: 'Man is not only what he has been; he is in the first place what he can and ought to be', writes Gajo Petrović. 'Marx's turn to praxis follows from this in the sense that his conception of man cannot remain a mere conception, but it is also a criticism of alienated man who does not realize his human possibilities and a humanistic program of struggle for humanness.' Hence, it necessarily follows that 'Marx's conception of man can thus not be separated from his humanistic theory of alienation and de-alienation' (1967, pp. 80–1). Full-fledged socialism is supposed to end alienation, whether economic or political; it is supposed to end the contradiction between human existence and essence. As Marx wrote, socialism would inevitably 'return man to himself' (1964, p. 135).

From this purely philosophical analysis, socialism would abolish both the anarchy of the market process and the hierarchy of the political structure. Abolishing the market in favor of despotic, command planning would merely replace many competing capitalist despots with a universal despot (the central planning board) that dictates the plan to the rest of society. Full de-alienation would require abolishing the market in favor of a *comprehensive yet decentralized* plan – a council-based, non-hierarchical planning network – grounded in radical democracy and self-management (see Marković, 1974).

WHICH MARX? (AND WHY AUSTRIANS MIGHT WANT TO CARE)

It is reasonable to believe, contrary to the orthodoxy, that Marx's scientific socialism offered some direction for socialism. Both the organization theory and praxis philosophy interpretations provide scholarly evidence of this, but we run the risk of making an exegetical mistake if we focus on one interpretation while ignoring the other. The organization theory approach, by itself, offers only an 'economistic' understanding of Marxian socialism – it deduces the economic logic of abolishing the market process, but at the cost of ignoring the praxis benchmark. Surely, organizational analysis is fruitful because it suggests that comprehensive planning must collapse into hierarchical centralism in the face of information scarcities and conflicts of interest (see Hayek, 1944; Prychitko, 1988). But that in itself does not mean central planning was an aspiration, let alone a 'defining' characteristic, of full-fledged Marxian socialism. Although the work of Roberts and Stephenson, for example, actually claims to comprehend the meaning of Marxian alienation, it is questionable because they ignore Marx's praxis concept, the fulcrum upon which the entire alienation issue rests. On the other hand, the praxis-philosophy interpretation, by itself, is much too 'philosophistic' – from the praxis benchmark it deduces a theory of alienation and de-alienation, which suggests an end to markets and hierarchies. It provides a nice *gedankenexperiment* which describes the parameters of a de-alienated, socialist society, but that society is dubious because it ignores organization theory and economic logic; the praxis-philosophy interpretation fails to comprehend the unintended consequences of decentralized planning.

Isolated, each interpretation tends to claim that Marx has a consistent, coherent vision of socialism. Yet, the visions contradict each other. This is a hermeneutical problem. Organization theory ignores the full implications of Marx's turn to praxis; praxis philosophy ignores the unintended organizational consequences of abolishing the market process in a world of scarcity. Both the organizational interpretation and the philosophical interpretation might instead shed more light on our understanding of Marx when juxtaposed. Each arguably represents two sides of a tension, a conflict, or struggle, in Marx's vision of socialism (see Prychitko, 1991). Perhaps Marx's vision of socialism is not nearly as coherent as we once thought.

This may interest more than historians of thought. It may also affect the way Austrians interpret the historical record. For instance, problematizing Marx's vision of socialism suggests three counterintuitive examples, upon which we shall conclude: (1) if central planning is ultimately inconsistent with Marxian *de*-alienation, then the failure of command planning would not *necessarily* establish a failure to implement Marxian socialism – for that is not its defining characteristic; conversely, (2) any theoretical (or practical) model of socialist planning that requires hierarchical centralization to work successfully represents a theoretical (or practical) *failure* to achieve

Marx's fully de-alienated Utopia (for instance, even if Lenin or Stalin centrally planned the USSR successfully, Marxism would still be a flop); and (3) if the Austrians are correct in arguing that the market *process* cannot be abolished in favor of rational economic planning – that the market system is here to stay – we are not 'stuck' with alienation. If comprehensive planning is humanly impossible, then Marx's claim that we are beings of praxis, whose essence is freely and creatively to design the society we live in, is patently false. If the achievable, as Marx saw it, is epistemologically unachievable, the gap disappears and *Marxian* alienation simply ceases to be.

6. Marx, postmodernism and self-management: reply to Abell*

I used the word 'post-modern' once in *Marxism and Workers' Self-Management. The Essential Tension* (Prychitko, 1991), in the Introduction. What a mistake. I hadn't realized it was open season, and that I'd possibly catch the attention of trigger-happy anti-postmodernists.

Peter Abell (1995) is skeptical of postmodernism, and he seems on the prowl, at least in this review, to expose the follies of post-modern philosophy as related to self-management, his area of expertise. He seizes on that one word, also notes my 'flirtation with a number of post-something or others' (1995, p. 342) (I used the words 'post-Marxist' and 'post-industrial' once each), and unfortunately charges after the wrong animal. Having only been grazed, I'd like to respond to Abell so that this doesn't become a real nuisance.

INTERPRETING MARX: FROM MODERN AND POST-MODERN TO UNITY AND TENSION

The first sentence of Abell's review reads: 'the time has come for a post-modern interpretation of Marx, one that helps explain the limits to his rational humanism' (1995, p. 341). This is supposed to be a quotation from my book, but I myself wrote: 'The time has come for a *post*-modern interpretation of Marx, one that helps explain the limits to his radical humanism' (Prychitko, 1991, xiii). The emphasis was in the original passage. So was the word 'radical' (not 'rational').

Abell casts me as some kind of postmodernist and antirationalist, but he makes two mistakes here: he misquotes and misrepresents me. Although I might now be charged with offering a number of mis-something or others, the misquoted statement raises the different issues of how we should interpret Marx, and where self-management fits in.

I claimed that there prevails a common (though by no means undisputed) interpretation of Marx, one that stresses an overall unity in his writings. I

* Originally published in *Critical Review*, **11**(2), 1997, pp. 301–10.

called this the 'modern' interpretation of Marx (Prychitko, 1991, xiii). In the modern view of Marx, there is no bifurcation between the young and the mature Marx, between the Marx of the 1844 Manuscripts and the Marx of the later writings, between Marx the philosopher and Marx the political economist. Throughout Marx's life work, according to the modern view, there unfolds a unified critique of capitalism and an implied vision of socialism. I tried to discuss what I see as a serious problem with this interpretation: the 'unity' thesis is defended by two heterogeneous groups of scholars; there are two different and in fact quite opposite sides to the unity thesis, which taken together, amount to a tension, evident in Marx's own work and in Yugoslav practice.

In Chapter 2 of my earlier book I discussed this tension in Marx (Prychitko, 1991, pp. 14–32). Contemporary Austrian economists such as Don Lavoie and Peter Boettke (familiar names to *Critical Review* readers) borrow from Paul Craig Roberts' and Matthew Stephenson's earlier arguments, which claim that Marx's work amounts to a remarkably unified and coherent case for hierarchical central planning, such as the command-planning and material balances models of Soviet socialism. The organizational requirements of a non-alienated socialist society dictate central economic planning; Marx, therefore, advocates (or envisions) a final socialist system planned from a single controlling center.[1]

The Yugoslav praxis philosophers, most notably Mihailo Marković and Gajo Petrović (and we could add Zagorka Golubović, Rudi Supek, and a host of others) interpret Marx's unity differently. To them, Marx's critique of capitalist alienation stems from a foundation in praxis philosophy, and that, in turn, leads us to envision socialism as, yes, comprehensively planned, but also radically democratic and self-managed. If so, Marx could not advocate the kind of centralized planning that Roberts and Stephenson lead us to believe he did; command planning would collapse a thousand and one competing capitalists into one *universal* capitalist: the central planning board. Alienation wouldn't dissipate, let alone disappear, in a Soviet-style model economy. In fact, it could become even more damaging.[2]

To the extent that it claims unity in Marx, the 'modern' view nevertheless struggles with two opposing sides. Each side claims that Marx's vision calls for socialism to be comprehensively planned. But (and here I'll state it even more clearly than I did in the book), each side calls for an opposite planning *method:* Roberts and Stephenson see Marxian socialism as necessarily centrally planned, while the Praxis Group sees it as necessarily decentralized and self-managed. These two methods are antithetical: central command-planning procedures can't be reconciled with socialist self-management.

Each side offers good arguments for its interpretation of Marx but, as far as I can tell, each seems unaware of the other. I suggested the time was right for a '*post*-modern' interpretation that exposes this tension in Marx: the Praxis philosophers are right in their claim that central economic planning would not eliminate alienation, and yet the economists are right in their claim that the organizational consequences of destroying market exchange could theoretically tend toward (but ultimately never fully achieve, due to knowledge problems) centralized command-based planning procedures. I attempted to bring both sides to light, and thereby expose a corresponding tension. I devoted Chapter 5 of my book to discussing how this tension sheds light on the contradictions in the contemporary theory of self-managed socialism (particularly Branko Horvat's model) and in Yugoslav practice, especially during Yugoslavia's attempt to implement its 1974 Constitution and the corresponding 1976 Act on Associated Labor.

Although Abell *seems* aware of my purpose (1995, p. 342), he shoots blindly when he writes that he is 'uneasy with lines of argument which purport to break with the canons of rational discourse'. Perhaps a postmodernist would try to break from the canons of rational discourse; I myself don't know. I haven't read many of them, and I don't purport to be one. (If Abell were sincere in his belief that I espoused irrationalism, his review should have tried to show how I *failed* to be irrationalist – how even Prychitko's [alleged] postmodernism cannot help but engage in rational discourse.)

The difference one word makes. But I must admit that I learned from Abell's pot shots, and in fact I thank him for it: I could have avoided confusing Abell (and perhaps others) if I had simply relied on the terms 'unity' versus 'tension' in Marx, rather than suggesting a 'modern' and 'postmodern' interpretive taxonomy.[3]

SELF-MANAGED SOCIALISM

In his abstract, Abell writes: 'Prychitko claims that by examining the humanist side of Marx, a socialist case can be made for both the LMF [labor managed firm] and markets in a postmodern world. Such a case rests upon an assumption that self-management confers competitive advantage by enhancing information sharing (increasingly important in postmodern conditions). The case, though interesting, is not yet made' (1995, p. 341). Elsewhere he states that mine is a 'salvage operation' (1995, p. 343) for the humanistic Marx.

Abell misunderstands my argument. I tried to take Marx (and the Praxis Group) seriously, not for the sake of salvaging any of them, but rather to assess the strengths and weaknesses of the economists' 'unity' thesis *and* to understand the Yugoslavs' call for self-managed socialism, which was rooted in their Marxist critique of Stalinism.[4] There was, admittedly, much untangling to do here, and even a careful reader or two might get confused.

Turning to Abell's claims: I don't argue that the humanistic side of Marx offers a socialist case for labor-managed firms and markets, in a post-modern or any other kind of world. I do claim that Marx's humanism (praxis philosophy) suggests that the ideal socialist system would be composed of democratic, labor-managed firms fully integrated through a comprehensive plan that is at once democratic, decentralized, and self-managed. Any and all markets would be *abolished* through the *ex ante* coordination embodied in a comprehensive plan (Prychitko, 1991, pp. 20–22). I thought I made my own stance clear when I summarized:

> From the praxis benchmark, the market system apparently created a gap between human existence and human essence. Praxis allows critics to condemn the market system *in toto*, to demand the abolition, the *aufhebung*, of the spontaneous market process in favor of democratic, fully participatory planning.
>
> In practice, however, revolutionary praxis has led to nothing short of chaos and disorder. We are not praxis beings in Marx's sense of the term. Part of what it means to be a human is to live within social institutions (most notably the market process) that have evolved as the unintended, undesigned outcomes of human action. To abolish the market system would be to destroy the *raison d'être* of advanced civilization. (1991, p. 118)

So, when Abell wonders how my discussion in the rest of the book (on the socialist calculation debate, the neoclassical debate over the feasibility of workers' self-management, Yugoslav self-managed socialism, and the American experience in successful self-managed firms) could 'amount to a validation of Marx's defense of praxis and self-realization' (1995, p. 343), I have one answer: I had no interest in validating Marx. In fact, I strove to draw the Austrian argument into new territory, that of self-managed (rather than centrally planned) socialism, a place where Austrian economists had yet to venture. Of course, along the way I pointed out that Austrians have some of it wrong. (Lord knows I engaged in much debate with my dissertation advisor, himself an Austrian, on these topics.)

'Nobody, as far as I am aware', writes Abell, 'is seeking to rehabilitate an unadulterated Langean model' (1995, pp. 343–5), so why bother with the socialist calculation debate? Well, first, there is in fact renewed interest in Lange and the calculation debate since the collapse of 'real existing socialism', as evidenced by the efforts of Alan Cottrell and W. P. Cockshot (1993) and others.[5] Second, and more important for the purpose of my book, applying the Austrian side of the socialist calculation debate – the 'knowledge problem' argument – to the 'humanistic' Marx allowed me to invalidate his praxis philosophy and its socialist implications.[6] It also led me to respond to Branko Horvat's theory of self-managed socialism (Horvat, 1982), which Horvat himself thought was an answer to the Austrians in the debate.[7]

SELF-MANAGEMENT AND MARKETS

If self-managed socialism cannot work, which was the main point of my book, must we also reject self-managed firms in a market system? After all, a good deal of neoclassical economics rejects the labor-managed firm, regardless of its institutional context. Austrian economists are inclined to do so, too. I therefore tried, in my book, to address related issues. For example, I devoted an entire empirical chapter to the experience of cooperage cooperatives in the United States. (Looking back now, the chapter fits badly into a book on Marxism and socialist self-management.) While I fully agree with Abell that case studies such as this 'do not enable us to answer the big questions' (1995, p. 345), I was trying simply (and clearly) to illustrate that cooperatives *can* and *have* survived (contrary to the claims of both Branko Horvat and the Austrian School's Murray Rothbard) in a dynamic, rivalrous market system. At least these cooperatives survived, and with no government help. This doesn't answer, of course, the important question of why cooperatives are not yet dominant (Abell, 1995, p. 343), and I still haven't got a full-blown answer. No doubt a large part of it has to do with the question of risk (Abell, 1995, p. 364), but also with the related issues of the evolution of cultural and organizational support structures (on this, see Prychitko and Vanek, 1996, pp. xvi–xviii).

Nor is Abell impressed with my speculations about the informational advantages of cooperatives in the postindustrial world (Prychitko, 1991, pp. 118–21), lamenting that he 'searched [the] book in vain for solid supporting evidence' (Abell, 1995, p. 347). (Since my brief discussion falls under the subheading 'Self-Management and Market Processes: Thoughts About The Future', and constitutes the last four pages of the book, I would hope the reader wouldn't waste time searching the rest of the book for solid supporting evidence.) Keith Bradley and Alan Gelb's (1981) study of several Mondragon cooperatives, which I've gathered in Prychitko and Vanek (1996, pp. 200–220), offers some good evidence about the informational and motivational advantages of self-managed firms. And although Abell is skeptical of the productivity of large-scale cooperatives (1995, p. 346), Defourny (1986), in his study of the construction sector in France, offers some empirical evidence that might make Abell more optimistic (see Prychitko and Vanek, 1996, pp. xii–xiv).[8]

POST-MODERN OR AUSTRIAN?

I wrote my book as an Austrian economist, not a postmodernist. (If anything, I've always thought of myself as a Romantic, though my wife disagrees.) I tried to show how Austrian economics offers a fundamental challenge to the theory of self-managed socialism, as well as to that *other* historical experiment in 'pure' socialism (using Boettke's term), the Yugoslav system of the 1970s. I also suggested that the empirical evidence should not lead Austrians to *reject* – as they do – the potential for self-managed firms in a true market system, especially as we enter the information age; and I suggested that the Austrian 'knowledge problem' argument against central planning might be turned against the traditional capitalist firm, Taylorism, and scientific management.[9] Since then I've become even more skeptical about the Austrian arguments against workers' self-management in a market system (Prychitko, 1996, 1997a). Abell, unfortunately, misunderstanding me as both a postmodernist and a salvager of humanistic Marxism, misses the real goal of my admittedly ambitious and, in places, insufficiently argued book.

To answer his question – 'Self-management: is it postmodernist?' – I'd have to say that I haven't really thought about it. But I wouldn't rule it out.

NOTES

1. One may question why I would focus on the Roberts–Stephenson (and Lavoie–Boettke) arguments. First, because I happen to be working within the Austrian School tradition, of which at least Lavoie and Boettke are leading figures; second, because I think the Roberts–Stephenson argument is the best developed within the economics profession, and although it is more than two decades old, they still manage to draw some obligatory citations in the field of comparative economic systems.
2. I have elsewhere noted that, once Austrian economists acknowledge the other side of the unity thesis (that of the Praxis philosophers), their interpretation of the Soviet experiment becomes more problematic: if central planning is indeed inconsistent with Marx's call for de-alienation, then the Soviet failure to establish full-blown command planning doesn't necessarily imply the failure of Marxian socialism, for central planning is not the *only* method of comprehensive planning – there is also self-managed planning. (Thus, the discussion of the Soviet experiment in 'pure' communism in Boettke (1988) might be enough to dismiss Marx as interpreted by Roberts and Stephenson, but it is not enough to dismiss the Marx of the Praxis Group.) Moreover, if a theoretical or practical model of comprehensive planning unintentionally *requires* central planning to work successfully, then that theory or practice would fail to achieve Marx's de-alienated system. (Hence, if the Soviets had been successful central planners, Marxism would fail to deliver its citizens out of alienation, as the Praxis Group warned us.)
3. I am pleased to report that Hilary Wainwright (1994, pp. 146–8, 182–4) tries to engage my argument, even if she gives my book two different titles and the wrong year of publication.
4. As a young Austrian economist I initially wondered how in the world Marxists could condemn Stalinism . . . perhaps for its failure successfully to centrally plan? I was some-

what surprised to see Svetozar Pejovich (1991) argue that I shouldn't have taken the Praxis Group seriously, for they were only bent on making an ideological case for the Yugoslav system. I felt that, at least in terms of understanding Marx, their ideological motivations could be safely bracketed or suspended, and that rejecting their arguments, as Pejovich seems to do, would amount to a mere *ad hominem* criticism.

5. For a criticism, see Horwitz (1996).
6. As I stated elsewhere: 'If comprehensive planning is humanly impossible, then Marx's claim that we are beings of praxis, whose essence is freely and creatively to design the society we live in, is patently false. If the achievable, as Marx saw it, is epistemologically unachievable, the gap disappears and Marxian alienation simply ceases to be' (Prychitko, 1994a, p. 521).
7. Abell suggests I'm paying too much attention to outdated theory when he states that Horvat 'can as late as 1982, be caught' offering a decentralized socialist answer to Hayek (1995, p. 344). Abell seems unaware that, as late as 1991, Michael Albert and Robin Hahnel (1991) offer a formal model of a fully decentralized, non-market socialist system. I had offered a criticism of their efforts in Prychitko (1988), also mentioned in Prychitko (1991, pp. 60–61 n. 37).
8. More generally, see Vanek (1996).
9. Austrians at George Mason University's Center for Market Processes have since run with the idea of applying the knowledge problem to traditional firm organization, in their notion of 'market-based management'. They have totally ignored, however, the feasibility of workers' self-management.

7. The critique of workers' self-management: Austrian perspectives and economic theory*

Four decades ago Benjamin Ward published the seminal criticism of the labor-managed firm (1958). Since then the economic theory of workers' self-management has exploded into hundreds of articles, and is now a research field of its own. But disagreement persists in the neoclassical literature: is the labor-managed firm productive? Will worker-managers possess optimal incentives? More generally, is a system of labor-managed firms workable, and if so, is it efficient? These questions have become relevant since 1989, with the collapse of the socialist governments in central and eastern Europe, as reformers consider the panoply of decentralized and market-based alternatives to socialist planning.

The critics answer 'no' to the above questions, and believe that self-management, in any form, is an impractical alternative for the former socialist countries. It should play no role in efforts toward privatization (see, for example, Pejovich, 1994). Austrians are, of course, prominent in the comparative systems literature. Yet as a group, we have not contributed directly to, nor follow, the theoretical and empirical self-management literature. Nevertheless, I think it is safe to say that Austrian School economists, again, as a group, tend to agree with the standard theoretical criticisms of workers' self-management.[1]

This position may be problematic as an a priori condemnation, for is there anything essentially 'Austrian' about the standard critique of workers' self-management? That is, what fortifies the Austrian stance against workers' self-management? Is it established by Austrian economic theory? If so, how? If not, are there elements of neoclassical theory imported into the Austrian criticism? If that's so, how are they justified? I will try to answer these questions by exploring whether Austrian economic theory – rather than something simply called 'free market economics' – provides a fundamental theoretical critique of workers' self-management, a critique that is independent of the concerns of neoclassical theory.[2]

* Reprinted from *Advances in Austrian Economics* (1996), **3**, pp. 5–25, with permission from Elsevier Science.

DEFINING WORKERS' SELF-MANAGEMENT

First, some definitions are in order.

Following Ward's approach, the standard literature defines workers' self-management (or the labor-managed firm, or producers' cooperative) by the nature of the firm's objective function, regardless of the surrounding institutional context. The labor-managed firm is modeled as a dividend maximizer, whereby worker-managers maximize net income per worker (for example), regardless of the state of the industry (which could range from perfectly or imperfectly competitive markets, to market-socialist, to decentralized yet fully planned socialist systems).[3] The merits of this approach are as strong as the merits of the neoclassical theory of the profit-maximizing capitalist firm. The weaknesses, however, which I will have opportunity to discuss later, may be even greater, because the institutional specifics – which are pushed far to the background if not assumed away completely – can span across entire economic systems and lead to confusion when interpreting and comparing labor-managed firms in institutionally different empirical contexts. Therefore we need to consider the broad definition of the labor-managed firm, one beyond the formal objective function and the narrow concerns of standard economic theory. The labor-managed firm is a productive organization whose ultimate decision making rights rest in the workers of the firm, on an equal basis, much like the case of political democracy, wherein individuals derive their right to vote from citizenship. The rights are equal irrespective of a worker's specific job, skill, age, or even capital contribution to the firm. Decision making rights accord to workers within the firm, *qua* workers, rather than as the possible owners of the firm. In this sense workers' self-management – as a basic principle – is about establishing control rights within a productive organization, while it leaves open the issue of *de jure* ownership (that is, who enjoys legal title to the physical and financial assets of the firm) and the type of economic system in which the firm is operating. The actual organizational structure within the labor-managed firm is open to experimentation as the worker-managers see fit: decisions can be reached directly or through elected representatives, whether by a majority rule or Quaker-style consensus or even a unanimity rule; operations can be completely decentralized or hierarchical; income distribution can follow any set of rules decided by the worker-managers; and so on.[4]

In general, the management and finance strategy is decided by the workers themselves, within the constitutional parameters (including rules of ownership) set by the system within which the firm is established (market, market-socialist or socialist). Thus defined, workers' self-management is not to be *equated* with socialism, or even syndicalism or workers' control.[5]

Self-management is about the design and the *ex ante* coordination within the firm (the enterprise division of labor) rather than the coordination of the inter-firm or overall economic order (the social division of labor or the economic system itself). Self-management is a particular way of managing a goal-related or organizational order, in Hayek's sense of the term.[6] If Austrian economic theory is to establish a critique – or defense – of workers' self-management, it shouldn't lose sight of this systems-independent definition. With this understanding in mind, let's briefly turn to workers' self-management within the specific institutional context of a socialist (and market-socialist) system. Here Austrian economic theory offers, in my opinion, a unique if not fundamental criticism (see Prychitko, 1988, 1991, pp. 51–5 for a more detailed argument). Then, after closely examining the neoclassical critique (and defense) of the labor-managed firm, I shall turn to the market-process based case where I hope to suggest that the uniquely Austrian criticism not only fades, but also that an Austrian defence, or at least a neutrality, can be proposed.

THE LABOR-MANAGED FIRM IN THE CONTEXT OF COMPLETE SOCIAL OWNERSHIP: SELF-MANAGED SOCIALISM

Traditional socialism strives to plan all economic activities comprehensively, both within and between enterprises. As such, it seeks to integrate the economic activities of society (the coordination of socially owned property) into a single coherent plan, rather than rely upon the spontaneous or anarchic ordering of the market system to coordinate plans. Hence, following Hayek's distinction between organization and spontaneous order, the socialist workplace or enterprise (itself an organization) would operate as a component of a much larger, integrated organization. It is perhaps less clearly understood that advocates of democratic socialism (who are committed to socialism in the above sense but opposed to Stalinist-style command planning) advocate a decentralized socialism, whereby the planning process itself (the integration of all productive units into one huge organization) would follow the workers' self-management principle.

Again, self-management is concerned with the method of establishing coordination within an organization. The socialist economy itself is considered a single organization, whose physical and financial assets are socially owned by society as a whole. In its purist form, then, the workers' self-management principle under *socialism* must consist of labor-managed firms that democratically (through elected representatives) contribute to the formation of inter-firm planning and coordination, on to overall industrial, regional, and macroeconomic planning. Ideally, the entire economy would be integrated by a single, comprehensive plan, developed dialogically from the bottom up, rather than the top down as in the Soviet or state-socialist model. The ultimate planning unit is the labor-managed firm (or, more precisely, the workers' council within the firm) as opposed to the central planning board, and self-management would extend so far beyond the walls of each enterprise unit that it would *completely* replace the market process. Rather than central or command-planned socialism, we can refer to workers' self-management within a socialist system as self-managed socialism.[7]

Advocates of this system (who, by the way, have rapidly shrunk in number) defend it epistemologically. That is, by giving workers the right to *manage* socially owned property and therefore dialogically participate in the entire planning function, this method, it is claimed, will disseminate more useful knowledge and create a more efficient and just allocation of resources than that captured by either authoritarian central planning procedures (such as material balances planning) or by the capitalist market system. Such is the contemporary argument of Albert and Hahnel, for instance.[8]

These claims, however, do not answer the knowledge problem argument of Austrian economic theory. Self-managed socialism replaces one planning method (central planning) with another planning method (self-managed planning). By retaining the goal of a comprehensive plan, the market for the means of production is intentionally destroyed, and with it the means to calculate scarcity-indicating prices. Social ownership replaces private or separable ownership. Although the planning process may actively encourage a dialogue concerning the worker–consumers' needs, wants, interests, and socially-oriented goals in a way that command planning wouldn't, there is still no way to assess the relative values of scarce factor goods. The relevant (and in most cases tacit) information can't be discovered through democratic council dialogue, without a competitive market processes. What is worse, it can be demonstrated that the decentralized process itself, upon facing inherent conflicts of interest and malcoordination that result from the scarcity of factor resources and knowledge, logically tends to collapse toward centralized methods of planning and control, endangering if not destroying its own self-management rationale. Clearly a move *de mal en pis* from the position of both workers' self-management and social ownership.

What about a market socialist variant? More sophisticated theorists, such as Branko Horvat (1982), admit that the Austrian criticism of central planning (if not, implicitly, comprehensive planning in general) is correct:

even the socialist system requires *some* market process to communicate otherwise untapped, yet crucial, information. Horvat explicitly acknowledges Hayek's influence when he admits that 'The market is a mechanism for communicating information' (p. 200), a useful system of 'organized information diffusion among economic decision makers' (p. 338). And, of course, by allowing a market in his model of self-managed socialism, Horvat thinks he refutes Hayek's criticism of socialism (p. 577, n. 56). But, as discussed in detail elsewhere (Prychitko, 1991, ch. 5), Horvat limits the extent of the market to consumer goods; his notion of social ownership of the means of production and his call for *ex ante* self-management planning of the capital structure precludes a market process in the means of production, and with it a way to discover their relative values.[9]

ITS IMPOSSIBILITY: A POSITION ESTABLISHED BY AUSTRIAN THEORY

The Austrian analysis of the knowledge problem under central planning can be extended to decentralized (yet comprehensive) planning, and its application against the Lange-type market socialism can also be extended to critique the (admittedly more sophisticated and nuanced) Horvat-type market socialism. Austrian economics does seem to offer, therefore, a solid a priori critique of workers' self-management when instituted under a socialist (or market-socialist as depicted above) system, independent of the criticisms that might be levied by neoclassical theory.

There is no reason to change the definition or basic principle of workers' self-management in light of this result. If my previous research, along with the Mises–Hayek knowledge problem argument from which it stems, is basically correct, then Austrian theory does seem to offer a strong theoretical position against implementing workers' self-management as a *socialist* corrective for centrally planned socialism or as a democratic twist on market socialism. In short: workers' self-management under conditions of complete social ownership may perhaps be theoretically conceivable, but only if one miscasts or assumes away the epistemological problem in the model. In any event, it appears impossible to successfully calculate the relative values of scarce means of production in practice.

Of course, this says nothing yet about the viability of workers' self-management within the radically different institutional context of the market process. Before we can assess whether a position is established by Austrian theory here, let's first consider the standard literature.

STANDARD CRITICISMS OF WORKERS' SELF-MANAGEMENT: THE THEORY OF THE LABOR-MANAGED FIRM

Neoclassical criticisms of the labor-managed firm seem to suggest that the institutional context, the structure of legal ownership rules or the economic system surrounding the labor-managed firm, won't make much of a difference. The labor-managed firm, by the very nature of its objective function, and its corroborating right of control rather than full ownership rights, will be riddled with poor incentives and, consequently, inefficiencies, regardless of whether it operates in a socialist or market system. If true, neoclassical opponents of self-management would not have to rely upon or even acknowledge those Austrian arguments against socialism mentioned above to sustain their objections; neoclassical economics could successfully avoid Austrian concerns. And, in fact, it generally does. The question for us is: do the following well-known neoclassical criticisms strengthen the Austrians' theoretical case against the principle of workers' self-management? That is, do they offer the Austrian theorist sound a priori reasons also to criticize, if not reject, the case for workers' self-management under a competitive *market* system?[10]

To answer this, let's first present, uncritically, the general textbook arguments against the labor-managed firm.

**1.   The labor-managed firm might generate market instability; a
    system of labor-managed firms will most likely generate system-wide
    instability**

This is Ward's original argument. To understand it, we must closely examine the narrow objective function of the labor-managed firm, compared to the traditional capitalist firm.

The capitalist firm is modeled as a profit maximizer with the objective function:

Maximize: Profit =
Total Revenue minus Labor Cost minus All Other Costs.

Formally, as any student knows, profit is maximized when marginal revenue equals marginal cost, according to the first order conditions.

Ward maintains that the labor-managed firm follows a different maxim, narrowly described by the following objective function:

Maximize: Net Income Per Worker =
(Total Revenue minus All Other Costs) divided by the number of Workers.

Notice that it could just as well be stated as 'maximize profit per worker'. The term 'profit' is changed to 'net income' because, traditionally, profit is considered the residual between revenue and all costs *including* direct labor costs. In the labor-managed firm, however, labor is not considered a direct cost of production, and thus it carries no 'minus sign' in the objective function.[11] Ward therefore offers the following formal objective function (assuming a labor-managed firm producing a single output with a single variable input in a perfectly competitive market):

$$y = \frac{pq - R}{L} \tag{7.1}$$

where: p is the perfectly competitive price,
q is the output associated with the short run production function
$q = f(L,K)$ and capital K is fixed,
R is the fixed cost of capital, and
L is the number of workers in the firm.

By differentiating the objective function with respect to L, we obtain the first order condition for a short run equilibrium:

$$\frac{dy}{dL} = p\frac{dq}{dL}\left(\frac{1}{L}\right) - pq\left(\frac{1}{L^2}\right) + R\left(\frac{1}{L^2}\right) = 0 \tag{7.2}$$

$$p\frac{dq}{dL} = pq\left(\frac{1}{L}\right) - R\left(\frac{1}{L}\right) \tag{7.3}$$

$$\frac{dq}{dL} = y \tag{7.4}$$

Notice the similarity between the economic behavior of the labor-managed firm and its capitalist counterpart: equation (7.4) suggests that the labor-managed firm produces to the point where the marginal value product of labor equals net income per worker. Likewise, it is easily demonstrated that the marginal value of capital will equal the price of capital when L is fixed and K is variable – in this case the exact same result as the capitalist counterpart.

Ward provides, however, a much more technically interesting result. Since equation (7.2) is set equal to zero, it necessarily follows that

$$q\left(\frac{1}{L}\right) - \frac{dq}{dL} = R\left(\frac{1}{pL}\right) \tag{7.5}$$

In other words, the average product of labor minus the marginal product of labor yields a non-negative number (since R, p and L are all non-negative). This not only means that the labor-managed firm produces under diminishing marginal returns to labor in the short run, which is no surprise, but it necessarily follows that an increase in the product price p will lead the firm to seek a new equilibrium characterized by a smaller number of workers, L, employed in the firm, and thus a lower level of output, q.[12] Hence, the labor-managed firm responds to favorable price increases by reducing output, just the opposite of its capitalist counterpart. Likewise, and by the same reasoning, a fall in the market price will motivate the labor-managed firm to increase its output. With equal precision, Ward also demonstrates that the labor-managed firm responds perversely – compared to its capitalist counterpart – to changes in the fixed cost of capital, R.

Thus, the quantity supplied by the labor-managed firm varies inversely with the product's price. An industry composed of labor-managed firms therefore generates a negatively sloped (or backward bending) market supply curve, which, depending on the relative elasticity of the market supply and demand curves, could lead to an unstable equilibrium, whereby any short run shortages or surpluses would tend to expand rather than disappear, and therefore any allocative inefficiencies generated by a temporary disequilibrium would tend to grow worse, assuming zero entry.

2. **The profitable labor-managed firm tends to restrict employment, compared to its capitalist counterpart; moreover, the labor-managed firm under less than perfectly competitive conditions would tend to restrict employment – and therefore reduce output – even further than the profit-maximizing capitalist counterpart**

These problems are already embedded in the perversity conclusion. Even under perfectly competitive *market* conditions, a profitable labor-managed firm would employ fewer workers (and also produce less output) than its capitalist counterpart (that is, a profit-maximizing firm facing exactly the same market conditions). Compared to the capitalist counterpart, the per capita income (dividend share) of workers in the labor-managed firm would be greater, as the dividend share consists not only of the (implicit) wage (equal to the marginal value product of labor) but also of the share of the (positive) residual. (These results would be just the opposite for a firm suffering a loss.) Worker-managers find, as discussed above, that the way to generate higher per capita income, particularly in the face of an increase in the price of their output, is by restricting – rather than expanding, as in the capitalist counterpart – employment (see Furubotn, 1971, pp. 194–5 for a somewhat different argument).

To the extent that labor-managed firms operate profitably in a market system that is less than perfectly competitive, the relative employment restriction will, *ceteris paribus*, imply a greater output restriction, and hence, a larger social welfare loss due to monopoly power.

On the basis of this analysis, the case for workers' self-management, in any context, doesn't seem promising.[13] Call it the Wardian Implication. The labor-managed firm is motivated to reduce membership (and output) when market conditions become more favorable, as this generates a greater per capita residual (greater net income per worker) for the workers who remain in the firm. Likewise, when market conditions turn less favorable, the labor-managed firm is motivated to expand membership (and output) in order to spread the losses. In either case the allocation of labor is Pareto inefficient. On top of that, the way is paved for a tremendous threat to the self-regulating features of the market even under the perfectly competitive case composed of labor-managed firms.

But this does not exhaust the neoclassical criticism. I will consider two more problems.

3. The labor-managed firm is riddled with suboptimal incentives that lead to shirking and therefore reduce work effort and productivity

This conclusion stems from the Alchian and Demsetz (1972) theory of the firm. Alchian and Demsetz argue that firms exist because team production is more efficient than non-team or purely individualized production and contracting. In their view, the firm is synonymous with team production.

Formally, team production is defined as the condition involving the use of two or more inputs (X_i and X_j) to produce an output Z such that

$$\delta^2 z / \delta X_i \delta X_j \neq 0 \qquad (7.6)$$

In other words, the essence of team production – and therefore the firm – is the non-zero condition of the cross partial. This means the firm's production function cannot be separable into (and thus considered the mere sum of) individual production functions for each of the inputs. (The productive firm will have, in fact, a positive cross partial, as the inputs cooperate in order to create something of value.) Alchian and Demsetz further suppose that information is neither free nor perfect, and thus there is a cost associated with metering the marginal products.

Alchian and Demsetz assert that, under these conditions, workers will have an incentive to shirk. The ith worker for example, enjoys the entire benefit from shirking, while externalizing some of the costs (considered as, for example, the reduction in total team productivity) among all the other (in this case jth) inputs.

Shirking can be reduced, and overall productivity increased, by establishing a particular and marketable property right for a specialist – a monitor – who is empowered to oversee inputs, meter the team's output, hire and fire the membership of the team, and last, but not least, also enjoys the right of residual claimant. For Alchian and Demsetz, this defines traditional capitalist ownership (1972, p. 85), and therefore they interpret the capitalist firm as a 'particular policing device utilized when joint team production is present' (1972, p. 90). In a world where metering inputs is costly, it creates optimal incentives against shirking.

The labor-managed firm, on the other hand, is a team without a central residual claimant. The team shares the residual as discussed earlier. As such, it lacks the 'policing device' established by traditional private property rights necessary to insure optimal work incentives.

This property-rights critique also suggests the final problem I shall consider.

4. The members of a labor-managed firm are likely to contribute a suboptimal level of self-financed investment

This incentives problem was advanced by the critical work of Furubotn and Pejovich.[14] Workers within the labor-managed firm enjoy rights to the firm's revenues, but not necessarily the firm's assets. Under conditions of social ownership (as in the 'Yugoslav' context) the workers have only *usufruct* rights to the firm's assets and, moreover, their rights to the firm's revenues are non-tradeable. Worker-members own only a portion of the firm's *current* residual, and enjoy no claim to the firm's future earnings upon exiting or being dismissed from the firm. Worker-members of the labor-managed firm therefore face two investment options. They may reinvest a portion of their incomes back into the enterprise, which allows the firm to enhance its capital stock and hopefully to fetch a larger residual in the future, which they may share only as long as they remain members of the firm. Their other option is to invest their incomes outside the enterprise, in personal assets such as a savings account with a contractual rate of interest, for example, of which individuals enjoy full ownership status. The individual would enjoy the contractual rate of return *in addition to* being free to recover the principal.

Of course, a combination of the two investment options is also permitted. But the incentive for a worker to reinvest in the labor-managed firm is stifled. Every dollar a worker plows back into the firm (and therefore converts to a capital asset) no longer belongs to him, but rather to 'society' at large. The opportunity cost of this is clear: the dollar could have been invested into an interest-bearing asset, such as a savings account, over which he and he alone would enjoy complete ownership. A priori, Furubotn and Pejovich (1970, p. 443) conclude that this property-rights arrangement shortens the time horizon of the worker-members and also raises their rate of time preference (compared to the case, *ceteris paribus*, of worker-members enjoying full ownership rights over the firm's capital assets).

The rate of return in a savings account is the market rate of interest, *i*. Pejovich (1992, pp. 470–71) suggests in per-dollar terms that the required rate of return, *r**, from a self-financed enterprise investment (one which would make worker-members indifferent between a savings account and self-financed enterprise investment, assuming equal risk) over the worker-members' time horizon, *t*, is

$$r^* = i(1 + i)^t/[(1 + i)^t - 1] \tag{7.7}$$

For example, if the market rate of interest is 10 per cent and the worker-members' time horizon is 1 year, worker-members would require at least a 110 per cent expected rate of return to induce them to plough some of their income back into the firm, rather than earn 10 per cent in a private savings account. If their time horizon is 20 years, they would require at least an 11.7 per cent expected return on self-financed investment. Because workers within the labor-managed firm would voluntarily opt to reinvest a portion of their income into the firm only if the expected rate of return on that investment exceeds the standard rate of return established by the market equilibrium rate of interest, self-financed investment is clearly inefficient.[15] This divergence in rates of return means, in other words, that workers are not indifferent between self-financed investment and their privately owned savings at the market equilibrium rate of interest, which necessarily leads to an inefficient level of self financed investment.

DO THE STANDARD CRITICISMS SUPPORT AN AUSTRIAN ARGUMENT AGAINST THE SELF-MANAGEMENT PRINCIPLE?

As a group, Austrians are sympathetic to the standard arguments against workers' self-management. This seems to clinch the Austrian case against self-management in principle, in any ownership context. But this may be a case of theoretical schizophrenia, or, if that is too harsh a term, a case of wearing different theoretical hats (one Austrian, the other neoclassical) to justify an a priori stance against something that does not fully fit the traditional institutions of a free market capitalist system. Moreover, there may even be a systematic bias in the type of neoclassical hat that is being squeezed onto the Austrian head.

I will try to demonstrate this by critically reconsidering the above arguments against workers' self-management. Rather than list them as conclusions drawn from established theory, I will list them as questions open to debate.

1. Is the Labor-managed Firm Allocatively Inefficient?

The first Wardian Implication may appear to be the most damning criticism of the workers' self-management principle. At the same time, however, it is also furthest removed from Austrian theoretical concerns: it reduces the firm to a short run objective function – and thus, among other things, precludes free entry or exit – and from that alone derives the formal equilibrium properties of the system and its short run efficiency. It says nothing of a rivalrous market process which is the chief task of Austrian theory. Moreover, the backward-bending supply curve seems to be of no alarm to Austrians: Rothbard (1970, pp. 515–17) considers such possibilities in the case of land and the *total* supply of labor with no alarm, since, if neoclassically perverse supply responses where practiced under real existing markets, such actions would simply represent, Rothbard suggests, the 'freely chosen values of individuals' regarding income and non-pecuniary forms of consumption. Presumably, such behavior, if practiced voluntarily by a labor-managed firm, would be consistent with the Austrian understanding of an efficient market process.[16]

Even if an Austrian theorist were willing to suspend his own methodological and theoretical objections to neoclassicism in general and that of the Wardian approach in particular, the fact is, even in neoclassical theory itself, the first Wardian Implication is highly questionable. There's a major defect of Ward's narrow objective function, for example. It is erroneously specified. Simply stated, if the single objective of the labor-managed firm is to maximize net income per worker, then how are the income-shares of those workers who are laid off or fired being maximized? Now non-members of the firm, their incomes are minimized instead (cf. Robinson's 1967 criticisms). Domar (1966), on the other hand, offers an alternative objective function (with two products and two variable factors) to conclude that the labor-managed firm's supply curve will be positively sloped, although not as elastic as its perfectly competitive capitalist twin. In the Domar case, the fear of market instability vanishes.

And whether we accept the Domar model or not, Meade formally demonstrates that, as long as market *entry* is allowed, the labor-managed market sheds any possible instability problem (see Meade, 1979; cf. Vanek,

1970, pp. 281 –8). Ward's conclusion precludes market entry or exit because it is concerned solely with the short run. Entry, however, is perhaps *the* essential characteristic of competition in the Austrian theory of the market process (see Kirzner, 1973, pp. 97–100; Hayek, 1979b, ch. 15).

2. Is there an Employment Problem?

Similarly, Austrian theory questions the second Wardian Implication. To show that a labor-managed firm will employ fewer workers, and also produce lower output, *compared to* a perfectly competitive capitalist firm in exactly similar conditions does not arm the Austrian theorist with an a priori argument against workers' self-management in a market process. It seems to me that an Austrian cannot claim, on the basis of this second implication, that the membership of a real-world labor-managed firm would necessarily be smaller than the workforce of a real-world capitalist firm under identical conditions.[17] Nor would this be the basis of an Austrian theory of overall employment in which the voluntary 'restriction' in the size of labor-managed firms would lead, say, to a problem of system-wide unemployment (see, for example, Mises, 1966, pp. 598–600; Rothbard, 1970, pp. 522–8).

What of the corresponding finding in neoclassical theory – that social welfare losses would be greater in a market system of less-than-perfectly competitive labor-managed firms? Should this cause concern for the Austrian theorist, who is well aware that the market process in the Austrian sense can never be perfectly competitive? Should this finding give the Austrian an a priori preference for the efficiency of the capitalist firm in the imperfectly competitive real world?

Austrian theory *rejects*, for the most part, the neoclassical claim of a social welfare loss of a monopoly when entry poses no legal barriers (see Rothbard, 1970, ch. 10; cf. Kirzner, 1973, ch. 3; O'Driscoll, 1982). Austrian theory does not use the perfectly competitive firm, or perfectly competitive industry, as the benchmark by which to judge the efficiency of a productive organization. This, I believe, is a central position of Austrian theory.[18] The standard neoclassical criticism[19] that labor-managed firms, in more 'realistic' conditions of imperfect competition, would create relatively greater inefficiency (compared to the capitalist twin) offers the Austrian theorist no grounds to believe that the labor-managed firm is allocatively inefficient.

I conjecture that Austrians cannot have it both ways here: we cannot borrow the Wardian Implications argument from standard theory and *also* defend the less-than-perfectly competitive capitalist market economy on process grounds, for the latter would lead us to dismiss the issue of the allocative inefficiency of workers' self-management.

3. Is there a Shirking Problem?

What of the Alchian–Demsetz criticism? First, I should note that the property rights theory of the firm – which ties the incentive to maximize profits to ownership rather than entrepreneurship – has already been chided by Kirzner (1973, p. 54). Kirzner's theory of entrepreneurship is neither equivalent to legal ownership nor to the 'policing device' established by the traditional capitalist firm to meter marginal products as suggested by Alchian and Demsetz. Surely Austrians do not define the firm, or equate its essence, with mere team production, that is, as a non-separable production function.

Suppose, just for the sake of argument, that Austrians explicitly adopt the team production definition of the firm to fortify their critique of workers' self-management. According to Alchian and Demsetz, workers in the labor-managed firm have an incentive to shirk – and will, in fact, probably act on that incentive – by the very nature of the production function.

There are two issues we can address. First, Alchian and Demsetz argue that the residual claimant will have an incentive to meter the firm's workforce adequately. They do not, however, show how the crucial and relevant information will be captured by the residual claimant. They simply claim (or imply) that the policing device works optimally because the claimant has an incentive to design it (see Putterman, 1984, pp. 172–5). To the extent that knowledge is tacit and dispersed in the skills and judgments of the enterprise workforce – a potential that is perfectly consistent with Austrian considerations of the knowledge problem in general – then the assumption that an optimal policing device will be discovered and successfully implemented assumes away the knowledge problem of the firm.

Second, and perhaps more important as part of an immanent critique, even if we heroically suppose an optimal policing device is found, and that a central monitor is so successful at perfectly metering the marginal products of all the firm's inputs – and thereby reducing shirking of the team – that he indeed earns a positive residual (his whole incentive for metering in the first place), this story runs into a contradiction. If the monitor pays all inputs, including his workforce, the value of their marginal products, then how is it that *any* residual is left over for the monitor to enjoy? As Aoki (1986, pp. 28–9) points out, if the monitor enjoys a residual after all factors are paid the value of their marginal products, then the residual must be explained by a firm-specific resource that is not specified by the cooperative inputs in the Alchian–Demsetz model. But if that is the case, then their claim that the traditional capitalist firm exists because of its efficient metering of cooperative inputs falls apart. Their case for the capitalist firm can be saved, of course, but at the cost of departing from the payment according to the marginal revenue product rule. (And if *that* goes, so does the traditional neoclassical case for free market distribution.)

Alchian and Demsetz admit that their team production theory is limited to the production of goods and services that do not require skilled or 'artistic' and 'professional' labor. When artistic or other forms of tacit knowledge is essential (such as, for example, in law firms, theatre troupes, music bands, many family owned and operated businesses) spontaneous self-monitoring may be much more effective than Alchian and Demsetz's proposed method of central metering. Moreover, if Austrians are correct in their claim that much of the knowledge of particular time and place is inherently tacit and inarticulate, this requires us not only to rethink the nature of organization theory. It suggests that, even if the Alchian–Demsetz model were immune to the above two criticisms, the extent of simple, non-artistic labor inputs may be vastly exaggerated, especially as we move into a 'post-industrial' economy.

4.   Is there an Investment Problem?

There seems to be some general agreement in the literature, by both critics and advocates of self-management, that self-financed investment will be sub-optimal under conditions of social (and perhaps market-social) ownership. The investment problem exists under conditions of *social* ownership – a case, as discussed above, that is discredited by Austrian theory independent of this criticism. The problem of social ownership is ultimately one of failing to overcome a fundamental knowledge problem implied in the system of social ownership and self-management planning. The Furubotn–Pejovich–Vanek criticism maintains that self-financed investment will be sub-optimal due to poor incentives. The Austrian criticism maintains that the problem is much more profound than that: the democratic planners would have little idea as to how to appraise the relative values of scarce factors of production, which products to produce, and how to produce them efficiently, in the first place. The context of the neoclassical debate already assumed all these things are known in principle (after all, the labor-managed firm exists as a clear organization, with clear goals and given factor endowments, and so on). The problem is simply the incentive to strike the optimal (and in principle, knowable) level of internal enterprise investment.

But what concerns us here is whether this investment incentives problem can fortify an Austrian case against labor-managed firms in a market economy. If the labor-managed firm operates in a non-socialist context, then a number of market-based investment possibilities arise that are consistent with the basic principle of workers' self-management addressed at the beginning of this chapter: workers may own equity shares – personal and redeemable claims – of their enterprise; the enterprise can sell bonds to its own workers or outside investors; non-voting equity shares (similar to pre-ferred stock) could be sold to prospective investors outside the firm.[20] The investment incentive problems in the socialist case could thus be avoided.

Acknowledging these market-based solutions, Pejovich relishes the fact that 'Vanek, Horvat, and other proponents of self-managed socialism have to search for and use various immunizing stratagems – most of which contain elements of private ownership – in order to deal with negative incentives and high transaction costs of self-managed socialism.'[21] So much the worse, perhaps, for those who advocate workers' self-management strictly within the socialist context,[22] but so much the better for at least a viable workers' self-management.

ON THE RHETORIC OF AGREEMENT

The questions raised in this chapter form perhaps a case study of the more general problem concerning the nature and scope of Austrian economics and its relationship to the neoclassical mainstream. I will keep strictly, however, to the case at hand.

In the absence of our own systematic research on the topic, Austrians don't seem justified sharing the criticisms of their free market neoclassical colleagues against workers' self-management in a market process. There are several issues in need of Austrian analysis: is the labor-managed firm better suited to resolve the knowledge problem compared to the traditional capi-talist firm? Does the more collectivistic notion of entrepreneurship within a labor-managed firm contradict the highly individualistic modeling of entrepreneurship in conventional Austrian theory? Is the distribution of entrepreneurship limited to an elite few, or is it much more dispersed than Austrians have traditionally admitted? These are questions that Austrians could begin to ask, rather than continuing to rely on the standard argu-ments against the labor-managed firm, arguments which remain too closely tied to precisely the features of neoclassicism that even mainline Austrian theory deems invalid.

Moreover, I have tried to show that different conclusions are generated within the neoclassical domain itself. If Austrians generally tend to agree with their free market neoclassical colleagues, this tendency suggests a bias tilted toward the theory's political conclusions as opposed to its immanent soundness. This is not to say, however, that Austrians are never justified in borrowing the neoclassical argument against the labor-managed firm.[23] If one offers an argument directly against a neoclassical opponent, it is surely reasonable, if not also necessary for scholarship, to adopt the other's techniques and assumptions and engage in immanent criticism. As McCloskey says, that may be required in order to join the conversation. On the other hand, the attempt to develop a rigorously *Austrian* position on the problems of post-socialist transformation, or third world development, or radical social theory guided by the theoretical vision of Austrian economics, is a different and terribly difficult task; and the temptation to pick and choose among the vast and conflicting array of neoclassical conclusions to support one's case can lead the theorist astray, in the sense that he or she may mistakenly believe neoclassicism has resolved certain issues, which apparently frees the Austrian theorist to concentrate on other demanding issues. This mistake seems to occur in the Austrian interpretation of workers' self-management. Perhaps a more serious inquiry into self-management would not only help Austrians overcome a mistake in theoretical interpretation: it may also offer new insights about the path to a freer, more democratic society.

NOTES

1. And thus workers' self-management receives no recommendation in Austrian proposals regarding socialist transformation (Boettke, 1993) or economic development (Boettke, 1994a). In a paper on economic democracy, Lavoie (1992) argues that 'Democracy should apply to all of our lives and should not be narrowly conceived as a form of government' (1992, p. 440) and it 'must subsume not only the situations of literal dialogues, but also the many ways in modern society in which we are able to communicate at a distance with one another' (1992, p. 446). But he is remarkably silent on whether the democratic impetus behind workers' self-management should be implemented – or even seriously considered – in his vision of a democratic, free society.
2. I am tempted to examine whether ideology might also be an influence at work, but instead I shall leave that judgment up to the reader. At any rate, I should make my own understanding of Austrian economics clear here. I do not believe Austrian theory has to be a verbal variant of free market, neoclassical economics, as some critics (and perhaps even some defenders) interpret it. Unlike neoclassical theory, which is concerned with the formal equilibrium properties (and their welfare characteristics) of a model economy, Austrian theory is concerned with the evolutionary and dynamic processes through which knowledge dissemination, plan coordination and order arise, a research project which could differ substantially from the methodology and puzzles of neoclassical economics and its free market practitioners. See Boettke, Horwitz and Prychitko (1994) for an example of my view on the subject, which is admittedly not in the mainline of the Austrian School itself. The comparative questions I raise in this present chapter, however, will be assessed from the perspective advanced by the Mises–Hayek–Kirzner–Rothbard mainline.
3. Just as the capitalist firm is modeled as a profit-maximizer, whose objective function is total profit, regardless of the competitive state of the industry (perfectly competitive, imperfectly competitive, monopoly, and so on). Of course, the capitalist firm is assumed to operate under a market-capitalist institutional umbrella. We can't imagine, for example, a capitalist firm operating in a web of comprehensive socialist planning. We can imagine, however, a producers' cooperative operating in an anarchic market environment.

In this sense, the institutional umbrella surrounding the labor-managed firm is much broader, including market systems and decentralized socialist systems, while perhaps only leaving out an authoritarian command-planning socialist system.

4. This general definition of the labor-managed firm is now accepted in the literature. See Bonin and Putterman (1987, pp. 1–3).

5. Syndicalism may be a variant, or a special case, of self-management, depending upon the strategies and tactics of the syndicalists. Workers' self-management, as defined above, however, is really not a subset of syndicalism. The syndicalist program would be considered a case of self-management only if the 'factories to the workers' and 'mines to the miners' confiscatory tactics were matched with the democratic principle above – with the principle that each worker within the factory or mine enjoys an equal right to *manage*. To the extent that syndicalist and worker control movements simply wanted to vest property in the hands of labor union leaders and other officials, or to declare workers the official 'owners' of their workplaces, without pursuing the democratic principle, they had nothing to do with workers' self-management as defined above. Hence, Ludwig von Mises' criticism of syndicalism (1981, pp. 239–44; 1966, pp. 812–20) may be appropriate for syndicalism, but it does not provide an a priori (or theoretical) case against workers' self-management. I mention this because I often find that Austrians tend to consider self-management synonymous with syndicalism, and they act as if the whole issue was refuted by Mises in his passages addressing syndicalism.

6. See Hayek (1964) and (1973, ch. 2) for the distinction between an intentionally designed order (organization) and an unplanned or spontaneous order.

7. See, for example, the collection by Horvat, Marković, and Supek (1975). Whatever else we may think of this literature, it does suggest a problem with defining socialism as *central* planning (that is, a comprehensive plan issued by a single commanding and controlling center), a definition common to the comparative systems literature in general, and the Austrian literature in particular (cf. Hayek, 1975, pp. 19–20), and see, for example, Mises (1966, pp. 695–6, 716). The definition of socialism as central planning has pervaded the Austrian literature ever since the 1920s and has continued in the recent writings of Don Lavoie and Peter Boettke, for example. While socialism's distinguishing feature is that of a non-market system based on a *comprehensive* (or coherent and all-encompassing) plan, it still leaves open the question of which methods are best suited (in the judgment of socialists themselves) for comprehensive planning. Command planning, material balance planning, and so forth are centralized methods that seek to create a comprehensive plan. The theory of self-managed socialism proposes an alternative method (a democratic, decentralized planning process), and its advocates, such as the Yugoslav group above, suggest that it best captures the emancipatory vision behind Marx's theory of alienation. See Prychitko (1991, ch. 2, 1994a) for a sympathetic yet critical interpretation.

8. See Albert and Hahnel (1978) and their more recent effort (1991), which is a formal restatement of their earlier work.

9. Cf. the similar attempt by Estrin and Winter (1989): 'Planning from our point of view does not concern the activities of agents or firms in the economy; it only applies at the level of the economy as a whole. It consists of an effort to provide a comprehensive and internally consistent account of the development of the economy, attempting to cover all demand and supplies in the economy and their relationship to each other' (1989, pp. 102–3). From this perspective, workers are not told precisely what to do and how to manage by some externally imposed plan. They are granted a good degree of *de jure* autonomy. On the other hand, they must coordinate their inter-firm activities through this comprehensive plan, whose chief characteristics include 'a decentralized, and preferably democratic, process of consultation and discussion concerned exclusively with plan construction and elaboration. . . . In itself, the plan does not contain an implementation procedure. It is left to individual agents to strike separate deals with one another within the planning framework, each deal enforceable like any other voluntary contract. Such a procedure contains rather more teeth then [sic] might first sight appear, because one of the major actors in a market socialist economy is the state' (1989, p. 116).

10. If my graduate-school memory serves me correctly, Don Lavoie used (in his Austrian-based comparative economic systems course at George Mason University in the mid 1980s) many of the following criticisms in his argument against workers' self-management. That doesn't imply, of course, that he still agrees with them today.

11. Do not let the terms fool us here: there is no a priori Austrian case against the labor-managed firm in general because it somehow 'abolishes' the profit principle. The convention that developed in the standard literature reserves the term 'profit' for the residual describing the traditional capitalist case where labor is considered a direct cost of production, and uses the term 'income' (or net income per worker) to discuss the residual of the labor-managed firm.

12. Because an increase in p reduces the right side of the equation, which means, in equilibrium, the left side must also fall, and thus the difference between the average and marginal product of labor must fall. This can only occur if the number of workers is reduced – that is, if some workers voluntarily relinquish their jobs or are fired – which necessarily reduces output under the constraints of the short run production function.

13. The same potential inefficiency appears in the market-socialist case, whereby the product price p (or rental price R) might be interpreted as parametrically given (as in the Lange model), or in the self-managed socialist case, where p (or R) might be interpreted as a given shadow price.

14. See for example Furubotn and Pejovich (1970) and Pejovich (1973, 1992). Although a defender of workers' self-management, Jaroslav Vanek agrees with the basic point raised in the above criticism, and thus calls for external financing as a complement to internal financing. See, for example, Vanek (1970, pp. 304–8) and especially (1977, ch. 8). Consequently, it has come to be referred to as the Furubotn–Pejovich–Vanek effect in the contemporary literature.

15. Again, for convenience we assume that either option carries equal risk.

16. In Rothbard's land example, a higher price (rent) for land may conceivably lead the owner to restrict the amount he offers for sale in the market, since he can enjoy more revenue from the sale of any particular parcel of land, the resulting income effect of which may further induce him to consume the natural beauty (for example) of his still-owned parcels.

17. See Rothbard's (1970, pp. 573–9) discussion of the limits of what economic theory can deduce about the optimal size of firms.

18. Rothbard: 'In the market, *there is no discernable, identifiable competitive price*, and therefore no way of distinguishing, even conceptually, any given price as a "monopoly price". The alleged "competitive price" can be identified neither by the producer himself nor by the disinterested observer' (1970, p. 605; original emphasis). Hence, 'we cannot use "restriction of production" as the test of the monopoly vs. competitive price' (1970, p. 607). The same, then can be said with regard to level of employment, size of firm, and so forth with regard to the firm, capitalist, labor-managed or whatever.

19. Itself theoretically questioned by Vanek in a number of places, including Vanek, Pienkos and Steinherr (1975).

20. In a lengthy footnote, Alchian and Demsetz (1972, p. 97 n.14) offer an interesting defense of non-voting common stock for capitalism, and question why it is necessary for participating investors to have voting rights in the firm.

21. Pejovich (1991, p. 329), in a review of my book (1991). He states that I fail to draw an important lesson from this move away from self-managed socialism: 'But if one could improve the efficiency of labor-managed socialism by introducing elements of private ownership into the system, then it would appear that *full* ownership rights could do even more for the system.'

22. Vanek, by the way, doesn't.

23. Or to make an argument for the labor-managed firm, as in the introductions to Prychitko and Vanek (1996).

8. Hayekian socialism: rethinking Burczak, Ellerman, and Kirzner*

In 'Socialism After Hayek', Ted Burczak (1996/1997) offers a theoretical alternative to both capitalism and comprehensively planned socialism. He concedes the Hayekian 'knowledge problem' and agrees that a technologically advanced economy requires competitive market pricing of the means of production to coordinate the plans of producers and consumers. He is also quite comfortable abandoning the labor theory of value in favor of an Austrian-style methodological subjectivism. He rejects, however, the traditional Austrian School's normative defense of the capitalist market system. Instead, Burczak hopes to show that one of the more important normative goals of socialism – the ideal of allowing labor to appropriate the whole product – can be theoretically preserved in a competitive market economy that constitutionally abolishes the wage–labor contract in favor of democratic, self-managed enterprise. With Cullenberg (1992), Burczak calls this a form of 'thin socialism', as opposed to comprehensively planned socialism. I would instead suggest 'Hayekian socialism', a more provocative label for obvious reasons.[1]

An Austrian might respond that Burczak's thin, Hayekian socialism is merely a semantic guise for interventionism (that is, a market economy with a great deal of state interference) rather than socialism. Many Marxists might respond similarly, and there is something to be said for such an argument. But that would miss a neat opportunity offered by Burczak: if comprehensive planning is both empirically and theoretically bankrupt, must socialists admit total defeat and abandon their solidarist ethics in favor of the hard capitalist ethics typically promoted by the Austrian School? Burczak challenges both Marxist and Austrian alike in sketching a vision of a market economy whose epistemic features – so brilliantly illuminated by Hayek, Mises and more contemporary Austrians – are preserved under a normative constitutional rule that grants labor the right to collectively appropriate newly created goods and services, a rule that I suspect no contemporary Austrian would embrace.

* Originally published in *Rethinking Marxism* (1998), **10**(2), pp. 75–85. Copyright The Guilford Press, New York.

Burczak imagines a market system composed of democratic, self-managed firms. There are markets in the means of production – a strong degree of private ownership – and perhaps simply a minimal state. The core feature is that people work together in the enterprise democratically, and appropriate the total result of their efforts, whether positive or negative. Individuals in society privately own the means of production (unlike the Yugoslavian system of self-managed socialism), but ownership does not in itself establish any right to control the firm. Commodities are produced for the market, but labor 'hires' capital. Private owners of capital are free to lend their assets to the democratic firm, but, like bondholders, they have no voice in the firm's operation.

This abolishes the wage–labor contract, and Burczak's proposed system is socialist in this regard.

Would Burczak's system tend toward calculational chaos? Would worker-managers face a bewildering throng of possibilities? Would there be no incentive to economize on the use of scarce resources? In other words, do Austrians have an a priori case to suggest that the system must collapse, like centrally planned socialism? Burczak believes not. So do I, but with some reservations discussed below.[2]

ELLERMAN AND KIRZNER ON RESPONSIBILITY, RIGHTS AND PROFITS

The scope of Burczak's paper is quite wide. To do it justice, I shall focus on Burczak's most insightful and challenging contribution – namely his clever juxtaposition of David Ellerman's Labor Theory of Property (1980, 1985, 1988) with Israel Kirzner's Entrepreneurial Theory of Profit, most recently summarized in Kirzner (1997), but also well developed in Kirzner (1973,1979,1990,1995). This topic alone would make for a fascinating chapter in the morality of profits. I shall only briefly address Burczak's criticism of Kirzner, so that I can concentrate more on the implications of Burczak's analysis.

To recall Burczak's discussion: both Ellerman and Kirzner trace the right to the whole product back to those responsible for its creation. Ellerman maintains that workers alone are fully responsible, but the capitalist legal system – especially the wage–labor employment contract – hides this fact by pretending that a worker can legally alienate his human identity. The fact that it is a voluntary contract is beside the point. Because it treats people as things, and denies their responsibility in the production process, it is a fraud and ought to be abolished: 'an *inalienable right* is a right such that the contract to voluntarily alienate the right is invalid on natural grounds. An inalienable right is not a right which may not be alienated without consent; it is a right which may not be alienated *even with consent* (1985, p. 318; original emphasis). Ellerman insists that, of all the factors of production, only labor can be held responsible for production, and therefore the entire product. Moreover, he points to Friedrich von Wieser, the Austrian economist, for being among the first to point out labor's responsibility for production (1985, pp. 308–9; 1988, p. 1114).

Kirzner, on the other hand, tends to treat labor as a passive factor of production. For him, it is only the alert entrepreneur who notices and acts upon price differentials in the market, who spots the opportunity to buy goods at a low price and sell them at a high price, and, therefore, who in fact *discovers* profit opportunities. This takes place in the markets for final goods and services as well as the markets for factors of production, including labor services. The residual – the profit – is the result of 'deliberate human discovery, not to be attributed to unaided luck but (at least in part) to the alert attitude on the part of the discoverer. It is the alertness of human beings that enables them to notice and profit by what they find' (1995, p. 39). Because others in the system fail to see the price gap, the arbitrage opportunity stares everybody in the face, 'the entrepreneur who notices the price gap is making the relevant discovery', and 'because he is the finder, the creator of what he has discovered', he is 'thus entitled to be its keeper' (1995, p. 42; cf. 1990, pp. 221–2).

Burczak mentions that Kirzner seems to follow Frank Knight's remark that the great mass of people, including workers, might as well be considered merely passive factors of production, and Burczak rightly points out that this is not only empirically false; it also flies in the face of Austrian theory itself, which purports that all human action contains an 'entrepreneurial' element.[3] Does Kirzner contradict himself?

It helps us to recall that Kirzner's goal is not to demonstrate that factor owners enjoy no entrepreneurial faculty – that they are merely passive agents – but rather to show how entrepreneurship ultimately does not, *in principle*, require factor ownership. That was the main point of Kirzner's argument (1979, pp. 185–99), which is purely analytical. He recognizes that, once we move out of the realm of pure theory and into real-world production and exchange processes, 'flesh and blood resource owners are, of course, also to *some* extent, their own entrepreneurs, just as flesh and blood entrepreneurs are likely to be owners of some factor services themselves' (1979, p. 198). Kirzner is well aware that his ethical case for profits is based squarely on an 'analytical device' (1979, p. 197) and consequently, 'to the extent that capitalist resource incomes involve a discovery element, they, too, may be held justified, at least in part, by the finders, keepers ethic' (1990, p. 225).

But he hardly discusses those cases. Kirzner seems most comfortable making the purely analytical case for the entrepreneur's exclusive right to the entire product, and indeed modeling labor as a passive factor of production. Ellerman insists that this is the *only* way that the case for the entrepreneur's sole right can be made. But Ellerman and Burczak remain unsatisfied, and wish to draw conclusions based on the existential, real-world, or flesh-and-blood cases that Kirzner himself admits to, but doesn't thoroughly examine.

SELF-MANAGEMENT AND MARKET CONTRACTS

Let us now suppose that a Kirznerian were to trace through the implications of the 'flesh-and-blood' case. If flesh-and-blood labor is entrepreneurial (as, again, every aspect of real-world human action carries an entrepreneurial element with it), the signing of a contract to sell certain goods and services at a specified price can itself be interpreted, by the Kirznerian economist, as an entrepreneurial act of grasping for 'profit' by laborers. It is a morally responsible activity, and the workers should enjoy the fruits (and bear the liabilities) of their creation.

With that in mind, I would like Burczak to consider the following four hypothetical cases and address whether he agrees with my own assessment:

- *Case A.* Suppose *n* flesh-and-blood workers establish a self-managed firm that produces pig iron. The pig iron is sold to the highest known bidder in an anonymous market, and the workers enjoy the rights to the entire product (whether profits or losses) democratically according to the traditional self-managed objective function, $(TR-TC)/n$.

It seems that a Kirzner and Ellerman (or, for our purposes, a Prychitko and Burczak) would agree that the workers are morally responsible for their actions, that they have discovered or tried to carve out an entrepreneurial opportunity, and that they should consequently enjoy the right to the entire residual as captured in their sales contract.

- *Case B.* Suppose *n* flesh-and-blood workers establish a self-managed firm that provides a service rather than a physical product – creating and selling, say, canned music programs to offices by subscription in an anonymous market. They will distribute the entire profit (or loss) according to the preceding objective function.

It seems that Burczak would again agree with me that they are morally responsible for their actions, that they have discovered or tried to carve out an entrepreneurial opportunity, and that they should consequently enjoy the right to the entire residual as captured in their sales contract. There seems to be no categorical difference between cases A and B.

- *Case C*. Suppose *n* flesh-and-blood workers establish a self-managed firm that provides a service not by subscription to an anonymous market, but rather seeks out a single buyer, the highest known bidder. An example might be a self-managed private protection agency that lands a year-long contract to safeguard a factory.

Surely the mere number of buyers in the market would not affect Burczak's willingness to agree with me that the workers are again morally responsible for their actions, that they have discovered or tried to carve out an entrepreneurial opportunity, and that they should consequently enjoy the right to the entire product as specified in their sales contract. Would Burczak maintain, like myself, that there is no categorical difference between cases B and C?

Perhaps the reader can see where I am trying to go with this. There is one more case to consider:

- *Case D*. Suppose *n* flesh-and-blood workers establish a self-managed firm that provides a good or service – call it X – to a single buyer (the highest known bidder), and the buyer combines something with it from a similar group – call it Y – such that $X + Y = Z$, and Z is sold in an anonymous market to the highest known bidder.

Would Burczak agree with me that there is no categorical difference between this case and case C: that the workers are morally responsible for their actions, that they have discovered or tried to carve out an entrepreneurial opportunity, and that they should consequently enjoy the right to the entire product as specified in their sales contract – in this case the residual from the sale of X? And would he also agree that the single buyer is morally responsible for her actions, that she has tried to carve out an entrepreneurial opportunity, and that she should enjoy the right to the entire product as specified in her sales contract – the residual from the sale of Z?

Or would Burczak insist on specific examples? The previous cases already provide a few.[4] Based on my reading of Kirzner, Ellerman, and especially Burczak's own application to thin socialism, I see no significant difference between the four cases. In these hypothetical 'flesh-and-blood' cases, labor is non-passive, it is entrepreneurial, and consequently labor 'should' enjoy the right to *the self-managed firm's* entire product.

It seems that, for Burczak's argument for commutative justice to hold, he must categorically distinguish between (a) different *kinds* of labor activity;

and/or (b) the number of n workers in the self-managed firm. Moreover, he oversimplifies the problem of just what constitutes the whole product of labor.

Should the Kinds of Labor Activity Matter?

Consider the type of good or service produced by labor. Producing pig iron is one thing, canned music programming by subscription is another, but what about offering janitorial services, or secretarial services, or, for the lack of a better term, assembly-line services? *All* of these activities are entrepreneurial in Kirzner's sense, and morally responsible in Ellerman's sense; therefore the n workers in the self-managed enterprise that provides these services should enjoy rights to the *self-managed enterprise's* entire product. It doesn't matter what *kind* of service the self-managed firm provides; what matters is that the workers within it are responsible for their actions, whether profitable or loss-making. If they sell music service, or nightwatchman's service, or janitorial service, they and they alone reap the rewards (positive or negative) established by their sales contract.

As responsible moral agents, workers enjoy membership rights within the self-managed firm, including those to the residual of the firm, $(TR-TC)/n$, and a control rule based not upon ownership but on the democratic basis of one worker, one vote (cf. Ellerman 1985, pp. 322–5). As a normative critique of capitalist production and the wage–labor contract, then, what really seems to matter in the above four cases is that the group of n workers be recognized as a set of entrepreneurial and morally responsible agents *within* a self-managed firm. The janitorial service workers are not *employed* by the owners of the factory within which they clean – they do not enter a wage–labor contract with owners of capital – rather, they are members of a self-managed firm that provides janitorial services to others at a mutually agreed upon price. They have not alienated their human identity. This, I take it, is perfectly acceptable in Burczak's world of thin, Hayekian socialism. After all, janitorial and a host of other *kinds* of services will still have to be provided, and competitively established market prices disseminate the kinds of knowledge people in society require to coordinate their consumption and production plans. What matters is that production activities contain (1) the incentives to 'switch on' entrepreneurial alertness to instances of economic malcoordination (in the form of hitherto unnoticed profit opportunities), which is the Hayekian dimension that I think can be supported, at least theoretically, and (2) the standards of commutative justice embodied in the systems of contracting entered into by self-managed firms, which is the socialist dimension that Burczak seeks to preserve.

Should the Number of Flesh-and-Blood Workers Matter?

Burczak challenges the conventional Austrian notion of entrepreneurship as too narrow, too analytically pure, and in fact simply too isolated. Kirzner often uses the device of the pure entrepreneur (1973, pp. 39–43) as the single discoverer of unnoticed profit opportunities within an economy composed of Robbinsian economizers. Burczak suggests, instead, that entrepreneurship can be extended, at least in the flesh-and-blood cases, to more collective activity, such as that which occurs in the self-managed firm. I believe he may be right, but I am little comforted by Burczak's claim that entrepreneurship is dispersed throughout society 'by definition' (that is, because all human action contains an entrepreneurial component).[5] We have to keep in mind that Kirzner is concerned with precisely the kind of entrepreneurship that would tend to improve the overall coordination of economic plans.

While Kirzner's analysis of entrepreneurship may be excessively individualistic, hesitating to consider notions of group or collective entrepreneurship, one wonders whether Burczak's is too collectivistic. Just what *does* Burczak have to say about individual entrepreneurs in his world of thin socialism? If thin socialism does not allow for individual acts of entrepreneurship, entrepreneurship would become too costly (not only would it be absurd for someone who spots a price discrepancy to have to get others together, form a self-managed firm, and only then act upon that opportunity by buying low and selling high; it would seem to violate the normative standard of the labor theory of property itself). Sensible Austrian analysis would predict, a priori, systemic plan discoordination, and thin socialism would flop. If, instead, thin socialism allows for individual entrepreneurs to profit from price discrepancies both within and between industries, then the coordinating feature of the market process would be preserved. Presumably, the individual entrepreneur should also enjoy the full product – in this case the full profit – of her efforts, even under the labor theory of property. But if *that* is allowed, perhaps even thin socialism might give rise to a handful of billionaires – another 'Hayekian' element!

Burczak doesn't address this issue. But we can take it one step further. I offered four hypothetical cases whereby n workers in self-managed enterprises act collectively to capture profit opportunities. All along we naturally assumed n was a stylistically large number. Now let $n = 1$. Isn't that the case of the individual entrepreneur, a 'self-managed firm' of one? If Burczak agrees with me that individual acts of entrepreneurship are necessary for the coordination of the market system – socialist or otherwise – then he must allow the possibility that $n = 1$ in any of the above hypothetical cases that he considers consistent with thin socialism and the commutative theory of justice.

It seems that we converge upon a consent theory of justice even in a flesh-and-blood case. Thin socialism requires the constitutional rule that whenever people work together in a common enterprise it is they, and not the owners of capital, who enjoy the rights to the entire product of their labor.[6] But this is true for a single entrepreneur, too, and it really wouldn't matter if he had to officially register his name as a 'self-managed firm' of one or not. He would be free to sell his services (whether that of a pig iron producer, a janitor, or an assembly line worker) to the highest bidder at a mutually agreed upon price. Although the wage–labor contract might be officially abolished, with the individual being self-employed and bearing rights to his 'firm's' entire product, this might not look all that different from the capitalist labor market, whose justice is based on the consent theory. But my critique is not yet exhausted. We have yet to consider the difficult issue of defining the whole product of labor.

THICKENING SOCIALISM: THE PROBLEM OF THE WHOLE PRODUCT OF LABOR

Burczak is willing to 'thicken' his socialist blueprint when he moves to his critique of Hayek's case against social justice, but for reasons of space and expertise I'll leave it to my Austrian colleagues to respond.[7] I would like, instead, to argue that Burczak's thin socialism may have a tendency to 'thicken' undesirably simply on the basis of the socialist self-management principle alone.

Burczak is unclear about just what it is that the workers are self-managing, or democratically and collectively appropriating. Workers are said to enjoy rights to the whole product of labor. But just what is the *whole* product of labor? Is it simply the commodity that a workers' collective happens to be producing? What if that commodity is used only as an intermediate good, an input in the production of another commodity? Workers who produce electricity, for instance, are producing an input that is crucial for steel production, which in turn is crucial for automobile manufacturing. Aren't workers in the electricity and steel cooperatives key players, then, in the creation of automobiles?

I am reminded here of Marx's (1968) discussion of the tremendous interconnectedness of production processes, his example being the production of cotton, which is the raw material for the spinner, who produces yarn, which in turn becomes the raw material for the weaver, and so on.[8] Although capitalism treats these as separate commodities with their own profit–loss systems of accounting – entities with apparent lives of their own – standard economic theory mirrors the system by modeling them as analytically separate entities. Does Burczak, as a proponent of socialism, accept this approach or would he consider it to be, like Kirzner's, a mere analytical convenience subject to ideological illusion? Can it be the case that the real interconnectedness of production processes within the structure of capital might serve to discredit an analytically clear distinction of the 'whole' product?

I do not think I am vainly stretching for a cute, parallel counter argument to Burczak's criticism of Kirzner, for my question is motivated by a vast theoretical, philosophical and empirical literature regarding the Yugoslavian example of socialist self-management. Yugoslav economists had long struggled over the complex issue of the analytical (and empirical) place of the self-managed firm in the process of social reproduction (Rakić, 1964; Vojnić, 1980; Vačić, 1982), as had philosophers (Marković, 1975). An official monograph states the point clearly: 'the income of a basic organization is the result not only of the current labour of workers in it, but also of the total social labour. In this sense it is in fact a kind of gross social income which may be claimed by the workers of other basic organizations and self-managing communities' (Trifunović, 1980, p. 116). In practice, indeed, workers in Yugoslavia often complained about being exploited by other self-managed firms further up and down the line of the structure of production (cf. Schrenk, Ardalan, and Tataway, 1979, pp. 29–30).

I don't wish to saddle Burczak with the Yugoslav system; he does not intend to replicate that blueprint. My point is, instead, that the 'whole' product is not self-evident in socialist theory or practice, and perhaps Burczak's blueprint might have to be thickened to account properly for the rights and responsibilities of workers in an expanded process of social reproduction. Doing that, of course, carries the risk of crowding out the Hayekian epistemological features embodied in a competitive market process, the very features that Burczak wishes to preserve.

THE 'VERY SHORT STEP' BETWEEN KIRZNER AND ELLERMAN

I commend Burczak for grasping an intellectual opportunity that stared the rest of us in the face but escaped our attention: he exposes the common link between Kirzner's defense of entrepreneurial profit and Ellerman's case against the traditional capitalist firm, which has important normative implications for comparative political economy. Both trace the right to the entire residual back to those responsible for its creation. Ellerman sees the worker, or workers, rather than the entrepreneur, as collectively responsible; Kirzner instead sees the entrepreneur, rather than workers or factor owners, as individually responsible. Burczak believes it is a 'very short step' for a

Kirznerian to abandon the entrepreneurial 'finders, keepers' ethic and instead accept the labor theory of property, for flesh-and-blood workers are, existentially, non-passive.

I hope to have shown that, in addition to raising the problem of what constitutes the whole product in a system of expanded social reproduction (and thus the potential for Hayekian socialism to thicken undesirably), Burczak's step can be walked in the other direction. One who holds a labor theory of property might be compelled to consider the consent theory of contract, for the existentially non-passive individual, behaving entrepreneurially and as a self-employed or self-managed firm of one, enjoys the same rights to his entire product, whatever that may be.

Perhaps this is the kind of tension that becomes most visible when either theory strains to support an absolute moral principle.

NOTES

1. I must admit I offer the term for selfish reasons. As an Austrian who defends the self-management principle (admittedly an outlier among my colleagues), my own work has been mistakenly labeled as an argument for 'Hayekian socialism' (Foster 1995). Because I don't consider myself a socialist, I'd be quite happy to pass the label to Burczak.
2. I do not believe self-management is a panacea, one that can solve the problems of comprehensive planning by offering an alternative method to hierarchical command planning, and I remain firm in my argument that comprehensive planning of any form – centralized or self-managed – will fail (Prychitko, 1991, 1997b). Nevertheless, I do agree with Burczak that a Hayekian or Austrian approach can support a system of self-managed enterprises operating within market processes (Prychitko, 1997a). I don't wish to repeat any of these arguments here. The key point is that Burczak and I envision the epistemic possibility of a spontaneous market process populated with self-managed enterprises. I believe this is at least theoretically conceivable by Austrian School standards, normatively desirable to some extent, and perhaps even an evolutionary possibility in some systems. Whether Burczak goes further and believes it is politically viable or morally necessary is beside the points I wish to address in this chapter.
3. Austrians stress that action necessarily occurs under uncertainty, and therefore every act has a 'speculative' or 'entrepreneurial' character. An individual strives to better himself *ex ante*, but only the *ex post* result will determine his success. In this way, Austrians consider human action in general to be 'entrepreneurial'.
4. *Case A*: suppose X is pig iron, Y might be an automated production process, and Z might be sheets of steel. *Case B*: X is the canned music programming, Y might be a dental office, and Z dental services. This wouldn't differ from case B, or from case C, which combines protection services (X) with factory resources (Y) to produce something else of market value, (Z).
5. My three children are 'entrepreneurs' in that they indefatigably seek 'psychic profit', but I would not expect that they are prepared to take the initiative in the rough and tumble world of market price discrepancies. This probably holds for millions of able-bodied adults, too.
6. In an earlier draft Burczak quotes my good friend Jaroslav Vanek, who has suggested: 'Whenever people work together in a common enterprise (whatever their number), it is they and they only who appropriate the results of their labors, whether positive (products) or negative (costs or liabilities), and who control and manage democratically on the basis

of equality of vote or weight the activities of their enterprise. These workers may or may not be owners of capital assets with which they work, but in any event such ownership does not impart any rights of control over the firm. Only possession of, and income from such assets can be assigned to the owners, to be regulated by a free contract between the working community (that is, the enterprise) and the owners (1996, p. 29).

7. Besides Boettke's (1998b) response in *Rethinking Marxism*, the reader may also wish to see the recent round of criticisms of Hayek's social theory, quite similar to Burczak's, by diZerega (1997), Johnston (1997), and Lukes (1997).

8. Also see Walliman's (1981, pp. 62–6) discussion, where he ties the theory of the whole product to Marx's theory of alienation.

PART TWO

Capitalism and the quest for Utopia

9. Formalism in Austrian School welfare economics: another pretense of knowledge?*

The hidden order, harmony, and efficiency of the voluntary free market, the hidden disorder, conflict, and gross inefficiency of coercion and intervention – these are the great truths that economic science, through deductive analysis from self-evident axioms, reveals to us.

Murray Rothbard (1970, p. 880)

It would be inappropriate to conclude that those Austrian approaches to welfare economics have simply been *ex post* rationalizations for some ideologically desired result. It is arguable that these conclusions regarding institutional efficiency are an inevitable consequence of consistently following the constraints imposed by Austrian methodology. The consistent focus on individual goal seeking, a theme of Austrian analysis beginning with Menger, coupled with the analytical constraints of radical subjectivism, may necessarily lead to [*laissez faire*] or something close to it, as an institutional touchstone for normative analysis.

Roy E. Cordato (1992, p. 87)

Welfare economics, for all its rigor, is still in trouble. The hope of developing a scientific benchmark by which to judge economic efficiency and social welfare, one that claims consistency, objectivity and relevance, has been dashed. The so-called New Welfare Economics – which held so much promise during Paul Samuelson's (1947) tenure – accomplished a technical feat that was nothing short of brilliant. But terrific technics produced poor praxis, and today's top welfare specialists, such as Amartya Sen, have rejected many of the foundations of New Welfare Economics in favor of cardinal, interpersonally comparable utility.

Neoclassical welfare economics has failed to provide a viable, and relevant, foundation on which to assess efficiency, growth and well-being in actual economic systems. It is a large leap from the realm of pure theory – say, Pigouvian externalities models – to determining, as an applied economist, an optimal Lindahl tax price. The question of how to calculate the tax

* Originally published in *Critical Review*, 7(4), 1993, pp. 567–92.

on free riders of public goods, or on polluters, in order to achieve a more efficient allocation of scarce resources, cannot be consistently answered by the neoclassical framework which gives rise to those questions. If actual market economies fail to achieve general economic equilibrium, then the going market prices do not reflect underlying marginal costs and benefits – either socially or privately. Neoclassical welfare theory cannot objectively and consistently ground the analyst, who has no way of measuring, for example, people's marginal rates of substitution in consumption, let alone predicting the intended and unintended consequences of such a policy scheme.[1]

What of the alternatives to neoclassical welfare economics? Austrian School economists are eager to present their views as remedying the deficiencies of the mainstream. Does Austrian welfare economics allow us to make meaningful, value-free, empirically rich statements regarding economic efficiency and social welfare? I will try to show that Austrian welfare theory, much like its neoclassical counterpart, cannot meet the canons of formal, a priori theory.[2]

AUSTRIAN CRITICISM

Austrians reject neoclassical welfare economics because it centers on the concept of general economic equilibrium, which requires appallingly unrealistic assumptions. These include, among others:

1. atomistic individualism, whereby each agent is modeled as a cultural eunuch, free from traditions, customs, personal relationships, and non-pecuniary interests;
2. perfect information, under which agents make perfectly rational utility maximizing and profit maximizing choices, knowing with full certainty the opportunities and constraints they face, and the consequences of their actions;
3. price taking behavior, whereby product and input prices are treated as parameters that cannot be influenced or manipulated by individual actors;
4. perfect competition, whereby rivalry over monetary profit is completely exhausted, and institutions that enable people to cope with uncertainty – such as money, firms, capital accounting – are assumed away, and
5. equilibrium prices which fully capture marginal costs and benefits, turning subjective assessments of utility and cost into objectively measurable data.

An economy under general equilibrium (assuming appropriate convexity conditions) is considered efficient because it fully exhausts opportunities for mutually beneficial exchange, and by definition is Pareto optimal: any redistribution of resources would make at least one party worse off. Since every agent is maximizing utility, social welfare is also maximized.[3] The free market system is said to maximize efficiency and welfare as long as these five conditions just listed (and others) apply. When a systematic general economic equilibrium is not achieved, however, a given distribution of resources may accordingly be deemed inefficient. Thus, under perfectly competitive conditions, more airline companies, stable prices, and other desirable features might supplant the market failures of the current airline industry. Monopolies, oligopolies, externalities and public goods are widely held to be examples of market failure. The presence of non-pecuniary interests, quasi-rents, and institutions designed to cope with ignorance are less obvious examples.

But how meaningful is the general equilibrium benchmark? Austrians argue, rightly in my opinion, that no real-world economy could achieve general economic equilibrium. It is safe to say that no society in the past, present, or relevant future can be characterized by the five conditions above. Many of the activities that a neoclassical economist deems market failures are, in fact, what the market process is all about. For example, real entrepreneurs aren't 'price takers': they engage in arbitrage (buying low and selling high), they discover new ways of satisfying consumer demand, they engage in rivalry. So, the issue is not only whether free rider problems or pollution externalities or even monopolies occur in actual capitalist economies. As long as uncertainty prevails, or entrepreneurial profits and losses occur, or even personal relationships exist, the economy is in disequilibrium and, if we remain true to the foundations of neoclassical economics, all actually existing economies must be judged inefficient, if they are to be judged at all. Austrians reject that conclusion because they reject the analysis. Of course, many neoclassical economists also reject that conclusion, and defend some policies and institutional arrangements as being more efficient than others (a monetary rule instead of discretionary monetary policy, for example, or airline deregulation instead of regulation, or the North American Free Trade Agreement instead of traditional protectionism). But neoclassical economists who make empirical welfare or efficiency claims about particular market processes are inconsistently applying their otherwise rigorous theory.[4]

This, perhaps, may help us better to understand Frank Hahn's (1981) criticisms of applied neoclassical economics. Hahn, an eminent neoclassicist himself, is unwilling to overlook the blatant inconsistency of applied equilibrium theory, or downplay its paucity of empirical content.

According to Hahn the role of general equilibrium theory is (or should be) very narrow: it addresses the question of whether or not a model decentralized economy composed of isolated agents who rely purely on price signals for utility and profit maximization can lead to a perfect coordination of plans. Happily, the answer is yes. Mathematical economics has shown that such an equilibrium exists (that is, it has a determinate mathematical solution) and that the model decentralized economy will tend to converge into a perfect coordination of plans.[5] For Hahn, one is mistaken to believe that general equilibrium describes any existing economy. General equilibrium is nothing more than an abstract solution to an abstract question. To even claim that actual free market economies tend toward general equilibrium (or to say that some economies – the US for example, are 'closer' to general equilibrium than others – that of Bangladesh, for example) is theoretically unfounded: tendency toward equilibrium has been demonstrated only under very extreme, and empirically unrealistic, assumptions such as perfect information, ergodicity, and so on. If participants in real-world economies face true uncertainty, or if they lack perfect information, or if indivisibilities exist, then at least some of the necessary conditions for convergence are violated, and the best one could say is that the 'real world' is in disequilibrium.

This lack of realism is the price paid by neoclassical economic theory in order to achieve value freedom, logical rigor and theoretical coherence. Of course, in order to study real existing economies many neoclassical economists depart from the assumptions necessary to meet such formalist criteria. In a sense, Hahn's insistence on upholding neoclassical formalism requires neoclassical economists to shut up when it comes to questions about real existing economies.

Austrian School economists contend, by contrast, that their methodology – deductive analysis from self-evident axioms – avoids Hahn's problem. They claim to offer an alternative method upon which to ground welfare economics. They claim their theory is founded upon empirically true assumptions, that they describe real phenomena, that their welfare conclusions are value-free, coherent and empirically meaningful. They claim to avoid the problems of neoclassical welfare economics. Do they – or perhaps, as one educated in this tradition, I should ask: do we?

THE FORMALIST TEMPTATION ABOUT PREFERENCES: AN AUSTRIAN CASE STUDY

In 'Toward a Reconstruction of Utility and Welfare Economics', Murray Rothbard offered the first extended Austrian criticism of the (then) New

Welfare Economics, and, more importantly, an alternative foundation for welfare theory.[6] Since Roy Cordato's *Welfare Economics and Externalities in an Open Ended Universe: A Modern Austrian Perspective* (1992) is strongly influenced by Rothbard's approach, it is worth taking a close look at Rothbard before turning to Cordato himself.

Rothbard's version of Austrian welfare economics is grounded in the praxeology of Ludwig von Mises. For Rothbard, as for Mises, it is incontestably true that humans act instrumentally (by arranging means to attain ends). Praxeology, a formal theory of human action, deduces logical implications from the action axiom. Rothbard claims that whatever is logically deduced from that axiom is absolutely and universally true.[7] Since, for Rothbard, the initial axioms are 'radically empirical', so, too, is the body of praxeological theory. Hence, the theoretical claims that Rothbard makes about the welfare-generating aspects of a market economy are at once apodictic *and* empirical, an epistemological status unrivalled by even the most sophisticated neoclassical welfare theory. 'It is the praxeologist who is truly empirical', proclaims Rothbard, 'because he recognizes the unique and heterogeneous nature of historical facts; it is the self-proclaimed "empiricist" who grossly violates the facts of history by attempting to reduce them to quantitative laws' (1976b, p. 33).

Rothbard's welfare economics can be summarized quite easily: action implies choice among alternatives. In acting so as to arrange scarce means to attain ends or goals, individuals will always act in a manner that will satisfy, *ex ante*, the ends or goals they value most highly. As a subjectivist, Rothbard argues that we cannot know the exact construction of each individual's scale of preferences. What we do know, scientifically (or praxeologically, which is supposed to amount to the same thing), is that people *demonstrate their preferences* in concrete, voluntary acts of choice. (A student majoring in economics, for example, demonstrates his preference over all other subjects of study available to him at the time of declaration. A Sunday morning churchgoer demonstrates she prefers the sermon to an extra hour of sleep. Your subscription to the *Times* shows you prefer it to the *Post*.) There is no need to reify tastes and preferences in terms of indifference curves, which are empirically empty hypotheses.

Rothbard's notion of demonstrated preferences reconciles his claim that value, utility and opportunity cost are inherently subjective with his desire to make objective, empirical claims about people's preferences. As long as the action is voluntary, individuals always and necessarily maximize utility, at least *ex ante*.

'This concept of preference, rooted in real choices', Rothbard believes, 'forms the cornerstone of the logical structure of economic analysis, and particularly of utility and welfare analysis' (1977b, p. 2). Demonstrated preference theory differs explicitly from Samuelson's formal notion of revealed preference in that Rothbard rejects Samuelson's assumption of constant tastes and preferences, which has no empirical justification.[8]

The move from each acting individual to overall social welfare is handled swiftly in Rothbard's analysis: because the free market is merely equated with the entire array of voluntary exchanges among individuals,[9] logic dictates that the free market necessarily benefits all its participants:

> the very fact that an exchange takes place demonstrates that both parties benefit (or more strictly, *expect* to benefit) from the exchange. The fact that both parties chose the exchange demonstrates that they both benefit. The free market is the name for the array of all the voluntary exchanges that take place in the world. Since every exchange demonstrates a unanimity of benefit for both parties concerned, we must conclude that *the free market benefits all its participants*. In other words, welfare economics can make the statement that the free market increases social utility, while still keeping to the framework of the [Paretian] Unanimity Rule. (1977b, p. 27; original emphasis; cf. 1970, p. 880)

Thus, by equating individual choices with social utility, Rothbard concludes that the free market maximizes it; 'And we can say this with absolute validity as economists', Rothbard claims, 'without engaging in ethical judgments' or interpersonal utility comparisons (1977b, p. 27, cf. 1970, 880–81, 1976c). Moreover, Rothbard argues that the free market not only maximizes *ex ante* utility, but, because of its competitive nature and incentives to satisfy urgent demands efficiently, it tends to maximize *ex post* utility as well (1970, pp. 772–7, 1977a, pp. 18–23).

Rothbard's approach apparently offers real solutions to neoclassical problems that are coherent, value-free, and empirically relevant. He avoids untenable neoclassical assumptions about quasi-concave social utility functions and the like, and he thinks he comes to terms with the real heterogeneity of history, the world of real choices.

COMPETITIVE JEALOUSY AND PSYCHIC LOSS

Let us re-examine Rothbard's claim that a free market necessarily maximizes *ex ante* social utility. Isn't it possible to conceive of third-party individuals to voluntary exchanges who, through fear, jealousy, envy or other common emotions, feel worse off by those exchanges? (Consider a yuppy who, having finally achieved his ambition to own a BMW, becomes truly depressed when he discovers that his neighbors have dumped their BMWs for Ferraris.) Doesn't this happen frequently in actual market processes, where people are highly motivated by conspicuous consumption and compete positionally?[10] Rothbard's answer to these criticisms, which were first raised by Melvin Reder (1952), is so clear, so simple, and so troubling that it deserves reproduction in full:

> But what about Reder's bogey: the envious man who hates the benefits of others? To the extent that he himself has participated in the market, to that extent he reveals that he likes and benefits from the market. And we are not interested in his opinions about the exchanges made by others, since his preferences are not demonstrated through action and are therefore irrelevant. How do we know that this hypothetical envious one loses in utility because of the exchanges of others? Consulting his verbal opinions does not suffice, for his proclaimed envy might be a joke or a literary game or a deliberate lie. (1977b, p. 27)

In his search for apodictic certainty, Rothbard summarily rejects the possibility of anomalies in his position. Because we 'have no ironclad proof' that those suffering psychic harm are not simply joking, telling lies, or playing sick mental games, then any 'person's "envy", unembodied in action, becomes pure moonshine from the praxeological point of view' (1977a, p. 18). He seems to assume that the 'praxeological point of view' has a monopoly on social knowledge: therefore he is entitled to reject all knowledge claims that cannot be deduced from first premises regarding action and demonstrated preference. Although he claims his formal theory is empirical – in fact, radically empirical – it provides no room for the very real people who, rationally or not, become frustrated or harmed and suffer utility losses in actual market processes.[11]

Despite Rothbard's rejection of positivism, his own demonstrated preference theory is thoroughly positivistic (or, better, behavioristic). As he would later write, 'we may know as historians, from interpretive understanding of the hearts and minds of envious neighbors, that they do lose in utility. But we are trying to determine . . . precisely what scientific economists can say about social utility or can advocate for public policy, and since they must confine themselves to demonstrated preference, they must affirm that social utility has increased' (1976b, pp. 99–100).[12] But if indeed we *can* learn something from history, as Rothbard suggests, then why discard that knowledge when we undertake scientific economics? Because of its source? Because it is not gained through a priori deduction alone? One suspects that the praxeological formalism to which Rothbard aspires rests upon a questionable view of science: we only scientifically 'know' that which can be deduced from 'absolutely true' axioms.

Whether Rothbard's welfare theory is a meaningful alternative to the mainstream depends, in part, on how well it can be applied to the pressing public policy issues of our time. Actual public policy questions occur in a specific time and place – that is to say, in *history* – so it does matter that some people will probably be psychically harmed with the introduction of freer markets – if one wants to analyze the effects of free markets on overall social utility. Rothbard's use of 'must' above is simply dogmatic, and suggests that his welfare economics might not be able to cope with the empirical complexities of actual policy analysis. If an actual public policy (say, NAFTA) is likely to impose a loss of utility on some (say, thousands of US factory workers who might be fired as a result of its enactment), and if we admit that indeed we 'know as historians' that they will lose in utility, then to ignore this knowledge and insist instead that, according to formalist criteria of science, social utility will necessarily *increase* is simply doctrinaire.

THE EXTRAORDINARY CLAIMS OF A PRIORI WELFARE THEORY

Even if we presume that Reder's challenge is met by praxeology, the additional claim that Rothbard makes about social welfare under interventionism – specifically, that no state intervention can ever increase social utility – is a careless self-contradiction.

His argument runs as follows. The free market maximizes *ex ante* social utility because it is nothing more than a nexus of voluntary trades. For the state to disrupt this nexus by, say, prohibiting two people from engaging in mutually beneficial trade, will make both parties worse off. The only one who gains utility is the state official(s) who demonstrated a preference for intervention. 'As economists', Rothbard concludes, 'we can therefore say nothing about social utility in this case, since some individuals have demonstrably gained, and some have demonstrably lost in utility, from the governmental action'. Rothbard suggests that Austrians should be agnostic here. Moreover, if the state forces two individuals to make a trade in a way they would not have done voluntarily, then at least one of the individuals is worse off, while the government official(s) gains utility. 'Again', Rothbard argues, 'economics can say nothing about social utility in this case'. Again, we must remain agnostic: we simply don't know.

Yet, his next sentence reads, 'We conclude therefore that *no government interference with exchanges can ever increase social utility.*' In fact, he goes so far as to proclaim that 'since some lose by the existence of taxes, therefore, and since all government actions rest on its taxing power, we deduce that: *no act of government whatever can increase social utility*'.[13] Somehow Rothbard has leapt from agnosticism to certainty: the state cannot increase social utility. His italics suggest we take his claim seriously, as an apodictic truth. But it's more apoplectic than apodictic.

Rothbard's conclusion directly contradicts his claims that Austrian welfare economics 'can say nothing' about social utility under state intervention. Rothbard now suggests that value-free science condemns *all* state intervention as utterly unable to increase utility. How does this claim logically follow from his own framework? It cannot, unless he inserts an implicit assumption – his libertarian 'nonaggression axiom' – to complete the step from agnosticism to certainty.[14] While such an insertion may plug the gap in Rothbard's logic, it contradicts his stated intention to produce value-free welfare economics; surely it violates Rothbard's formalist canons to clinch his indictment of state intervention by means of a value-laden deontological libertarian ethic.[15]

If Rothbard's formalism cannot consistently answer the question of whether *ex ante* social utility rises or falls in simple hypothetical thought experiments (such as the one that Reder suggested), how can it possibly be expected to help assess the complex questions raised by actual state interventions and externalities?

Equally problematic is Rothbard's claim that the market process both maximizes *ex ante* social utility *and* tends toward equilibrium. His welfare analysis explicitly rejects the notion of constant tastes and preferences, but his claims about the free market's equilibrating tendencies requires constant tastes and preferences. Rothbard makes it clear that since general equilibrium implies unchanging value scales, static technology, and so on, we can say that the market process tends toward equilibrium only as long as we hold value scales and technology constant (1970, p.275). To the extent that demonstrated preferences reject the notion of constant tastes, Rothbard cannot claim (however tenuously) that the market process both maximizes *ex ante* social utility and tends toward equilibrium, for the assumptions required for him to make the welfare claim are inconsistent with those required for the tendency claim.

My criticism is immanent: as a formalist who asks that his claims be tested only by their logic (1976b, 1979, pp.19–22, 31–43), Rothbard's ultimate conclusions about state intervention do not follow. To achieve coherence, Rothbard must rely on natural rights libertarianism. This is not only dubious in itself, but necessarily violates Rothbard's stricture which is the basis of his critique of the neoclassical alternative that welfare economics be completely independent of value judgments if it is to be a science at all. This formalism allows Rothbard to ignore utility losses due to envy, power, positional competition, poverty, even inept entrepreneurship. But there is nothing self-evident about Rothbard's assumption that 'purely' theoretical, ahistorical knowledge exhausts the realm of science.

A NEW FORM OF WELFARE THEORY?

Roy Cordato's work (1992) is something of a landmark in Austrian economics. It is the first book-length Austrian attempt to provide an alternative paradigm to neoclassical welfare theory by creating a general theory of welfare and efficiency that is 'divorced from perfect competition or any notion of general equilibrium' (1992, p. 1).[16]

It is also marked by the author's refreshing discomfort with the Rothbardian framework. Cordato offers the following criticisms of his demonstrated preference approach:

1. Rothbard fails to include psychic utility losses in his free market benchmark;
2. Rothbard ignores the problem of interpersonal utility comparison: 'In order to conclude that a market exchange unambiguously increases "social utility"', writes Cordato, 'the effects on everyone's satisfaction must be considered and compared, even those whose preferences are not being demonstrated' (1992, p. 43);
3. Rothbard studies only *ex ante* utility effects, and 'rules out all consideration of costs and therefore the possibility of utility loss' (1992, p. 43), which, in effect, implies that
4. Rothbard constructs 'an error free world of perfect knowledge, where expectations necessarily coincide with results . . . He rules out the possibility of utility loss in constructing his model' (1992, p. 43);[17]
5. Rothbard's framework is ultimately static, and leads him to 'conclusions with regard to both individual and social welfare that are obviously incorrect' (1992, p. 44).[18] Concerning externalities, for example, 'a strict [Rothbardian] interpretation would have to conclude that any harms or benefits that are not demonstrated do not actually exist', which seems preposterous. 'In light of these criticisms', Cordato concludes, 'Rothbard's welfare economics does not offer much promise as a general guide for externalities theory or policy' (1992, p. 44).

Despite these promising sentiments, unfortunately, Cordato is not interested in revamping (let alone rejecting) Rothbard's demonstrated preference theory; he wishes to merge it with his neo-Kirznerian assertion that the market process is at once efficient and equilibrating, in order to provide, finally, a general Austrian theory of efficiency and welfare. The key to doing so is found in Cordato's contribution of a new concept, 'catallactic efficiency'.

Cordato acknowledges that this concept requires the 'wholesale adoption' of Israel Kirzner's theory of individual efficiency, but adds that the individual faces a more 'open-ended' knowledge problem than Kirzner allows. Indeed, since Cordato wants to create a welfare economics that is divorced from any notion of general equilibrium, one would expect him to have trouble with Kirzner's approach. What, then, is Cordato's criticism of Kirzner?

Kirzner's notion of a perfectly coordinated general equilibrium leads him to claim that improvements in knowledge are always both equilibrating and coordinating. But Cordato notes that 'while knowledge improvements may be equilibrating, in that, *ceteris paribus*, they move us closer to a world of "perfect knowledge"', Cordato writes, 'they may not always be strictly coordinating' (1992, p. 52). For example, a successful entrepreneur may unintentionally frustrate some people's plans (for example, those of his competitors), at least in the short run, in the process of profiting from his coordination of the plans of others (for example, his customers). Cordato, in making this loosely Schumpeterian argument, is justifiably troubled with Kirzner's claim that each step in the process must be, overall, a step toward greater plan coordination. But Cordato agrees with Kirzner that the logic of this process *is* always *knowledge-enhancing*: market participants continuously learn from their successes and failures, and thus the market process, while not strictly coordinating in the short run, is in the long run a strictly equilibrating process, as it tends toward but never reaches a world of perfect knowledge. 'Since the entrepreneurial process is always knowledge enhancing, even though at different stages it may be discoordinating, my conclusion is Kirznerian in that, I believe entrepreneurship is always equilibrating but may not always be coordinating' (1992, p. 55 n. 7).

Cordato contends that the equilibrating tendency of entrepreneurship provides a 'partial benchmark' and 'logical starting point' for a thoroughgoing Austrian welfare theory. This contradicts Cordato's expressed hope of providing a welfare economics divorced from any notion of general equilibrium (e.g. 1992, pp. 1, 4, 5, 15, 19, 36, 73). After all, to claim that market processes tend toward (but never quite reach) equilibrium necessarily requires a clearly developed notion of general economic equilibrium. Moreover, in claiming that a catallactically efficient market continuously generates new knowledge, but doesn't continuously coordinate individual plans, it is hard to discern what *type* or *kind* of knowledge Cordato has in mind. To be sure, the market produces some forms of new knowledge. But so does the state, the household, the Elks Lodge, the Little Sisters of the Poor, and all other institutions.

Cordato also differs from Kirzner in recognizing that tastes and preferences change continuously in light of new knowledge (1992, pp. 60, 62, cf. 70). But this insertion of 'open-ended' knowledge into a Kirznerian framework leaves Cordato hard pressed to show that the market is still strictly equilibrating. Indeed, for all his references to open-ended knowledge, Cordato does not come to terms with the complexities of such knowledge or the possibility of its varying qualities; he fails to explain how and why market processes continually generate the type of knowledge that would create efficiency and tend to converge toward equilibrium. At best, he simply asserts that market prices and rivalrous competition will provide as much of this knowledge as possible (e.g. 1992, pp. 21, 64, 67, 69, 82, 97–8). To claim, as he does, that the market is therefore 'equilibrating', but not necessarily coordinating, is a tautology at best.

One may infer that Cordato must mean by 'knowledge', information about matters that will help individuals satisfy their own plans, that is, knowledge that enhances *coordination*. Cordato invites this interpretation by claiming, for instance, that a market system promotes catallactic efficiency 'to the extent to which the catallaxy encourages individuals existing in a social context to pursue their own goals as consistently as possible' (1992, p. 62). This sounds like enhanced coordination. Elsewhere he writes: 'mutually agreed upon market prices will reflect as much information about market participants' preferences, expectations, and perceptions of resource scarcities as possible' (1992, p. 67). This, too, sounds like the type of knowledge that better coordinates, rather than disrupts and discoordinates individual plans. Cordato even goes so far as to claim that 'all of Kirzner's concerns with regards to the individual's means–ends framework and the ability of the price system to capture and disseminate accurate information are embraced within this theory of catallactic efficiency' (1992, p. 70). Similar assertions resound throughout the book. But they remain assertions, since Cordato offers no scholarly demonstration (theoretical or empirical) of their validity.[19]

Despite his appeal to 'open-ended' knowledge, one wonders if Cordato's 'catallactic efficiency' concept has added anything new to Kirzner's analysis.[20] Although he 'rejects' equilibrium-based analysis, he suggests convergence (equilibrating) tendencies in the traditional sense; that is, the market produces not merely new knowledge, but precisely the type of knowledge that leads to greater and greater coordination of individual plans. Can such a 'rejection' of equilibrium analysis offer any special solutions to the potential problems in Kirzner's equilibrium-convergence theory?[21] On the other hand, if Cordato does not really intend to claim that the market process fundamentally converges toward general equilibrium, in the traditional sense of full plan coordination, then at best, we are left with his uninteresting claim that markets generate 'knowledge', and one wonders how Cordato can deduce a priori the efficiency of the market process on the basis of that claim alone. While Cordato might have tried to come to terms with a post-Keynesian kind of 'open-endedness', one that employs radical subjectivism *and* suggests a fundamental indeterminacy of economic processes,[22] he completely ignores the issue.

THE RETURN OF RADICALLY SUBJECTIVIST FORMALISM

Cordato's (undemonstrated) case for the catallactic efficiency of the market process provides a (very shaky) bridge to his additional claim that markets increase social welfare because market participants find it easier to satisfy their plans than they would in alternative institutional settings (1992, pp. 62–4). Cordato similarly contends that social welfare is not reduced in the presence of simple negative externalities. Yet Cordato believes that traditional welfare theory notions of 'social' benefits and costs are unfounded: they are 'not only arbitrary, but simply fabrications of the economist's mind' (1992, p. 111, cf. 43, 59, 65, 78, 81, 87). He therefore rejects interpersonal utility comparisons and embraces a radically subjectivist methodology, whereby 'the full implications of subjective value are taken seriously' (1992, p. 111, cf. 4, 87). Cordato attempts to reconcile his welfarist claims with his repudiation of neoclassical welfare theory by turning to Rothbard's theory of demonstrated preference:

> The two fundamental tenets of Austrian economics, methodological individualism and subjectivism, must be part of any operational theory of efficiency.
> In conjunction with and as an implication of subjectivism, any analysis of people's preferences must be based on a recognition and acceptance of the guiding principle behind Rothbard's theory of social utility, i.e., revealed or 'demonstrated' preference. Since the economist cannot project a value scale onto individual actors within the catallaxy, preferences can only be deduced by observing activities. Furthermore, since states of knowledge can and do change with the passage of time, preferences that are revealed at a point in time cannot be assumed to remain constant over time. Again, this is an important part of Rothbard's analysis that can and should be used as a building block for the theory being presented here. (1992, p. 59)

How does Cordato propose to square his reliance on Rothbard with his earlier criticisms of Rothbard's position? As far as I can tell, he fails even to try to do so. One searches in vain for any fundamental differences between Cordato's ultimate position and Rothbard's. True, Cordato does mention that his own theory rests on imperfect knowledge, and he tries to come to terms with the dynamics of an 'open-ended universe', but this does not create an iota of difference between the two authors' embrace of demonstrated preference analysis. On the basis of this analysis, Cordato fundamentally agrees with Rothbard's conclusion that '"no government interference with exchanges can ever increase social utility . . . whenever government forces anyone to make an exchange which he would not have made, this person loses in utility as a result of the coercion"' (Rothbard quoted, 1992, p. 87). Whatever became of Cordato's earlier conclusion that Rothbard's position is 'obviously incorrect'?

Cordato's equivocation is evidenced in his repeated references to a hypothetical homeowner, A, who stores junk cars in his back yard, upsetting his next-door neighbor, B. This hypothetical situation is first raised in order to explicate Rothbardian welfare economics. As Cordato recognizes, a Rothbardian would have to conclude that there is no way to enhance welfare in this example by means of intervention: 'Since the satisfaction levels of A and B cannot be observed or measured', writes Cordato, 'it would be meaningless for any outside observer to compare A's utility losses to B's utility gains. In fact, there would be no way of knowing an externality even exists' (1992, p. 17). At this point, it is hard to say whether Cordato approves or disapproves of the Rothbardian position.

Cordato explicitly criticizes Rothbard the second time he considers this story (Cordato now unwittingly places the junk cars on A's front lawn). Cordato argues that

> if only external effects that are demonstrated can be evaluated by Rothbard's normative criteria, a strict interpretation of his approach would have to conclude that any harms or benefits that are not demonstrated do not actually exist. For instance, an example of a negative externality that does not involve a violation of property rights was discussed in chapter 1. In this example, individual A imposed psychic harm on his neighbor, individual B, by storing junk cars on his front lawn. As was pointed out, the standard Austrian conclusion with respect to this type of situation is that a non-voluntary remedy to this problem could not unambiguously improve social welfare. But if Rothbard's welfare criteria was guiding the analysis the fact that an externality was even being generated would have to be denied.
>
> In light of these criticisms [(1)–(4) above], Rothbard's welfare economics does not offer much promise as a general guide for externalities theory or policy. His approach begs many of the questions that would have to be answered if an analysis of externalities were to be considered complete. (1992, p. 44)

Yet by the time Cordato resurrects the story the third time (now being considered in light of Cordato's own general welfare economics), he draws exactly the same conclusion for which he earlier chided Rothbard:

> First, it should be pointed out that from a strictly subjectivist perspective, the presence of such externalities would be unverifiable by an outside observer, such as a policymaker or an economist. There is no way of telling what the actual impact of such an effect is on the utility of those living in the neighborhood; no way of knowing whether such effects are necessarily negative. For example, other

older car enthusiasts or automobile hobbyists in the neighborhood may find such circumstances aesthetically pleasing. For them the cars on their neighbor's lawn could represent a positive externality. Furthermore, even if utility were observable, in cases where cars might be generating both positive and negative effects, there is no way of telling, since utility is not comparable, whether, on net, they represent a positive or negative externality. (1992, p. 81)

This final oscillation leads Cordato straight into Rothbardian dogmatics. In the 'real world', the one that Cordato claims to address, we can usually learn with relatively little trouble whether or not people dislike junk cars on a neighbor's lawn. They may dislike it so much that they volunteer the information (to the owner, the local government, and so on). Or, we can ask them. But that fails, of course, to meet the formalist criteria for knowledge: Cordato asserts that we have 'no way of knowing'; for as Rothbard warns us, we have no 'ironclad proof'.

It is true, of course, that we have no 'unambiguous' or 'apodictic' method to measure costs (or benefits) imposed on (or donated to) the neighbors. The real world is a terribly fuzzy place. But acknowledging this does not justify Cordato's absurd statement that we have no way of learning who is harmed by an externality and who isn't. The *unmeasurability* of utility gains and losses in no way entails their complete *inaccessibility* to analysis.

If utility gains and losses *were* inaccessible, however, then Cordato would be unable to claim that his framework can scientifically assess the costs of alternative degrees of state intervention in the market.[23] Cordato cannot have it both ways: if costs and benefits are so fundamentally subjective that we cannot even know if an externality is present, then we can hardly know if an intervention is more costly than beneficial, or that, in general, a free market is the 'Ideal Institutional Setting' (IIS) for maximizing efficiency and social welfare. Yet he writes that

it seems that . . . the IIS will be the logical outcome of any comparative institutions analysis done from an Austrian perspective, regardless of the specific definition of efficiency guiding the analyst.

When externalities are viewed in light of the IIS the Austrian conclusions as originally put forth by Mises are automatically implied. Only externality 'problems' that involve the conflicting use of property are inconsistent with that institutional arrangement. . . . The point is that the general normative analysis of externalities found throughout the Austrian literature can be interpreted as an attempt to establish or maintain a widely agreed on 'ideal' institutional arrangement. In addition, viewing the analysis from this perspective gives it an overall coherency that cannot be seen when discussing it strictly from the perspective of any of the separate welfare criteria. (1992, p. 88)

Cordato's welfare economics imports the most untenable features of Rothbard's theory. While Cordato criticizes Rothbard for implicitly accepting some type of perfect knowledge assumption, he fully accepts the bulk of Rothbard's demonstrated preference theory, which is theoretically incoherent, if not largely ideological. And while Cordato tries to criticize Kirzner for arguing that the market process continuously coordinates plans, he must ultimately side with Kirzner's claims that the market process is fundamentally equilibrating and efficiency enhancing. If Cordato has done anything new, he has used Kirzner's convergence theory as a way to save Rothbardian welfare conclusions.

A FAREWELL TO FORMALISM IN WELFARE THEORY?

Cordato (like Rothbard before him) believes he deduces *laissez-faire* capitalism as the ultimate benchmark for normative welfare analysis. He concludes, in the comfort of pure, a priori theory, that only free markets can increase social welfare and efficiency, that deviations and interventions which restrict free market processes necessarily reduce welfare and efficiency. He does not seem concerned that these are empirical claims that require detailed, historical case studies. As a formalist, he thinks such studies unnecessary. Like Rothbard's, Cordato's claims are said to be deduced from self-evident axioms, his conclusions are perhaps even 'an inevitable consequence of consistently following the constraints imposed by Austrian methodology' (1992, p.87). ('Constraints' is a very interesting word choice.)

But, if my argument is correct, Austrian welfare economics does not provide any solutions to the problems of neoclassical welfare economics. It, too, is inconsistent, value-laden, and empirically questionable. It, too, fails to live up to its own formalist criteria – which could not sustain, without careful historical case study the assertion that any and all acts of the state necessarily diminish social welfare (even though one may have good reasons to believe that envy may lead to disutility, or that people are indeed harmed by negative externalities, or even that a dollar may provide more utility to a homeless person than to a millionaire to whom it legally belongs). While their formalism allows them to argue that we must dismiss this knowledge and instead uphold a naive relativism on such issues in the absence of 'ironclad proof', neither Rothbard nor Cordato has ironclad proof that the market process maximizes social utility and catallactic efficiency, or that any act of the state necessarily reduces utility and efficiency, or even that their methodology or choice of tenets is the most appropriate way to address welfare questions. Austrian School welfare economists have tried to offer apodictic knowledge by appealing to the formal and a priori epistemological status of praxeological theory, but have failed to meet their own standards.

Put differently, if the 'constraints' of Austrian formalism demand of its practitioners that they uphold value relativism, then they also demand that Austrians embrace the same relativism (or nihilism) about the effects of markets and states upon social welfare and efficiency (at least until all the inconsistencies and value-laden arguments are jettisoned, so that what remains can truly enjoy an apodictic status). Failing to do so amounts to an unwarranted 'pretence of knowledge'.

If, on the other hand, one rejects relativism, it may be necessary to conclude that the effort to create a grand, conclusive, relevant welfare theory through formal a priori reasoning alone probably hinders, rather than enables, a truer understanding of society. Perhaps formalist philosophies of science (whether Austrian, neoclassical, or other) are questionable in themselves, and perhaps should be abandoned, because they unnecessarily constrain the chances for better argument, improved dialogue, and greater empirical relevance.

NOTES

1. The Pigouvian norm in standard welfare economics is theoretically inconsistent. Under conditions of general competitive equilibrium, which necessarily presume an absence of externalities, prices equate and objectively measure marginal benefits and marginal costs. There is no need to distinguish between 'private' marginal costs or benefits and 'social' marginal costs or benefits. In this way general equilibrium prices allow for an objective assessment of costs and benefits. In the event of an externality – say, a profit-maximizing firm that pollutes and ignores the costs it imposes on others – general competitive equilibrium is not achieved. Hence, the problem becomes more than a divergence between 'private' and 'social' costs (generated by the externality). Because the system is now outside general equilibrium, the prevailing disequilibrium prices fail to measure private costs and benefits objectively (marginal rates of substitution can no longer be unambiguously compared). It is theoretically inconsistent, then, to presume that the internal and external costs can be objectively measured and that an efficient corrective tax can be formulated. See Buchanan (1969, chapter 5). Vaughn (1980a) develops this criticism further. For the value-laden and ideological underpinnings of traditional welfare economics, see Myrdal (1991) and Sen (1987). Sen (1982) also questions the empirical relevance of traditional welfare economics. For a criticism of alternative, non-traditional welfare theory, see Cowen (1990).
2. *Critical Review* readers may recall the recent debate between F.M. Scherer and Dominick Armentano on the scientific and ideological status of Austrian economics as applied to industrial organization. See Scherer (1991, 1992) and Armentano (1992a). This chapter may be seen as something of an extension of that debate, by offering an immanent critique of the methodological presuppositions which guided Armentano's position. It also critically extends the themes discussed some years ago in Prychitko (1987).
3. This can be shown only under specific convexity conditions. A group or social utility function must exist, which, although perhaps composed of non-quasi-concave individual utility functions, is itself a family of convex hulls that is necessarily quasi-concave. This allows the theorist to assume comparable marginal rates of substitution in consumption among all consumers. See, for example, Malinvaud (1972, pp. 96–9, 165–70).
4. Relying upon Chicago School partial equilibrium theory (particularly with its Tight Prior assumption) gets the analyst no further. See Fink (1984–85).

5. Not everyone agrees with Hahn. See, for example, Fisher (1983), esp. ch. 2.
6. The essay first appeared in a 1956 festschrift for Ludwig von Mises, and was resurrected over 20 years later as an occasional paper (Rothbard, 1977b). Rothbard's welfare theory also reappears with minor revisions in (1970, pp. 768–7, 1977a, pp. 13–23). Rothbard (1992, p. 7) claimed that his reconstruction of welfare theory was a creative development and advancement of Misesian economics. For a spirited defense of Rothbard's general approach, see Hoppe (1991).
7. 'Economics, or praxeology, has full and complete knowledge of its original and basic axioms. These are axioms *implicit in the very existence of human action*, and they are absolutely valid as long as human beings exist. But if the axioms of praxeology are absolutely valid for human existence, then so are the consequents which can be logically deduced from them. Hence, economics, in contrast to physics, can derive absolutely valid substantive truths about the real world by deductive logic. The axioms of physics are only hypothecated and hence subject to revision; the axioms of economics are already known and hence absolutely true' (1977b, pp. 3–4; original emphasis). This theme of the apodictic status of praxeology (pure theory) is repeated throughout Rothbard's later works. See, for example, Rothbard (1957, 1970; esp. ch. 1, 1976b, 1976c, 1979, 1985, 1992). A more recent restatement of praxeological economic theory comes from Rothbard's student, Hoppe: 'Indeed, the Austrian school represents the most ambitious of all forms of social relationalism with its unyielding contention that nonhypothetical, a priori, empirical knowledge within the field of the social sciences exists, and that it is ethics and economics (which contain this knowledge), which are analogous to logic and protophysics as the absolutely indispensable foundation for all empirical social research. Furthermore, the Austrian school alone has substantiated this contention by offering a completely developed, consistent, and all-comprehensive *positive* theory of ethics and economics' (Hoppe, 1991, p. 81; original emphasis).
8. 'The prime error here is the assumption that the preference scale remains constant over time', writes Rothbard. 'There is no reason for making any such assumption. All we can say is that an action, at a specific point of time, reveals part of man's preference scale *at that time*' (Rothbard, 1977b, p. 5; original emphasis).
9. This notion of the free market runs throughout Rothbard's later works. In *Man, Economy, and State*, for example, Rothbard claims that exploitation cannot occur in the free market. Reminiscent of nineteenth century liberalism, Rothbard goes so far as to say 'on the market all is harmony' (1970, p. 769). Of course, most free market economists share Rothbard's view that the market is simply, and only, the total nexus of voluntary exchanges and chide critics of the actual market processes for not understanding this. See, for example, Wagner (1989, p. 510).
10. I have in mind the discussions of Hirsch (1976, esp. ch. 3) and Kassiola (1990, ch. 6). On the more general social influences upon tastes and preferences, see McPherson (1983).
11. Traditional neoclassical theory tries to avoid these questions by allowing only pecuniary arguments to enter the individual and social utility functions, which is admittedly unrealistic. But Austrian theory, including Rothbard's, purports to study human action in its rich and wonderful complexity, rather than arbitrarily restricting it to pecuniary and traditionally 'economic' motivations. See, for example, Mises (1966, pp. 62–4, and especially 651–2) and Rothbard (1970, p. 63).
12. Cf. Robbins (1935, pp. 141–2). Citing *Toward a Reconstruction*, Armentano accepts Rothbard's argument that the market increases *ex ante* social utility. For example, when considering horizontal price agreements, Armentano claims that they 'always signify unambiguous evidence of benefit (utility) to the parties involved. We know that the parties to the agreement expect to benefit – else why did they make the agreement? On the other hand, we do not know if there is a loss to society as a whole, since costs are ultimately subjective and incapable of aggregation and exact measurement. Thus we could always assert that in our judgment the benefits exceed any possible costs, and not vice versa, as neoclassical analysis has consistently assumed' (Armentano 1982, pp. 137–8).
13. All quotes are from Rothbard (1977b, p. 29; original emphasis). Also see Rothbard (1976c, p. 100).

14. I thank an anonymous *Critical Review* referee for initially reminding me of this.
15. Elsewhere Rothbard (1970; p. 777, cf. 1977a, p. 23) claims that intervention into the market is likely to create unintended consequences that the interveners eventually find undesirable. Therefore, although state officials enjoy *ex ante* gains when they first interfere with the market (demonstrating a preference for coercion), they will nevertheless become frustrated over time and suffer *ex post* utility losses: 'As we analyze the *indirect* consequences of intervention . . . we shall find that, in every instance, the consequences of intervention will make the intervention look worse in the eyes of many of its original supporters. . . . *Ex post*, many of the interveners themselves will feel that they have lost rather than gained in utility.' So Rothbard would have us believe even the proponent of coercion will ultimately suffer utility losses. Of course, if the coercer loses along with the coerced, then everybody loses and the state can't increase social utility. If Rothbard is willing to count the imagined *ex post* utility losses of state officials, however, then he should also be willing to entertain thoughts of coerced citizens enjoying *ex post* utility gains (for example, when an attempted suicide fails because of intervention, the individual may be happy that his life was saved). Moreover, if Rothbard is willing to claim that the bungled projects of bureaucrats who monkey with markets unexpectedly create *ex post* utility losses, for the sake of consistency he should be willing to treat the foiled projects of free market entrepreneurs similarly. After all, an entrepreneur who suffers monetary losses most probably suffers *ex post* utility losses, too. But Rothbard instead throws the issue out of the door: 'Take, for example, the buggy manufacturer who faces a shift in public demand from buggies to automobiles. Does *he* not lose utility from the operation of the free market? We must realize, however, that we are concerned only with utilities that are *demonstrated* by the manufacturer's action. In both period 1, when consumers demanded buggies, and in period 2, when they shifted to autos, he acts so as to maximize his utility on the free market. The fact that, in retrospect, he prefers the results of period 1 may be interesting data for the historian, but is irrelevant for the economic theorist. For the manufacturer is *not* living in period 1 any more. He lives always under *present* conditions and in relation to the present value scales of his fellow men' (Rothbard, 1970, p. 770; original emphasis).
   Were Rothbard to use the same analysis he applied to the inept entrepreneur when analyzing bureaucrats, he would have no grounds for claiming that state intervention tends to create *ex post* utility losses on behalf of the bureaucrats themselves. If he uses the same analysis he applied to bureaucrats when analyzing inept entrepreneurs, he has no grounds for claiming that the free market tends to maximize the *ex post* utility of all its participants. Perhaps fearing that the first option would weaken his criticism of the state while the second would undermine his defense of the market, Rothbard arbitrarily applies two different theoretical standards, and therefore violates his own claims that his praxeological theory is 'a formal but universally valid science based on the existence of human action and on the logical deductions from that existence' (Rothbard, 1977a, p. 203). As far as I see it, Rothbard can't deduce both stories from the same set of axioms.
16. I found Cordato's overview of the earlier Austrian School (1992, chapter 1) and his criticisms of Coase (1992, chapter 5) to be quite informative, but unfortunately I cannot discuss every aspect of Cordato's book. My inquiry is more narrow: I shall critically focus upon the foundations and claims behind Cordato's reformulation of Austrian welfare economics.
17. Cordato's claim is questionable. No matter how badly argued, Rothbard thinks he examines *ex post* utility losses – at least for bureaucrats.
18. Cordato says that (1) is the 'most common criticism', (2) is 'readily apparent' once (1) is recognized, (3) and (4) are 'even more damaging criticisms,' while (5) is 'another fundamental problem.'
19. I would not expect Cordato to demonstrate this himself if he were simply reiterating Kirzner's position. That would be like asking him to reinvent the wheel. My point is that Cordato's 'catallactic efficiency' concept intends to depart from Kirzner's argument that the market is a strictly coordinating process, but it relies almost fully on Kirzner's *knowledge* claims, the very claims that point toward the market as a fundamentally coordinating

process. Kirzner has been very careful to discuss the kind of knowledge necessary for the market to have coordinating properties. See Kirzner (1979, chs. 2, 9) and (1992, chs. 8, 9, 10).

20. Cf. Armentano (1982, p. 275). He writes (1982, p. 29): 'Social efficiency, if the expression has any meaning whatever, is to be associated with a society that allows full scope for free and voluntary exchange agreements. Social arrangements are efficient if they provide the widest opportunity for private plan fulfilment and private plan coordination. A free society is both the necessary and the sufficient condition for efficient action and efficient resource allocation. . . . The efficient accomplishment of ends in a social context requires that particular planned activity dovetail or coordinate with the planned activity of other market participants.' Here Armentano is thoroughly Kirznerian in that social efficiency is tied to the market's tendency to equilibrate (to tend toward a complete coordination of individual plans). In his forward to the Cordato book Armentano embraces, without hesitation, Cordato's concept of catallactic efficiency, and considers price agreements as an example of increased social efficiency in Cordato's sense of the term. See Armentano (1992b, pp. ix–xiii). It seems that Cordato's 'open-endedness' is not really of a loosely Schumpeterian, creatively destructive variety after all. In the end, Cordato's story has strictly Kirznerian results.

21. See, for example, High (1986, 1990), O'Driscoll and Rizzo (1985), Vaughn (1992), Buchanan and Vanberg (1991), and Boettke, Horwitz and Prychitko (1994).

22. See, for example, Boulding (1981), Davidson (1989, pp. 467–87), Lachmann (1976), Samuels (1993), and G.L.S. Shackle (1992).

23. 'To the extent that such decisions are made through the state apparatus, economics can help clarify some of the opportunity costs associated with transferring additional resources from the private to the public sector, and some of the benefits that might accrue for the market process as a result of enhanced property rights enforcement' (Cordato 1992, p. 86). Which costs are those, the objective ones?

10. Expanding the anarchist range: a critical reappraisal of Rothbard's contribution to the contemporary theory of anarchism*

ANARCHISM'S RELEVANCE

In *For Anarchism*, David Goodway (1989) claims that, considering the political implications of everything from the new social movements to the upheavals of communist regimes, 'anarchism seems currently to be in the process of removing itself from its consignment to the scrap-heap of history' (1989, p. 2). While this may be a bit far-fetched, there is some evidence that the theory of anarchism does seem to be enjoying a reawakened interest, particularly among the disenchanted Left.[1]

Supposing that the theory of anarchism is relevant enough to warrant some serious inquiry and critical reflection, I would like to ask the following question. To what extent is Murray Rothbard's economics and anarchist vision relevant to the contemporary literature? Rothbard, after all, devoted his professional career to developing a case for a radically libertarian or 'anarcho-capitalist' vision, captured positively in the pure theory of an unhampered market economy (1970), and negatively in his critique of any and all forms of government intervention (1977a, 1977b). More than a pure theorist, Rothbard was a political economist in the broadest sense, one who engaged in revisionist history, natural rights ethics, and ideological pamphleteering to buttress his case further for anarchism.[2]

It takes no effort to inquire if Rothbard's work has had any impact on the anarchist theories of the Left. Although some have occasionally nodded to Rothbard in accounts of the history of anarchist thought (DeLeon, 1978, pp. 126, 129–30), and even though Rothbard has contributed to collections spanning the gamut of Left and Right radicalism, Rothbard's work is virtually ignored by the leading theoreticians of the contemporary anarchist Left.[3] When Rothbard does receive an all-too-rare

* Originally published in *Review of Political Economy* (1997), **9**(4), pp. 433–55. http://www.tandf.co.uk.

citation from the Left, it is unfailingly of the 'contemporary apologist of *laissez-faire* capitalism' variety (Marshall, 1989, p. 134).

Among the Left, anarchism is more than a stateless society, more than simply allowing free market capitalism to blossom (or explode) without the constraints of the state. While a society without a state is necessary for full-fledged anarchy, it is nevertheless insufficient. Goodway sums up the contemporary stance of mainline anarchism:

> I consider it helpful to view anarchism as a socialist critique of capitalism with a liberal critique of socialism, a (*laissez-faire*) liberal rejection of the state, both as status quo and as a vehicle for social change, with a socialist insistence upon human solidarity and communitarianism. In total, then, anarchism can be understood as the most extreme form of libertarian socialism, the term so frequently employed as its synonym. (1989, p. 1)[4]

The question I wish to address is what, if any, features of Rothbard's theory are compelling enough to revise this largely accepted understanding of contemporary anarchist theory?

I will not consider Rothbard's ethical case for anarchism (he rejects the state on natural rights grounds, independent of his own economic theory). Instead, in the first part of this chapter, I critically reappraise Rothbard's economic vision – his general claims of anarcho-capitalism as a welfare-maximizing system of economic organization – rather than his more detailed arguments regarding, say, the system of legal justice or the provision of public goods (although we will find that these issues cannot be ignored). This builds on my arguments in the preceding chapter. Then I discuss Rothbard's and the contemporary Austrian School's understanding of the 'anarchy' of the social division of labour and the calculative rationality provided by the pricing system of the market economy. I also consider the contemporary Left-anarchist moral rejection of the market system, paying particular attention to Murray Bookchin's anarcho-communist ideal. Next I reconsider the viability of self-managed enterprise against both Rothbard's anarcho-capitalist and Bookchin's anarcho-communist visions, whereby I articulate my notion of an expanded anarchist range of market-oriented producer organizations. I conclude with a brief reflection on the problem of law and contract under anarchy.

DOES ROTHBARD'S WELFARE ECONOMICS JUSTIFY ANARCHO-CAPITALISM?

Rothbard's economic argument against any and all forms of state activity is found throughout his major theoretical works, including *Man, Economy, and State* (1970, pp. 765–890) and *Power and Market* (1977a). The core of his argument is contained in Rothbard's welfare economics (1977b), where he argues that any and all acts of the state cannot make people better off (that is, state policy cannot increase social welfare).[5]

Rothbard's welfare theory, which underpins his formal critique of the state, is well known among Austrian and subjectivist economists, and can easily be summarized. Insofar as an action is voluntary, the individual always and necessarily maximizes *ex ante* utility. Rothbard's demonstrated preference principle 'forms the cornerstone' of his deductive welfare theory (1977b, p. 2).[6]

Because Rothbard defines the free market as simply the arena where free, voluntary exchange takes place, it follows that the market necessarily benefits all its participants (*ex ante*) and necessarily increases social utility. Rothbard feels that 'we can say this with absolute validity as economists' (1977b, p. 27) – independent of one's ethical stance – because that conclusion is validly deduced from the true axiom of demonstrated preference:

> The very fact that an exchange takes place demonstrates that both parties benefit (or more strictly, *expect* to benefit) from the exchange. The fact that both parties chose the exchange demonstrates that they both benefit. The free market is the name for the array of all the voluntary exchanges that take place in the world. Since every exchange demonstrates a unanimity of benefit for both parties concerned, we must conclude that *the free market benefits all its participants* (1977b, p. 27; original emphasis).

Does Every Act of the State Reduce Social Welfare?

The utilitarian benefits of market exchange imply nothing about the value of state interference. Claiming that the market system benefits its participants is not enough to reject the state. (What if, for example, the state provides the law and order that makes market exchange possible, or more prevalent, in the first place?) While Rothbard could try to provide empirical evidence to the contrary, he instead attempts to formally deduce that *no* act of the state can ever improve social utility. Believing that his logic is valid, and claiming that the demonstrated preference axiom is absolutely true, he believes his economic case against the state is absolute, certain, and scientifically irrefutable.

Yet it seems to follow that, because any and all state actions are coercive actions, benefiting the coercer but harming the coerced, *ex ante*, and because we have no scientific measure whether there will be a net increase or decrease in overall utility, formal economic theory must remain agnostic about the state's ability to influence social welfare.

Rather than call for scientific agnosticism, however, Rothbard maintains that the state cannot improve social welfare: 'We conclude therefore that *no government interference with exchanges can ever increase social utility* . . . [S]ince some lose by the existence of taxes, therefore, and since all government actions rest on its taxing power, we deduce that: *no act of government whatever can increase social utility*' (1977b, p. 29; original emphasis).

In a now classic paper on individualist anarchism, Laurence Moss (1974, pp. 28–30) interpreted Rothbard as claiming that all state action decreases social utility. While Rothbard tries to suggest that this may be likely, *ex post* (when the bungled projects of bureaucrats finally create utility losses among the state officials), he nevertheless does not validly deduce this as a praxeological certainty. Instead, Rothbard argues that no act of the state can improve social welfare.[7] Rothbard's a priorism has not established a value-free, scientific case for rejecting the state outright.

Does Every Market Exchange Improve Social Welfare?

Rothbard seems to stress the market's social welfare properties over its knowledge disseminating and spontaneous order characteristics. He tries to show that 'on the market all is harmony' (1970, p. 769) (harmony meaning the undertaking of voluntary exchanges), and hence that social welfare can only be 'maximized' under a full-blown system of private-property market exchanges, a capitalist system without a state – anarcho-capitalism. But this comes perilously close to a tautology.

The market exists, according to Rothbard, whenever a voluntary exchange occurs. Because voluntary exchange is assumed to be mutually beneficial, all gain on the market. Rothbard flatly dismisses questions of envy, jealousy, or psychic loss because, although an individual in the market system may appear envious or upset by the financial successes of others (or, one might add, the stress of competition, the monotony and meaninglessness of Taylorist production processes, the endless pushing of advertisers, marketeers, and telemarketing agents, or the financial failures, lost jobs, or questionable employment prospects of their friends and loved ones), these may be mere mental states 'divorced' from the realm of action. He argues:

> We cannot, however, deal with hypothetical utilities divorced from concrete action. We may, *as praxeologists*, deal only with utilities that we can deduce from the concrete behaviour of human beings. A person's 'envy', unembodied in action, becomes pure moonshine from the praxeological point of view. All that we know is that he has participated in the free market and to that extent benefits by it. How he feels about the exchanges made by *others* cannot be demonstrated to us unless he commits an invasive act. (1977a, p. 18; original emphasis)[8]

Rothbard borrows from Mises the strict dichotomy between a deductive-theoretical 'conception' and the application of deductive theory to create historical 'understanding'.[9] Praxeology, for Rothbard, is deductive, pure theory, and Rothbard would not have us contaminate praxeology with mere historical inferences. This is why Rothbard stresses above that, as praxeologists, we can only deduce utility on the basis of demonstrated preference. At times it seems that, for Rothbard, praxeology is prepared only to deduce claims regarding *ex ante* utility (because, after all, *ex post* utility is something realized in history, and thus the praxeologist cannot make definite statements regarding *ex post* personal as well as social utility).

I find this discussion unpersuasive for two reasons. First, what if envious people express dissatisfaction 'voluntarily' by talking with others (family, friends, shrinks and so on) or screaming (if not jumping) out of the window? Rothbard categorically rejects these non-invasive demonstrations of preference with a simple 'Even if he publishes a pamphlet denouncing these exchanges, we have no ironclad proof that this is not a joke or a deliberate lie' (1977a, p. 18). His insistence upon ironclad proof is not only ridiculous, it can also be turned against Rothbard. As observing economists we generally do not enjoy ironclad proof that sentiments *are* insincere. That being so, we cannot insist that the market system necessarily improves (let alone maximizes) social welfare. We would have to conclude instead that, because utility (or disutility) is immeasurable, we do not know, as deductivists, whether the market system improves (let alone maximizes) *ex ante* social welfare.

Second, Rothbard himself jumps from strict *ex ante* reasoning to theoretical deductions about *ex post* utility within the free markets *and* within coercive state institutions. His *Power and Market* offers a theoretical discussion of both expected and realized utility. Although he could perhaps draw empirical–historical evidence to reinforce his claims that the market tends to increase both expected and realized utility (and, conversely, the state reduces realized social utility), he instead seems comforted by a theoretical treatment.[10]

Would Reducing the State through Political Means Improve Social Welfare?

Even if Rothbard were right in his insistence that all voluntary acts among individuals necessarily increase *ex ante* social welfare, and that no act of government can ever improve social welfare, we face some interesting paradoxes if we ask what should be done in the real world.

Suppose, not unlike the political–economic reforms in Eastern Europe, or the British Public Choice movement, or some kind of so-called

'Contract With America' scheme, state officials enact policies to privatize industry, reduce deficits, and bring about a freer market economy. It seems that Rothbardian welfare economics must insist that these policies cannot improve social welfare, for they are established through the institutions of the state (and the tax-supported incomes of politicians). *Ex ante*, society can't be better off, for a 'hegemonic principle' is still at work here. (And, amusingly, if Moss is right about Rothbard's position, the Rothbardian welfare economist must conclude that such reform would make society worse off, *ex ante*.)[11]

Rothbard's welfare economics has not established that the state is unable to improve social welfare, nor that the market system is singularly welfare-maximizing, even in the absence of negative externalities. He has not proven what he set out to prove. Although his subjectivist critique of standard cost–benefit analysis (and the corresponding neoclassical model of a social welfare function) might lead us to seriously examine and question the ability of state bureaucrats to engage in scientifically 'optimal' welfare policy, he has not established that a market-based anarchism (his anarcho-capitalism) is a utility-maximizing alternative.

ROTHBARD'S LEGACY: THE KNOWLEDGE PROBLEM AS A LESSON FOR THE ANARCHO-COMMUNIST LEFT

Having said that, however, Rothbard draws the market-process approach of Mises and Hayek into the anarchist conversation; and it is precisely the Austrian theory of the knowledge-generating properties of the market process, rather than Rothbard's formal welfare economics, that offers a solid criticism of anarchist theory. Let us, therefore, review the traditional Austrian position.

Society Requires an 'Anarchy' of Production

The challenge to centrally planned socialism first appeared in the economic calculation debate. Mises (1920) understood socialism to be a system that abolishes private property in favor of state or social ownership; money as a general medium of exchange would be abolished, as well as commodity production (production for profit). The coordination of production and consumption plans would be accomplished through a central planning board. The *ex post* coordination accomplished by spontaneous or anarchic market processes (both Fourier and Marx complained about the 'anarchy of production' under capitalism) would be replaced by *ex ante* coordination through rational, scientific planning directed by a single controlling center.

Because socialism abolishes private ownership of the means of production (higher-order capital goods) in favor of state or social ownership, Mises recognized that the market for capital goods would be destroyed. Factors of production would not be freely exchanged. Without markets, Mises continued, socialism abolishes the prices that reflect relative scarcities among capital goods. And without these prices, Mises concluded, rational economic calculation is impossible. Socialism as a system of central planning (and thus centrally directed calculation, production, and distribution) must fail.

By destroying capitalism's anarchy of production, socialist central planners would unwittingly (yet necessarily) destroy their own ability to calculate relative scarcities and values. Although the central planning board might enjoy a wealth of statistical data regarding both the quantities of existing factors of production and perhaps even historically 'given' technological information (such as production functions), quantitative data and mathematical formulae (as important as they are) cannot be enough to judge and calculate relative value, for value is not inherent or embodied in capital or consumer goods. The central planning board would be bogged down with so much technical information that they would face, as Mises put it, nothing less than a 'bewildering throng of possibilities'. Planners might know, for example, that they can use existing stockpiles of pig iron to make enough steel for a railroad line of a given distance, or so many cars, or bridges, or refrigerators, and so on, but the planners would not be able to calculate whether cars are more highly valued than refrigerators, or whether bridges are less valued than cars, or whether any of these should be produced with steel as opposed to other metals, or other technologies, or, indeed, whether it is sensible and efficient to produce any of these goods (including the steel itself) at all.

Market prices and monetary calculation 'aid the mind' by allowing individual enterprises to judge, *ex ante*, the relative efficiency and expected profitability of their activities through cost accounting. The prices need not be (and, indeed, in the real world they cannot be) perfectly competitive equilibrium prices, and it is entirely misleading to even theoretically postulate general equilibrium to describe the market system. Actual, spontaneously established disequilibrium prices are enough to allow individuals to accomplish *ex ante* appraisals of potential profitability *and* later to calculate and assess realized, *ex post* results. Because individuals face genuine uncertainty, market processes can never hit a state of general equilibrium; the market system is indeed 'anarchic' in the sense of being unpredictable and out of anybody's control, but it is not anarchic in the sense of being necessarily chaotic. The market process continuously shuffles and reshuffles capital goods, as entrepreneurs learn of their errors through the *ex post* determination of economic losses, and are informed of their success through the *ex post* determination of profits.

Hayek (1945) added to these arguments by stressing the knowledge-disseminating features (as opposed to the purely calculative properties) of the market process. He argued that market prices inform 'the man on the spot' about what to do with the resources in his possession. Disequilibrium prices communicate knowledge (perhaps tacit in nature) to participants in the market system, knowledge that cannot, even in principle, be collected by a central planning board, because the knowledge is itself discovered and generated by the market process. By seeking to destroy private ownership, markets, and the monetary calculation of the means of production, central planners also destroy the set of institutional processes that make this knowledge available in the first place.[12]

The problem of abolishing the calculative and knowledge-disseminating features of the market process applies not only to socialist systems of central planning (the original focus of the Mises–Hayek literature), but also to decentralized and self-managed socialist systems. The problem lies not simply with the *state*, or with a *central* planning procedure, as Left anarchists (and even some Austrians) would have us believe. I have elsewhere argued that decentralized, democratic, and self-managed socialist systems (of the ideal Yugoslavian, as opposed to Soviet, variety) also confront the knowledge problem that arises when the market for the means of production is abolished. *Comprehensive planning*, whether in the form of central planning or self-managed and democratic planning, is itself the problem.

The Austrian argument that advanced society requires markets in the means of production in order to evaluate their relative scarcities, has become, after a long hiatus following the socialist calculation debate, increasingly accepted among socialists since the late 1980s.[13]

A Note on the Heterogeneity of the Current Austrian Discourse

While Austrians generally agree on the necessity of markets, it would be a mistake to present the argument as a unified, seamless theoretical contribution. I agree with Boettke (1998a) that the issue of economic calculation and the knowledge problem provide '*The* Austrian contribution to political economy' (his emphasis). If Austrians have anything to add to modern economics, it is precisely their case against comprehensive economic planning. Yet, although contemporary Austrians ground their current work in the solid Mises–Hayek tradition, much of the recent literature is methodologically and theoretically varied. Austrians themselves diverge (if not disagree) over the nature of the calculative and knowledge-disseminating properties of markets.

For example, Rothbard (1976a, 1991) and Salerno (1990, 1994) uphold the Misesian emphasis on calculation, and they tend to separate, if not downplay, Hayek's more epistemological emphasis. Kirzner (1992) and Thomsen (1992), on the other hand, emphasize the discovery component of the entrepreneurial market process (the market process exposes error by acts of entrepreneurship which discover price differentials and the potential profits that they generate), while Cordato (1992) attempts to synthesize Rothbard and Kirzner in a notion of 'catallactic' efficiency.

The Kirznerian entrepreneurial-discovery thesis is also extended by Machovec (1995) and Ikeda (1996) to expose and criticize the dynamic, unintended consequences that develop under any state interventions into the market process. Boettke (1993, 1995) has attempted to supplement this analysis by adding a Hayekian Public Choice twist.

Harper (1994) attempts to model the learning-discovery features endogenously, drawing from the Popperian Growth of Knowledge literature in the philosophy of science. O'Driscoll and Rizzo (1985), on the other hand, draw from the phenomenologies of Bergson and Schutz to explain intertemporal plan coordination. Outside economics, Lavoie (1985a) has argued that the communicative properties of market prices are analogous to pheromones in an ant colony, and both Lavoie (1990a) and Horwitz (1992a, 1996) have stressed that a competitive market process is an extended 'dialogue' among all market participants. Horwitz, for example, sees market prices functioning like individual words, and argues that they communicate knowledge and have meaning only against the background of the rest of the market text, that is, an individual price makes sense only against the market backdrop of all other prices.

These rather disparate explanations reflect the greater specialization of interests and concerns among the current generation within the Austrian School. The growing heterogeneity of methodology and theoretical substance is, perhaps, also a symptom of more fundamental tensions that have developed within post-war Austrian economics in general (see Vaughn, 1992, 1994). I would nevertheless suggest that, based upon our theory of the epistemological features of the market process (and its confirmation in the experience of the state socialist countries in Eastern Europe and elsewhere), the Austrians are generally correct in their claim that the market process is a necessary feature of modern society.[14]

Guerin, Bookchin and the Moral Rejection of the Market

But the Left anarchists (that is, the bulk of contemporary non-Rothbardian anarchists) continue headstrong and unaware of this literature. They seem to consider (either explicitly or implicitly) the state as the source of crisis in socialism. Presumably the problems of both capitalism and socialism can be abolished through a self-managed, thoroughly decentralized anarcho-communism.

Consider Daniel Guerin. He sees his own classic work, *Anarchism* (1970), as 'the first to put self-management back on the agenda' (1989, p. 124). For Guerin, the problem with socialism was its Marxian foundations; the failure of socialism lies, as Bakunin warned, in the creation of a 'red bureaucracy', its explosion into authoritarianism and statism. In his more recent work Guerin continues to claim that the solution to capitalism and state socialism lies in a 'libertarian and self-management communism' (1989, p. 125) – a decentralized, worker-managed society that abolishes *both* the state and the market system.

The arguments of the 'other' Murray – Murray Bookchin – are most illustrative of the adamant anti-market stance in contemporary anarchist theory. Bookchin, who will undoubtedly go down as the most brilliant anarchist theoretician of the twentieth century, attacks economic theory by positing a moral basis for a non-market anarcho-communism, supported in part by Kropotkin's decentralized communism.[15] In *The Modern Crisis* Bookchin rejects the accounting for costs and benefits as 'bourgeois calculation' (1986a, p. 5), and offers a clear and especially readable distinction between the market economy and his anarchist alternative, the 'moral economy'. It is worth quoting at length:

> Care, responsibility, and obligation become the authentic 'price tag' of the moral economy, as distinguished from the interest, cost, and profitability that enter the 'price tag' of the market economy.
>
> Care, responsibility, and obligation, we are told, are 'ideological' concepts which have no place in a scientistic notion of economics. This criticism points to the very heart of the issues raised by a moral economy. A moral economy – a participatory system of distribution based on ethical concerns – is meant to dissolve the immorality that the modern mind identifies with economics as such. Its goal is to dissolve the antagonism between 'buyer' and 'seller', to show that in practice both 'buyer' and 'seller' form a *community* based on a rich sense of mutuality, not on the opposition of 'scarce resources' to 'unlimited needs'. (1986a, pp. 89–90; original emphasis)

These images of the moral economy and its ethical preconditions are not abstractions. They imply concrete institutions and specific forms of behaviour. Institutionally, they presuppose a new form of productive community, as distinguished from a mere marketplace where each buyer and seller fends for himself or herself – a community in which actual producers are networked and interlocked somewhat like the old medieval guilds in a responsible support system. . . .

Like all real communities, they form a family that provides for the welfare of its participants as a collective responsibility, not simply a personal responsibility. . . .

This sense of moral complementarily – this social 'ecosystem', so to speak – encompasses all members of the productive community. Price, resources, personal interests, and costs play no role in a moral economy. Services and provisions are available as needed, with no 'accounting' of what is given and taken. (1986a, pp. 91–2)

I quote Bookchin not to indict him as an unsophisticated thinker (much of his work is iconoclastic and thought-provoking), but rather to draw out a core element of his system – the hostility towards the calculative properties of the market-pricing system. He hopes to replace individualist, competitive, and hierarchical institutions with collectivist, cooperative, and decentralized institutions, a stateless system that engenders 'community self-management based on a fully participatory democracy – in the highest form of direct action, the full empowerment of the people in determining the destiny of society' (Bookchin, 1990, pp. 3–4).

Libertarian Municipalism Doesn't Beat Statist Central Planning

Bookchin's anarcho-communism allegedly frees itself from the problems of statism by municipalizing rather than nationalizing and collectivizing property. His is thoroughly and ecologically decentralized, upholding face-to-face communication through participatory democracy, the maintenance of appropriate technologies, and a contextual, localist emphasis on community values. In a sense, Bookchin, too, is concerned with the particular knowledge of time and place. His libertarian municipalism offers a knowledge-based, decentralized politics in the classical sense, whereby individuals coordinate and plan together as citizens rather than managers, workers, consumers, or bureaucrats.[16] Rather than consolidate power in the grip of a state-backed central planning board, Bookchin's communist society is confederalist – a network of administrative councils peopled with delegates elected by popular, democratic assemblies. His system of confederated municipalities would not only restrict, but outright abolish, private property and the market process, for 'a market economy, conjoined with "socialism", "anarchism", or whatever concept one has of the good society, would eventually dominate the society as a whole' (1991, p. 97).

Bookchin thereby offers yet another procedure for comprehensive economic planning. His is radically democratic – going far beyond the ideals of Yugoslavian socialist self-management, for example – by rejecting the nation state (and, by implication, a coercive planning structure) itself.

Again, however, the thrust of the Austrian argument, in my view, is that it is not the state, *per se*, that belies the problem of economic calculation under socialism. It is, rather, the destruction of the discovery properties of the dynamic market process. *That* creates a knowledge problem under any system of comprehensive planning – statist, centralist, self-managed, or municipalist. While Bookchin is probably right to emphasize that the knowledge embedded within the context of an individual's locality provides the basis for rational politics, he refuses to acknowledge that private or separate ownership of the means of production, and the spontaneous series of exchanges and monetary calculations of profit and loss, are crucial for economic coordination. The delegates within the various levels of Bookchin's municipal planning councils must also face a bewildering throng of economic possibilities. They may have the political freedom to debate, criticize and engage in genuine dialogue about the nature and movement of society, but they will not have the ability to calculate the relative values of the scarce resources at their disposal.

The market process is necessary for the success of the collectivist and cooperative enterprises that anarchism, in general, has valued so highly.[17] Viable workers' self-management requires a market process. This brings us to a re-examination of Rothbard's attack on self-management in the name of anarcho-capitalism.

MUST THE SELF-MANAGEMENT PRINCIPLE BE REJECTED? QUESTIONING THE ANARCHO-CAPITALIST RIGHT

We hear little from Rothbard on the possibility of workers' self-management at the enterprise level. His few (and brief) statements are entirely negative. Recall that Rothbard's ideal is anarcho-capitalism. He sees little reason to extend the decentralist-anarchist critique into the organizational principles of the capitalist firm.

The Meaning of Self-Management

To judge the validity of Rothbard's dismissal of workers' self-management, it is necessary to define the meaning of the term carefully.

Workers' self-management has to do with the organization of enterprise. Also known as a producer cooperative or labor-managed firm, the self-managed enterprise is a productive organization whose ultimate decision-making rights rest equally among the workers of the firm, on the basis of one person, one vote, irrespective of a worker's specific job, skill, age, or even capital contribution to the firm. These decision-making rights accord to workers within the firm, *qua* workers, rather than as the possible owners of the firm. Workers' self-management seeks to establish participatory control rights within a productive organization, but leaves open the question of legal, *de jure* ownership. The firm's assets may be owned by the workers, or they may be owned by others outside the firm (or, in its socialist variant, by the state, or by society as a whole). Legal ownership is not the chief issue in defining workers' self-management – management is. Worker-managers, though not necessarily the legal owners of all the factors of production collected within the firm, are free to experiment and establish enterprise policy as they see fit. Decisions can be reached directly or through elected delegates, whether by majority rule, unanimity rule, or consensus; operations can be totally decentralized or hierarchical; income distribution can follow any set of rules decided by the worker-managers, and so on.[18] Thus, the principle has to do with the design and *ex ante* coordination within the firm (the enterprise division of labour) rather than the coordination of inter-firm plans and the overall social division of labor. Hence, it is a mistake to equate self-management with socialism, or syndicalism, or even worker control.

A blueprint for socialism may include self-management as an ideal. To the extent that socialism strives to abolish the market system in favor of comprehensive economic planning (treating society as one huge, rationally integrated enterprise) then self-management within the framework of socialist ownership would imply that all aspects of society would be planned and managed democratically according to the principle defined above. In this context, self-managed socialism proposes an alternative planning procedure (though not as radical as Bookchin's) to the hierarchical command method of the Soviet variety.

However, a blueprint for workers' self-management need not adopt a socialist ideal. Nor is self-management synonymous with syndicalism or worker control.[19] As a democratic method of enterprise organization, workers' self-management is, in principle, fully compatible with a market system.

Slouching Towards Socialism? Rothbard's Rejection

In his only extended treatment of the topic (amounting to a full paragraph) Rothbard, however, argues that a system composed exclusively of self-managed enterprises is impossible, and would lead, like socialism, to calculative chaos and complete breakdown (1970, pp. 543–4).[20] But there is a

problem with Rothbard's presuppositions. He equates producer cooperatives (self-managed enterprise) with worker or socialist ownership of the
means of production. His is simply a case 'in which each firm is owned jointly
by all its factor-owners' (1970, p. 543). From which he jumps to the following conclusion:

> In that case, there is no separation at all between workers, landowners, capitalists,
> and entrepreneurs. There would be no way, then, of separating the wage incomes
> received from the interest or rent incomes or profits received. And now we finally
> arrive at the reason why the economy cannot consist completely of such firms
> (called 'producers' cooperatives'). For, without an external market for wage rates,
> rents, and interest, there would be no rational way for entrepreneurs to allocate
> factors in accordance with the wishes of the consumers. No one would know
> where he could allocate his land or his labor to provide the maximum monetary
> gains. No entrepreneur would know how to arrange factors in their most value-
> productive combination to earn greatest profit. There could be no efficiency in pro-
> duction because the requisite knowledge would be lacking. The productive system
> would be in complete chaos, and everyone, whether in his capacity as consumer or
> as producer, would be injured thereby. (1970, pp. 543–4)

Rothbard clearly misunderstands the general principle behind producer
cooperatives and self-management in general. Self-management in no way
requires that workers within a firm own all the firm's factors; it only requires
that they manage the firm's factors on the democratic and participatory
basis of one worker, one vote regardless of the worker's capital contribution (if any) to the firm. Non-labor factors can be supplied by the workers,
or they can be purchased in the market, or rented from others. Workers
may, if they wish, make capital contributions to the firm, or the firm can
borrow funds (or sell, say, variable income debentures) in financial markets
at competitively established rates of interest. An economy of producer
cooperatives would not, as Rothbard erroneously claims, abolish 'external
markets'.[21]

This theoretical criticism is not a criticism, as Rothbard believes, of the
self-management principle. Rather, it is a confused understanding of what
a producer cooperative is. Rothbard does not establish an a priori, praxeological case against an anarchist community composed exclusively of self-
managed enterprises that compete, cooperate, exchange and produce
commodities in a dynamic market process.[22] There is nothing necessarily
socialist (or communist) about it.

Slouching Towards Capitalism? Bookchin's Rejection

And yet, it is precisely the *market*-embedded feature of cooperatives that
leads Murray Bookchin to question, if not reject, self-managed enterprise

in the name of anarcho-communism. He laments that the radicals among the ecological Left 'too often end up advocating a kind of "collective" capitalism, in which one community functions like a single entrepreneur, with a sense of proprietorship toward its resources' (1991, p. 93). Bookchin will have nothing to do with this, for 'Such a system of cooperatives once again marks the beginnings of a market system of distribution, as cooperatives become entangled in the web of "bourgeois rights" – that is, in contracts and bookkeeping that focus on the exact amounts a community will receive in "exchange" for what it delivers to others' (1991, p. 93, cf. p. 96). By rejecting the calculative properties of the market exchange system, even if loaded with self-managed enterprises, Bookchin's anarchism becomes hopelessly utopian and epistemically impossible.

FINDING A HOME ON THE ANARCHIST RANGE

Although economic theory should not reject all utopian thinking, it nevertheless places parameters around our Utopias. The Austrian notion of the knowledge problem significantly constrains the contemporary theory of anarchism. An anarchist community must allow for a market in the means of production, for prices and cost accounting, and for money as a general medium of exchange. The communist and libertarian-socialist impulse within the theory of anarchism must take the Austrian argument seriously. Comprehensive, participatory planning will fail under anarcho-communism and libertarian socialism for the same reasons that it will fail under centrally planned state socialism. Contrary to mainline anarchism, the abolition of the state (or the market, for that matter) is not enough to provide the requisite knowledge to coordinate the intertemporal production and consumption plans of the anarchist community. On this issue, Rothbard is generally right.

At the same time, I'd like to suggest that Rothbard's own insistence that anarchism makes theoretical sense only as a stateless *capitalist* society is unfounded. Neither Rothbard, nor the Austrian School in general, has established a sound theoretical case against a market economy composed exclusively of self-managed firms. Although Austrian economic theory constrains anarchism to some kind of dynamic market system, the theory may, if properly informed of the self-management principle, also expand the organizational range of enterprises within the stateless market order. Moving along a spectrum from right to left, we could imagine at the right end a system composed largely of capitalist-type enterprises (Rothbardian anarcho-capitalism), then passing through a middle range of capitalist and worker-managed firms, and finally on the left side to firms operating on the self-management principle.[23]

In a sense, the 'relevance' of Rothbard himself is still open to question. For the most part, I am critical of Rothbard's a priori case against both the state and self-managed enterprise. I have suggested that Rothbard's vision is not as solid as he himself believed. But at least this can be said: market-based anarchism is Rothbard's theoretical legacy in the contemporary theory of anarchism. Rothbard was the first to draw upon market-process economics and apply the insights of Mises and Hayek to contemporary anarchist theory. The same cannot be said of anarchism's leading thinkers. Guerin, Bookchin and a host of others seem unaware of the market-process literature, including Rothbard's, and continue to insist that anarchism must be anti-market and transcendent.

While anarchist thought might well carry on with a liberal (*laissez-faire*) critique of the state, it no longer persuades as a socialist–communist critique of capitalism. Forsaking its socialist framework (specifically, its totalistic, anti-market ideology) anarchist theory could conceivably reconstruct a decentralist and solidarist critique of state capitalist production, by allowing for competitive commodity production and the spontaneous ordering of the social division of labor, while reorganizing the enterprise division of labor on the basis of the self-management principle, properly understood.

MAKING AND BREAKING ANARCHISM: A (MORE PESSIMISTIC?) CONCLUSION

The market must, in my view, make anarchism. That is, market processes are a necessary organizational feature of an even remotely viable stateless system. But, of course, market processes work only if ownership rights are acknowledged and enforced, and if contracts are generally obeyed. Property rights require some system of law and contract.

Although the anarchist Proudhon called for *usufruct* rights and a system of contractual exchanges, much of modern, mainline anarchism follows Kropotkin's communist impulse, which denies the validity of Proudhon's contractarian position (see Graham, 1989). Exchange based upon a mutually agreed price does not, as Proudhon erroneously believed, represent an exchange of equivalents. Moreover, the contracted price offers no measure or indicator (recall Bookchin's complaints above) of moral worth. Following Kropotkin's lead, anarchist communities are to be organized under a structure of free agreements that arise through mutual aid, as opposed to competitively contracted obligations. In this view, law as a rule-based enforcement of agreed upon obligations is unnecessary. In fact, any legal code (and contractual obligation) is considered an illegitimate infringement of human freedom.[24]

Law does matter, however, to an anarcho-capitalist. Here's another Rothbardian legacy in the contemporary theory of anarchism. Rothbard does not deny the need for appropriate monitoring and enforcement of private property rights, and the support of mutually agreed-upon contracts. Rather than deny the need for law, Rothbard claims that systems of law and legal enforcement (ensuring that a 'Libertarian Code' is effectively followed) would spontaneously arise within the market process itself. In Rothbard's anarcho-capitalism, police protection is supposed to be supplied by free market subscription (1978a, pp. 215–22); private court-judicial services would be competitively supplied, for profit, through monthly subscription or the payment of fees when these services are in demand, or perhaps through vertically integrated enterprises that offer customers a combination of police and judicial services (1978a, pp. 222–7); and the libertarian legal code itself (consisting of a non-aggression axiom against person or property) would be observed in common law fashion, except that particular for-profit courts would survive on the basis of a competitive market process that weeds out inefficient court procedures (1978a, pp. 227–34).

What about corruption, fraud, racketeering and other problems? A competitive market process, Rothbard insists, provides all the appropriate incentives:

> What keeps A & P honest is the competition, actual and potential, of Safeway, Pioneer, and countless other grocery stores. . . . What keeps them honest is the ability of the consumers to cut off their patronage. What would keep the free-market judges and courts honest is the lively possibility of heading down the block or down the road to *another* judge or court if suspicion should descend on any particular one. What should keep them honest is the lively possibility of their customers cutting off their business. These are the *real*, active checks and balances of the free-market economy and the free society. (1978a, p. 236; original emphasis)[25]

No matter how much we accept the Austrian argument that markets and monetary calculation are necessary for an advanced social order, and no matter how much we might even agree that there are instances in which market processes can overcome certain public goods and externalities problems, it takes quite a leap of faith to maintain that a market process is both necessary *and* sufficient for a full-blown and stable legal–political–economic order. Of course, if Rothbard believes that all is harmony on the market; if he believes that social welfare is necessarily maximized on the free market; and if he believes that people's preferences can only be demonstrated by acts of free contracting, then we can begin to understand why he concludes that only anarcho-capitalism can possibly generate welfare-maximizing and efficient production of law and judicial service. It may already be contained in his presuppositions.

Anarchism requires markets, monetary calculation and contractual exchange. Thus, anarchism also requires law. Whereas Bookchin and mainline anarchism deny the need for courts, police and enforcement of contracts (the anarcho-communist Left considers these systems of hierarchy and domination inherent in both capitalism and statist socialism), Rothbard and the anarcho-capitalist Right subsume them completely under the calculative, profit-seeking institutions within the market process itself – just another industry within the market's competitive provision of services. But if we stick to careful analysis, and resist drawing Rothbardian conclusions based on a faith in market processes, three possible conclusions follow.

First, it remains to be shown that market processes can spontaneously supply a viable legal order on the basis of the profit–loss principle. Although I have argued that Rothbard's relevance to contemporary anarchism is twofold (markets are necessary for anarchism, and so is law) we have no clear demonstration that markets can spontaneously generate a stable, non-coercive legal structure.

Second, perhaps a council-based, administrative and intentionally designed set of municipalist legal institutions might arise on the basis of solidarity and mutual aid, operating outside the profit–loss principle. A feature of Bookchin's classical political vision based upon a rational discourse among citizens might therefore be preserved, or might even be necessary (even though we must reject his call for abolishing markets and calculation among the means of production). This, too, however, remains to be shown.

Or third: perhaps, following Nozick's (1974) argument, anarchism must invariably break apart from an inability to generate, individually or collectively, spontaneously or purposively, stable non-coercive institutions of rights provision and enforcement.

NOTES

1. For example, I had the pleasure of attending and participating in what must have been the first above-ground scholarly conference on anarchism in Eastern Europe in over four decades, 'Political Theory and Political Education – Anarchism: Community and Utopia', Inter-University Centre for Postgraduate Studies, Dubrovnik, Yugoslavia (20–31 March 1989). Organized by Laslo Sekelj, the two-week conference drew many theorists and historians of anarchism, including: H.-M. Bock, April Carter, George Crowder, Christa Dericum, Marianne Enckell, Walter Euchner, Thom Holterman, Yaacov Oved, Milan Podunavać, Ivan Prpić, Žarko Puhovski, William Reichert, Alan Ritter, Dimitrios Roussopoulos, and Rudi Supek.

Contemporary economists and political scientists have also demonstrated an interest in the theory of anarchism, beginning with Tullock (1973, 1974), Buchanan (1975) and Taylor (1976, 1982). These works, and especially the more recent literature, have pursued a rational-choice and game-theoretic approach which, though interesting, is not the approach taken in this present chapter.

2.   Rothbard penned hundreds of polemics in libertarian publications, many of which he served as an editor. See Gordon (1986) for a comprehensive bibliography through the mid 1980s.

3.   Rothbard had no influence on the work of the leading contemporary theoreticians among the Left, as evidenced by the works of Guerin (1970), Ward (1982), and perhaps most glaringly, the other Murray from New York City, Bookchin (1986a, 1986b, 1986c, 1989). Rothbard has influenced right-wing libertarians such as Robert Nozick (1974) and David Friedman (1989).

4.   Alan Ritter (1980, pp. 25–39) argues that the classic goal of anarchism (among Godwin, Proudhon, Bakunin and Kropotkin) is neither purely libertarian individualism nor absolute freedom, but rather a 'communal individuality'. Ritter agrees with Buchanan's (1977) criticism of Rothbard and other anarcho-capitalists who erroneously claim that a robust individualism does not require some commitment to the ties and traditions of community (1980, p. 180, n.28).

For my present purpose, I will not focus on the goals of anarchism. Following Frank Harrison's suggestion that 'anarchism is better understood not in terms of any specific goal, but rather as a set of organizational principles' (1991, p. 102), I shall try to explore the broadest of economic organizational principles – the role of the market exchange and pricing system under anarchism.

5.   Rothbard's original paper, 'Toward a Reconstruction of Utility and Welfare Economics' was first published in Sennholz (1956). This statement would become a foundation for his subsequent theoretical works, reappearing with only minor revisions in Rothbard (1970, pp. 768–77) and (1977a, pp. 13–23). The original paper was republished, without revision, as a monograph (1977b).

I should point out that anarchists among the Left, of course, also view the state as a crippling monstrosity that harms social welfare, but they would not consider the neo-conservative (and the Rothbardian) criticisms of the state to be in accord with anarchism. As Harrison recognizes, the neo-conservative criticisms are 'an attack by the economic hierarchy upon the State hierarchy at a point where their interests conflict. It is very much a rebellion of capitalism against the State, seeking to remove State controls. In this way they wish to replace dependence on the State by dependence on the capitalist employer by *expanding the arbitrary power of employers*' (1986, p. 53; original emphasis). Cf. Bookchin (1986a, pp. 66–7).

6.   It is also based upon a dubiously strict dichotomy between a voluntary act and coercion, or, in the social setting, what he calls the 'market' principle and the 'hegemonic' principle. To anticipate what follows, Rothbard tries to demonstrate that the consequences of following either principle are also strictly dichotomous: Rothbard (1977a, p. 263) provides a table listing the polar outcomes of following the market vs. hegemony: individual freedom vs. coercion; general mutual benefit (maximized social utility) vs. exploitation; mutual harmony vs. caste conflict and war of all against all; peace vs. war; power of man over nature vs. power of man over man; most efficient satisfaction of consumer wants vs. disruption of want-satisfaction; economic calculation vs. calculative chaos; and incentives for production and advanced living standard vs. destruction of incentives combined with capital consumption and regression of living standards.

This strict separation follows Rothbard's treatment of socially situated individuals as simply a collection of Crusoes and Fridays. Its simple dualism, rooted in an almost atomistic individualism, is open to the criticism leveled by Sciabarra (1987).

7.   I think Moss was mistaken: Rothbard does not conclude that the state decreases social welfare; rather, he insists that the state cannot *increase* welfare. Yet this, too, is an invalid conclusion. Perhaps it could be supported by sneaking in the 'non-aggression axiom' from Rothbard's natural rights ethics, but that would unquestionably 'contaminate'

Rothbard's attempt to construct a value-free economic theory, independent of his libertarian ethics.

8. Thus, envy and other purely subjective mental states can be definitively demonstrated, but only through invasive or coercive acts, according to Rothbard. Recall that, for Rothbard, 'the free market is the name for the array of all the voluntary exchanges that take place in the world'. By this definition, the free market excludes invasive acts. Presumably, for Rothbard, envious mental states become 'embodied' (and thus become data for the praxeologist) only through coercive actions, and therefore cannot become 'embodied' (whatever that means) within the market process.

9. For more on the conception–understanding distinction, see Koppl's (1997) discussion.

10. For example, Rothbard devotes an entire section of chapter 2 of *Power and Market* to the *ex post* dimension (1977a, pp. 18–24), from which he concludes: 'In sum, the free market always benefits every participant, and it maximizes social utility *ex ante*; it also tends to do so *ex post*, since it works for the rapid conversion of anticipations into realizations. With intervention, one group gains directly at the expense of another, and therefore social utility cannot be increased; the attainment of goals is blocked rather than facilitated; and, as we shall see, the indirect consequences are such that many interveners themselves will lose utility *ex post*. The remainder of this work is largely devoted to tracing the indirect consequences of various forms of governmental intervention.' (1977a, p. 24; original emphasis)

Rothbard does not examine the indirect consequences – and subsequent *ex post* benefits and losses – historically. In the remainder of the book he continues largely in the realm of praxeological 'conception', or pure economic theory. Indeed, he would later reflect upon his contribution in the following way: 'We cannot outline here the entire analysis of this volume. Suffice it to say that *in addition* to the praxeological truth that (1) under a regime of freedom, everyone gains, whereas (2) under statism, some gain (X) at the expense of others (Y), we can say something else. For, in all cases, X is *not* a pure gainer. The indirect long-run consequences of his statist privilege will redound to what he would generally consider his *disadvantage* – the lowering of living standards, capital consumption, etc. X's exploitation gain, in short, is clear and obvious to everyone. His *future loss*, however, can be comprehended only by praxeological reasoning. A prime function of the economist is to make this clear to all potential X's of the world' (1977a, p. 262; original emphasis).

Thus, Rothbard believes he has an a priori set of praxeological truths regarding both *ex ante* and *ex post* benefits and losses, with little need for historical analysis. Theory informs history, no doubt; but for Rothbard, historical understanding need not inform theoretical conception. This problem was also recognized by Moss (1974, pp. 22, 29–30).

11. Although I disagree with Moss's (1974, p. 30) interpretation that 'at best, Rothbardian anarchism can prove that state action always decreases social welfare' (Rothbard's welfare theory does not prove that, neither does it prove that the state can never improve well being), I do agree with Moss that 'it fails to support the argument that anarchism necessarily maximizes social economic welfare even when the fundamental Libertarian Code is diligently enforced', because it ignores questions of envy, interdependent utility functions and the like, and because it only deals haphazardly with questions of *ex post* – actualized – utility and social welfare.

12. The Austrian argument would, of course, be challenged by Oskar Lange and others during the famous socialist calculation debate, in which the proponents of socialism answered the Austrians by providing a model of market socialism grounded in a competitive, general equilibrium. They failed to understand, however, that the Austrian case for capitalist calculation rests (and continues to rest) on the market as a disequilibrium process, as opposed to the neoclassical notion of perfect competition and general equilibrium conditions. See Steele (1992), Kirzner (1992, esp. chapter 6), Vaughn (1994, esp. chapter 3), and Lavoie (1985b) for careful discussions of these confusions and misunderstandings within the socialist calculation debate. But new confusions have arisen, in the socialist proposals of Stiglitz for instance, which I discuss in Chapter 12.

13. The influence of the Mises–Hayek argument is clear in Miller (1989), Plant (1989),

Wainwright (1994), and Burczak (1997). Some among the Left, however, remain unpersuaded. See, for instance, Devine (1992), Cottrell and Cockshott (1993), and Foster (1995).

14. One need not, however, subscribe to all the above embellishments of the basic Mises–Hayek argument to accept the general Austrian insight. For example, Murray Bookchin rightly criticizes sociobiology for using economic categories – based upon will and intention – to explain insect and animal colonies. He states that 'The widely touted "division of labor" which is falsely imputed to all kinds of animal communities, particularly the "social insects", is an *economic* fact – a specifically *human* one – not a variegated constellation of complementary functions and activities' (1994, p. 57; original emphasis). I suspect, therefore, that Bookchin would find little use for Lavoie's (1985a, pp. 67–78) 'Austrian' explanation (which, ironically, and perhaps unwittingly, turns sociobiology on its head). Lavoie uses categories that were developed to explain insect behavior (pheromones, for instance) to explain *human* society, in which, for instance, 'The human analogue of the insects' pheromone', Lavoie suggests, 'is the expenditure of money in market exchanges' (1985a, p. 70). It is certainly understandable for someone to reject this *specific*, sociobiological explanation of the knowledge-generating features of the market system, but I don't think that is enough to reject the entire Austrian claim.

15. Actually, Bookchin has already earned such accolades: David DeLeon (1978, p. 199) states that Bookchin is 'Probably the most systematic and intelligent of all anarchist theoreticians, past and present'. Goodway (1989, p. 11; original emphasis) states that 'There can be no doubt that the foremost contemporary anarchist thinker is the American Murray Bookchin, an outstandingly original theorist, almost certainly the most innovative since Kropotkin, with whom he merits comparison [cites DeLeon]. Here is the anarchist theorist today whose work *should* be read with real interest by non-anarchists.'

16. Bookchin: 'Instead of nationalizing and collectivizing land, factories, workshops, and distribution centres, an ecological community would *municipalize* its economy and join with other muncipalities in integrating its resources into a regional confederal system. Land, factories, and workshops would be controlled by the popular assemblies of free communities, not by a nation-state or by worker-producers who might very well develop a proprietary interest in them. Everyone, in a sense, would function as a citizen, not as a self-interested ego, a class being, or part of a particularized "collective". The classical ideal of the rational citizen, engaged in a discursive, face-to-face relationship with other members of his or her community, would acquire *economic* underpinnings as well as pervade every aspect of public life. Such an individual, presumably free of a particularistic interest in a community where each contributes to the whole to the best of his or her ability and takes from the common fund of produce what he or she needs, would give citizenship abroad, indeed unprecedented, material solidarity that goes beyond the private ownership of property' (1989, pp. 194–5; original emphasis).

17. See, for example, Lindenfeld (1986) and Cahill (1989).

18. This is the generally accepted definition in the literature. See, for example, Bonin and Putterman (1987, pp. 1–3), and Prychitko and Vanek (1996, vol. I, pp. xiii–xxiii).

19. Syndicalism may be a subset of workers' self-management (that is, some syndicalists may allow for the self-management principle defined above), but self-management is not a subset of syndicalism. To the extent that syndicalist and worker-control movements simply want to vest property in the hands of labor union officials and other labor-oriented institutions, or simply to legally declare workers the official owners of their enterprises, *without* pursuing the democratic principle, they are not adopting the workers' self-management as defined above.

20. More specifically, he argues that a *world* of producer cooperatives would collapse, rather than a given system. This may hark back to Mises's argument about socialism: if a given society abolished their own market and adopted socialism within their own borders, planners might still be able to calculate factor values by resorting to world-capitalist prices. But a world-socialist system (which Marx had predicted must appear) would have no 'external' market prices to guide it, and must surely be impossible to achieve.

Presumably, for Rothbard, a given economy of producer cooperatives might similarly overcome calculation problems if surrounded by a sea of world-capitalist prices, but, in his own words, 'It is clear that a world of producers' co-operatives would break down for any economy but the most primitive, because it could not calculate and therefore could not arrange productive factors to meet the desires of the consumers and hence earn the highest incomes for the producers' (1970, p. 544).

21. And, in a comparison of the former Yugoslavia to the market socialist models of Lange and Lerner, Rothbard claimed that 'firms in Yugoslavia engage in genuine exchanges and therefore in a genuine price system' (1976a, p. 68). If Yugoslavia did have a genuine-enough price system even under its socialist notion of ownership, then surely the kind of workers' self-management that I am in favor of above is clearly feasible, by *Rothbardian* terms alone, in a market anarchist system. I must admit, however, that I am much more skeptical about the rationality of the former Yugoslavian economy than Rothbard was.

22. What about the 'standard' (that is, neoclassical) arguments against the efficiency of self-managed firms? While the theoretical and empirical literature is huge, both pro and con (see Prychitko and Vanek (1996) for a large and representative sampling), the standard arguments against the self-managed enterprise are questionable from the perspective of Austrian economic theory. Austrian theory does not employ, as this standard literature does, perfectly competitive equilibrium as an efficiency benchmark. The neoclassical criticism of workers' self-management, and the implicit willingness of Austrians to agree with the neoclassical critics without, however, adopting the neoclassical equilibrium model, was discussed at length in Chapter 7.

23. This expanded organizational range in a theory of anarchism is not meant to suggest that all places on the spectrum would be, or should be, equally valued. Even if the anarcho-communist Left, for example, were eventually to agree on a dynamic market process, I would not expect them to endorse anarcho-capitalism, nor, similarly, would I expect Rothbardians equally to endorse anarchic self-management. Having said that, my own biases would suggest that the Left end of such a range might carry greater moral suasion, to the extent that anarchist and other forms of utopian theorizing are attempts to envision people emancipated from existing yet unnecessary political–economic constraints, and acting in solidarity as opposed to merely narrow self-interests.

24. Law has consequently been thoroughly downplayed in the Left anarcho-communist literature. See, however, Holterman and van Maarseveen (1984) for the only contemporary exception.

25. Also see Rothbard (1978b). Although a non-Austrian, neoclassical economist, David Friedman provides remarkably similar arguments. See Friedman (1989, especially pp. 114–26, 183–208). Randy Barnett's discussion (1985,1986) is in a similar vein.

11.   The welfare state: what is left?*

> When the Left, in Europe and America, can conceive of no solution to the crisis other than state-managed capitalism, and still looks to Keynes for remedies which, already ineffective under Roosevelt, have become inapplicable, then it is clearly about to die from lack of imagination.
>
> Andre Gorz (1985, vii)

The autumn of 1989 ushered in the collapse of 'really existing' socialism. Previously, one would never have known from most leftist theoretical work that socialism was in such dire straits as to call its basic presuppositions into question. Now, with the massive shift of Western intellectual opinion away from socialism and toward the market-based welfare state, we seem poised to forget that it, too, is in serious trouble. Welfare programs, that, little more than a year ago, were widely considered to be deeply, if not intractably flawed, are now held up as models that Eastern Europe should emulate. On the Left, the formerly excoriated welfare state, once assumed to be an instrument of class hegemony, has suddenly found legions of new supporters.[1]

Jürgen Habermas and especially Claus Offe are among the few leftist writers who have attempted to offer a critical, systematic analysis of the welfare state. Offe, who upholds a sophisticated, post-Marxist methodological holism, has exposed the contradictory nature of welfare-state intervention in the market. His conclusions weaken the assumption that the welfare state is a viable corrective to the economic problems of capitalism. Yet Offe does not realize that implication of his work: he shares the assumption that the welfare state is a necessary response to capitalism. Thus, Offe is convinced that for all its contradictions and undesirable consequences, the welfare state is an irreversible development. In this chapter I wish to reappraise Offe's somewhat puzzling contribution to the fiscal sociology of the welfare state.

THE CRITICAL THEORY OF THE WELFARE STATE

The strength of the Habermas–Offe approach is in its attempt to explain economic crises in general, and the problem of the welfare state in

* Originally published in *Critical Review*, 4(4), 1990, pp. 619–32.

particular, from a systems perspective. They maintain that crises issue from systematically inherent contradictions in society. Habermas writes, for example, that 'crises in social systems are not produced through accidental changes in the environment, but through structurally inherent system imperatives that are incompatible and cannot be hierarchically integrated' (1975, p. 2). He adds that crises arise from 'unresolved steering problems'.

Habermas develops his argument in the following manner. In liberal capitalism, voluntary exchange of private property through the medium of money works as the fundamental 'steering mechanism'. The market process has two functions (1975, pp. 25–6). First, it serves an organizational purpose: economic exchange brings about a far-reaching, complex allocation of scarce commodities. Purchases and sales motivated by personal gain are integrated through the use of monetary price signals and profit-and-loss accounting. The second function, argues Habermas, is ideological: private property and market exchange institutionalize a class relationship between owners and non-owners of capital. As long as the market runs smoothly and society is near or at full employment, the working classes have little occasion to question the system.

An economic crisis (such as a recession), however, may lead to mass loyalty problems. That is, an economic crisis may create a social or political crisis as well, because the fundamental organizing principle itself – the market process – can easily, if not inevitably, become the focus of discontent. As a recession deepens, conflicts of interest will worsen between owners and workers. Those laid off or thrown out of work may go beyond simply blaming their former managers and businesses if they find no jobs available elsewhere. They may become discontented with the economy as a whole, and in the long run may question the market system itself.

For Habermas, the welfare state is a response to such crises. He writes: 'The bourgeois state could not rely on the integrative power of national consciousness alone; it had to try to head off the conflicts inherent in the economic system and channel them into the political system as an institutionalized struggle over distribution. Where this succeeded, the modern state took on one of the forms of social welfare state mass democracy' (1979, p. 193). Even today, in the late twentieth century, 'the origins of the crisis still lie in the economic system of capitalism, but . . . the Welfare State no longer allows the crisis to explode in an *immediately* economic form. Instead, when there is a recession and large-scale unemployment, the symptoms of the crisis are displaced into strains within the cultural and social order' (1986, pp. 57–8).

Habermas argues that the market system, if left alone, will ultimately lead to a series of incompatible claims on behalf of workers and owners of capital. Swings in the business cycle, and especially the downturns that generate lengthy recessions or depressions, tend to incite the laboring classes to call for something other than the market 'alone' to generate jobs or, more generally, incomes. Short of totally abolishing the market system, state intervention is expected to improve market performance and economic conditions. Hence, a second 'steering mechanism' appears – administrative power, or bureaucracy.

And yet, Habermas is quite aware that the modern economy is too complex to be bureaucratically controlled. Counter to intuitive expectations, such complex orders are fundamentally anarchic; the economy cannot be 'run' by anybody. State interference, then, must yield a series of unintended, even undesirable consequences.

Hence the potential for a legitimation crisis. The welfare state remains legitimate only if it renders the anarchic organizational principle stable by compensating for business cycles (neither Habermas nor Offe consider the possibility that cycles may result from centralized state banking institutions in the first place) and for the economic disturbances that are unintentionally caused by state intervention.[2] (In the new vogue of the welfare state, it has been temporarily forgotten that over the last two decades, Western economies have been in turmoil as the welfare state has become both overloaded with growing claims and increasingly chaotic in its effects.)

Offe, like Habermas, recognizes that the welfare state faces a 'precarious double function'. It must intervene in market exchanges in order to deter what are thought to be inherent instabilities, yet it must also abstain from intervening in order to ward off the undesirable consequences of intervention.[3] A legitimation crisis of state and system arises when, in the name of stabilizing the market system, state intervention unintentionally encourages greater instability. Offe (1984, p. 38) writes: 'If the dominant organizational principle of the social processes of every capitalist society is that of exchange, a theory of the crises of capitalist society can identify those processes which challenge the dominance of this central principle.'

Offe tries to abandon the traditional approach of historical materialism, an approach that views crises as inevitable contradictions of the system of commodity production and exchange (something that still haunted the early Habermas).[4] As an alternative, Offe calls for a theory that approaches crisis as the unintended result of a clash between fundamentally different systems of organization (namely the anarchic market process and the planned intervention of the tax-based welfare state): 'Not the self-negation of the exchange principle but its restriction and questioning. . .would serve as the criterion of crisis processes' (1984, p. 38).

Offe's approach to the problems of welfare-state capitalism is something of a rarity among the post-Marxist Left. He sees neither economic crises, nor crisis management, as the fundamental problematic of the welfare state. Rather, for Offe, the Left must come to terms with the continuous failure of crisis management:

> Today . . . the tantalizing and baffling riddle (in a political as well as theoretical sense) is why capitalist systems have so far been able to survive – in spite of all existing contradictions and conflicts – even though an intact bourgeois ideology that could deny these contradictions and construct the image of a harmonious order no longer exists . . . A theoretically useful and practically relevant way out of this dilemma may lie in the attempt to see neither 'crises' nor 'crisis management' but rather 'crises of crisis management' as a constant – in the attempt, in other words, to systematically anticipate and analyse the deficiencies and limitations of the stabilizing activity of the state. (1984, p. 36)

Interventionism – the idea that the monetary, fiscal, and welfare measures of the state can rationalize and ward off major economic problems – is itself in crisis. 'Everyone is convinced of the facts of the crisis', observes Offe, a bit prematurely (1984, p. 74). Welfare-state interventionism has failed to create a viable middle ground between unbridled markets and hierarchical central planning. Even though he does not seem to consider recent claims that free markets with competitive note issue (free banking) might reduce the likelihood of business cycles, Offe rightly observes that Keynesian-type monetary and fiscal policies, which seek to enhance economic growth and secure full employment, combined with welfare-state transfer-payment programs that try to compensate for the contingencies and inequalities of markets, have created nothing short of 'the worst of both worlds': namely, high unemployment and recurrent inflation (1984, pp. 198–9). The Keynesian welfare state antagonizes and threatens the market process: it undermines incentives to save, invest, and produce efficiently. It thus undermines its own legitimacy.

OFFE'S NEO-SCHUMPETERIANISM

Offe's theory of the crises of crisis management recognizes the incompatibility between Plan and Market, broadly considered. The purpose of the welfare state is at once to restrict, reorganize, and redefine the rules and outcomes of the market process, without threatening the fundamental spontaneity of that process. For example, Keynesian monetary and fiscal policy does not attempt in any way to replace the spontaneously generated market process with detailed, comprehensive planning. Keynes considered himself a realist in the classical liberal tradition (recall, for instance, his concluding notes in the *General Theory*). The idea was, and still is, for state officials to provide planned, rational intervention in order to improve the working outcomes of the unplanned market process. The problem, as Offe sees it, is that Keynesian welfare-state policies attempt to do the impossible. First, the expenditures of the welfare state are generally not self-financing (notwithstanding the imaginative but fictional notion of budget-balancing multipliers); consequently, Keynesian welfare-state policies must create a chronic fiscal problem. Second, the disposal of relevant and useful information and the ability to forecast the effects of intervention have not proved possible, despite an ever-growing bureaucracy. The growth of the welfare state has, in fact, undermined administrative rationality. Third, although the welfare state arose in order to maintain mass loyalty to the capitalist system by improving its outcomes, it is instead quickly losing mass support as it continually fails to deliver the goods (Offe, 1984, pp. 57–61).

Offe points out that the problems of the welfare state emerged from the structural incompatibility between tax-based interventionism and the spontaneous order of the market. Interventionist policies seek to maintain and improve the overall market system, but they consistently and systematically deprive producers of a portion of their capital value. This unintentionally creates disincentives to save and accumulate capital, which in turn diminishes economic growth. Diminished growth places an even greater responsibility on the officials of the welfare state to improve the situation for which they are largely responsible in the first place. Moreover, diminished growth reduces the flow of fiscal resources going to the state.

Although the welfare state is not designed to abolish the market process as the dominant organizational principle, Offe contends that the welfare state has, over time, restricted and limited the principle to such an extent that the welfare state has threatened its ability to reproduce itself. By exacerbating the problems of the market, the welfare state itself has become self-paralyzing and self-destructive.

Offe's notion of self-destructiveness is plausible in light of recent history, but it is not very well developed.[5] His focus on the structural problems and incompatibilities of welfare-state intervention into the spontaneous ordering of the market economy could benefit from explicit comparison with the similar views of Joseph Schumpeter.

In his unduly neglected article, 'The Crisis of the Tax State', Schumpeter (1918) tried to come to terms with the growing fiscal burden incurred by the post-World War I Austrian state.[6] Influenced by Rudolf Goldscheid's appeal to develop a 'fiscal sociology' of the 'tax state', Schumpeter proceeded to analyze the origin, nature, and prospects of the modern state. Schumpeter observed that the modern tax state has its origins in private property. The tax state that he speaks of, and that we face today, was created and formed by revenues appropriated from the use of private property. In other words, the modern tax state arose with the development of both state and civil society, the public and private domains.

Schumpeter clearly saw that the modern state is maintained by the productive activities that comprise the market process. A growing market allows for a greater division of labor and enhanced productivity, and thus the extent of the market affects the state's fiscal potential. The tax state is 'derived' from the market system: 'In this world', Schumpeter writes, 'the tax state lives as an economic parasite.' Hence, 'the tax state must not demand from the people so much that they lose financial interest in production or at any rate cease to use their best energies for it' (1918, p.112).

Long before the 'supply-siders' rode a short-lived wave of popularity, Schumpeter observed that levels of taxation in 'almost all countries have shot way beyond the mark in this or that case of indirect taxation and have burdened some articles to such an extent that the fiscal interest of the state itself has been hurt and a tax reduction would lead to an increase in revenues' (1918, p.113). Worse, taxing entrepreneurial profit hinders innovation and destroys the discovery-making potential of the market process. The state faces limits to its fiscal potential. When it pushes against those limits, it exacerbates the problems it originally set out to relieve:

> The fiscal capacity of the state has its limits not only in the sense in which this is self-evident and which would be valid also for a socialist community, but in a much narrower and, for the tax state, more painful sense. If the will of the people demands higher and higher expenditures, if more and more means are used for purposes for which private individuals have not produced them, if more and more power stands behind this will, and if finally all parts of the people are gripped entirely by new ideas about private property and the forms of life – then the tax state will have run its course and society will have to depend on other motive forces for its economy than self-interest. This limit, and with it the crisis which the tax state could not survive, can certainly be reached. Without doubt, the tax state *can* collapse. (1918, p.116; original emphasis)

There seems to be, therefore, a strong parallel to Schumpeter in Offe's analysis of the contemporary welfare state. Furthermore, by recognizing the modern welfare state as a set of institutions that *contribute* to the problems of working people and the poor, as well as to the wealthy, Offe's contribution would appear to have a neoliberal quality, which may surprise anyone familiar with other neo-Marxist pronouncements on the topic.

THE ISSUE OF IRREVERSIBILITY

But Offe's iconoclasm ends there. While he recognizes that both neoliberal therapy for the present crisis (privatization, deregulation, monetary and fiscal policy based upon rules rather than authority, and so on) and neo-conservative traditionalism fail to come to grips with the core of the problem, Offe is trapped, by his assumption of the objective need for the welfare state, into being unable to offer any more realistic solutions.

He argues persuasively that

> On the one hand, there is a diffuse lament regarding the societal conditions produced in the political and economic process of modernization; on the other hand there is an appeal to politicians and actors in the public sphere, urging them to leave behind their conventional scruples and to set out on the path back to stability and 'order'. In the conservative world view, the crisis of governability is a disturbance in the face of which the false path of political modernization must be abandoned and 'non-political' principles of order (such as family, property, achievement and science) must again be given their due. The polemic against political modernization – against equality, participation and socialism – therefore appears to require no consistent justification, no political program, and no theory of political transition. Its proponents are content to forge a negative political coalition of those who (actually or purportedly) are threatened by reform. They do so through nebulous appeals to authoritative powers – which serious theoretical consideration would show to be either without substance or altogether subversive of their own appeals. (1984, pp. 79–80)

Yet, because we need an interventionist welfare state, we are stuck with its growth and self-destructiveness:

> State institutions which assign legal entitlements to citizens become relatively 'rigid' or even irreversible. Not constrained by a definite index or 'stop rule' that would ensure they do not develop beyond the extent functionally required for the absorption of risks and uncertainties connected with wage labor, decommodified state institutions tend to develop an independent life of their own. (1984, p. 264)

Offe maintains that individuals within welfare-state systems have come to expect a panoply of legal claims, services and entitlements, irretrievably committing the welfare state to their provision. That, combined with Offe's (and many neoconservatives') incomplete appreciation of interventionist causes of poverty, and of the real potential for 'private' forms of welfare provision – through market provision of such services as education and housing, as well as mutual aid and non-profit and charitable organizations – leads Offe to conclude that: 'The welfare state is indeed a highly problematic, costly and disruptive arrangement, yet its absence would be even more disruptive. Welfare state capitalist societies simply cannot be remodeled into something resembling pure market societies' (1984, p. 288).

Offe contends that the standard neoconservative response to the growing problems of the welfare state is not likely to bring about fundamental and lasting change. He correctly points out that neoconservatives and even neo-liberals (he does not distinguish between them) largely seek to restore the authority of the state by reducing its range of responsibilities, but do not call for an unhampered market process. (The appeal to a central banking system managed by an appropriate monetary authority is a case in point.)

Offe, however, is unable to provide an alternative to the welfare state. He had entertained hopes for a tripartite corporatism as a non-state institutional arrangement to reconcile markets and planned intervention. But more recently Offe has concentrated on the development of such new social movements as feminism, environmentalism and pacifism, which express a greater concern for the quality of the social and ecological conditions of modernity than with class interests in the usual Marxian sense. He seems to anticipate a possible alternative in the alliance of these diverse movements and a growing trend toward eco-socialism, but provides no systematic idea of how they can overcome the welfare state (1984, p. 299). In fact, these movements have themselves been eager to appropriate the welfare state to their own ends, and they tend to exacerbate the very problems Offe describes.[7]

WHAT IS LEFT?

Agnes Heller and Ferenc Feher (1989, p. 375) have recognized that, with the recent collapse of 'socialism' in Eastern Europe, 'we are living in an age of the explosion of political fantasy', of which the new social movements in general, and a renewed faith in the welfare state in particular, are examples. But the economies that collapsed in Eastern Europe and the USSR were not, despite traditional socialist rhetoric, comprehensively planned systems. The fundamental organizing principle in 'really existing socialist' countries was still the spontaneous exchange of *de facto* private property. The central planners had neither the power nor the knowledge rationally to control the myriad production and consumption decisions they claimed were part of the plan. Although they successfully created a 'myth of the plan', as Peter Rutland (1985) calls it, they failed to achieve a true, rational and comprehensive plan.[8] Perhaps Julian Le Grand and Saul Estrin, themselves market socialists, said it best when they observed that although socialist ideology sought to destroy the 'anarchy' of the market process, socialist practice could not avoid the 'anarchy of central planning, with a perpetual sellers' market, speculation and corruption in black markets, and extensive waste and poor quality outside priority areas' (1989, p. 12).

Such observations have enormous implications for the interventionist welfare state. They imply that socialist comprehensive planning is not falling apart in Eastern Europe – where it never existed – but rather that it is state interference with a perverted market system (backed by the rhetoric and ideology of socialist planning) that has recently failed (cf. Friedman, 1989).

While the socialist-interventionist state faces a legitimation crisis, the Left has turned toward the 'triumphant' welfare state. East European 'socialism', however, was but a vastly exaggerated version of the Western interventionist welfare state; the fact that socialism has failed does not imply that the welfare state is a viable alternative, for the welfare state differs only in degree, and not in kind, from its miserable East European counterpart. This does not dictate the imminent or even the eventual disintegration of the welfare state, though it does raise that possibility as it grows ever larger. Even short of its collapse, however, the welfare state's contradictions, viewed in light of the Habermas–Offe analysis, might explain a good deal about the failings and dynamics of the welfare-state version of interventionism that appears to be victorious as the century turns.

NOTES

1. See, for example, Heilbroner (1989), Heller and Feher (1989), and Walzer (1990). *Dissent* has become an exemplary forum for the Left's turn to the welfare state – so almost any recent issue will do – but perhaps the best exchange of opinion has appeared in the Winter 1991 issue, which includes a symposium by Robert Heilbroner, Joanne Barkan, H. Brand, Mitchell Cohen, Lewis Coser, Bogdan Denitch, Ferenc Feher and Agnes Heller, Branko Horvat and Gus Tyler on 'From Sweden to Socialism.'
2. Steven Horwitz (1989) argues that expecting politicized central banks to maintain monetary equilibrium has proved to be in vain (as is hoping they can be insulated from politics). Giving power over the money supply to a centralized authority may appear to make the system more flexible by centralizing decision making, but the unintended consequence is to subject the system to the incentive structures of the political marketplace. Any recognition of this is absent from Keynesian thinking about the desirability of discretionary monetary policy. Horwitz maintains that, even if central banking institutions could somehow get beyond public-choice incentives problems – which, for example, monetarism theoretically tried to do by advocating an appropriate monetary rule (which failed miserably during the Paul Volcker years) – central bankers of whatever persuasion would still confront a more fundamental problem. They would lack the knowledge necessary to coordinate the supplies and demands for money effectively. Horwitz, following the recent work of White, Selgin, Glasner and Dowd, calls for free banking and competitive note issue in order to overcome both incentive and knowledge problems. His argument is more fully developed in Horwitz (1992b), White (1984, 1989) and Dowd (1989).
3. 'The precarious double function of the capitalist state continuously demands a combination of intervention and abstention from intervention, of "planning" and "freedom" – in short, it demands an "opportunism" (Luhmann) whose adherence to its own principles is absolutely unswerving' (Offe, 1984, p. 50). It is clear that Offe (like Habermas) breaks from classical Frankfurt School critical theory on the issue of administrative control of society. Individuals who live within modern welfare-state societies are not victims of a complete administrative complex that controls nearly every aspect of their lives, as Adorno and the classical Frankfurt theorists would have us believe. Rather, Offe insists that although the

state must stabilize the economy to remain legitimate, its interventions tend to destabilize the economy further. Administrators of the welfare state may enjoy positions of power, but their ability to control social processes is still very limited. Thus, Offe concludes that an approach which views state administrators as dominating society, as the earlier Frankfurt School did, 'is nowadays misleading and perhaps dangerous, and must in my view be questioned' (1984, p. 255).

4. Offe turns to systems theory because he believes that the 'managers' of socioeconomic systems now understand how each system or subsystem (the market, the family, the state, and so on) is related to the others. The Federal Reserve, for instance, is entrusted with a tremendous degree of power and responsibility to manipulate the supply of money and credit and thereby ward off economic recessions. Offe maintains that bureaucratic institutions have emerged in order to control, regulate, and guide market processes. Hence traditional historical materialism is no longer relevant: 'It is basically wrong to assume that contemporary capitalist society continues to be the kind of anarchic liberal society considered from Mandeville to Marx. Welfare capitalist society has less the character of an anarchic interplay of unconscious forces, in which order is an unintended byproduct. Order, in the sense of a complex and integrated coherence between different subsystems, is something that is consciously pursued by agents within the system. Of central importance is the capacity of state power to regulate and integrate discrepancies and conflicts. Whether state power is able to manage and reproduce the highly oppressive, irrational and self-contradictory capitalist system is of course an open question' (1984, p. 257, cf. 49).

    Offe apparently contradicts himself. At times he describes market exchange as anarchic; here he says it is not nearly as anarchic as Marx believed. But the contradiction is only apparent. Offe points out that modern, capitalist governments are increasingly entrusted with the responsibility of 'guiding' the market system – order is indeed consciously pursued. In this sense contemporary capitalism differs from that of Marx's generation. On the other hand, though people within governments intend to create order, they rarely do so. They disrupt the system instead. Hence the recurring crises of crisis management: although agents of the welfare state try, bit by bit, to guide the anarchic market process, they always seem to fail. The fundamental organizational principle is still out of control.

5. There are other problems as well: Offe's reliance upon the notions of surplus value, the valorization of capital, and other categories of Marxist thought have been discredited by a century of economic criticism. In spite of that, I believe he offers something of value to readers in search of a realistic theory of the welfare state.

6. Although this article has been neglected in the past, the growing welfare state crisis has brought about a reawakened interest in Schumpeter's general thesis. See, for example, Bell (1978, pp. 227–32), Musgrave (1980), and Zimmermann (1980).

7. Cf. Bell (1978, p. 226; original emphasis): 'While much of this came pell-mell and piecemeal, what was not completely recognized and still is not, is that the government had made a commitment not only to create a substantial welfare state, *but to redress the impact of all economic and social inequalities as well.* Much of this was faltering; in actual fact, little as yet may have been accomplished. But the historical watershed is the fact that a normative societal commitment has been made, and it, too, is largely irreversible.'

8. Michael Polanyi recognized this decades ago in his criticism of Soviet material balances planning. Polanyi argued that, as opposed to the theoretical model, the Soviet economy has been composed of numerous, conflicting planning centers – a 'polycentric' as opposed to 'monocentric' order. Coordination, to the extent that it occurred at all, took place not at the center of the planning hierarchy, but at the lower levels, among the individual enterprise managers who used their own discretionary authority and engaged in black market exchanges. Though the quantity and quality of outputs chosen and produced at the enterprise level became aggregated into a so-called central plan, and indeed were later published as a unified, centrally issued plan established by the directives of GOSPLAN (the Soviet central planning bureau), in fact the coordination of economic activities took place at the enterprise level, at the bottom of the hierarchy. True, production was traditionally geared to satisfy the demands of the officials of the socialist state. But production decisions were ultimately coordinated in a spontaneous (black) market setting. Thus Polanyi

(1951, p. 134) remarked, 'in reality such an alleged plan is but a meaningless summary of an aggregate of plans, dressed up as a single plan'. Cf. Roberts (1971), Zaleski (1980), and Lavoie (1986–87). Peter Boettke (1988, 1990) argues that the only sincere attempt to plan a second-world society comprehensively seems to have been immediately after the Bolshevik Revolution, during the so-called War Communism era (1918–1921) in the Soviet Union, and that was a grand failure.

12. Does market socialism have a future? From Lange and Lerner to Schumpeter and Stiglitz

Joseph Stiglitz dropped a bomb on the post-communist literature with the publication of his *Whither Socialism?* in 1994. I had argued in the previous chapter that the modern welfare state has emerged as the Left's ideal, and yet Stiglitz, an eminently respectable economist, published a defense of market socialism shortly thereafter. Surely Stiglitz must be taken seriously.

In this chapter I shall explore Stiglitz's general case for a renewed vision for market socialism.[1] I think, of course, that Stiglitz still misunderstands the Mises–Hayek case against socialist planning. But I also believe Stiglitz focused too much on Lange's idealized model of market socialism, and failed to consider Schumpeter's. In fact, the market socialist models of Lange and Schumpeter seem to be treated as complementary in the literature on socialist calculation. (Perhaps this is one reason why Stiglitz focuses almost exclusively on the Langean variant and offers *no* citations to Schumpeter's model.) I shall attempt to disentangle and critically compare the two models. By doing so, we shall find that many of Stiglitz's present concerns, and flaws, are remarkably similar to Schumpeter's. We shall also find that Stiglitz is really much more mainstream than the title of his book suggests: he is really trying to save, in the name of 'market socialism', the modern welfare state.

ARROW, DEBREU, AND STIGLITZ

Stiglitz (1994, pp. 15–26) argues that market socialism failed in Eastern Europe because it was based upon a faulty model, that of Lange and Lerner. And the Lange–Lerner model was faulty because, in turn, it was founded upon a notion of general economic equilibrium which (at least implicitly at the time of the socialist calculation debate) required Arrow–Debreu notions of a *complete* set of perfectly competitive markets – not only spot markets but futures markets as well. If Arrow–Debreu really describes the capitalist system, Stiglitz argues, it would *also* provide an empirically feasible case for market socialism, if not outright central planning (1994, p. 10). But:

> Casual observation would suggest that market socialist economies are not identical to capitalist economies, not even remotely so. The model of market socialism underlying that theorem is seriously flawed.
>
> But our contention is that it is equally important to observe the model of the market economy – underlying not only that theorem but also the fundamental theorems of welfare economics – is seriously flawed. With a bad model of the market economy and a bad model of the socialist economy, no wonder that any semblance of the equivalence of the two could, at most, be a matter of chance! (1994, p. 24)

Stiglitz proceeds to criticize the standard model's welfare claims, reacquainting us with the now well-known Greenwald–Stiglitz theorems which demonstrate that a world with imperfect information (leading to incomplete markets, moral hazard problems, and so on) vitiates the First Fundamental Theorem of Welfare Economics: the purely free market can *never* reach a constrained Pareto optimum under such conditions, but government intervention can *potentially* create Pareto improvements in the economy. (Compare this to Rothbard's and Cordato's praxeological position, which reaches opposite conclusions.) Stiglitz calls into question the Second Fundamental Theorem, which otherwise establishes a general case for decentralization of the economy, by raising further questions about the prevalence of nonconvexities and externalities (including in some cases what are otherwise considered mere pecuniary externalities).

Stiglitz further explores these criticisms by discussing how, *contra* Arrow–Debreu, decentralized plans are often coordinated by more than prices in actual capitalist economies, that the presence of rents, significant sunk costs, strategic barriers to entry and so forth all call into question the Arrow–Debreu concept of competition, and finally, that the Arrow–Debreu concept of a complete set of markets (including forward markets for each commodity) leaves out the entire question of innovation. In a chapter titled, 'The Socialist Experiment: What Went Wrong?', he argues that these theoretical limitations of the Arrow–Debreu model (and, thus Lange–Lerner) go a long way to explain why the market-socialist experiences in Eastern Europe failed.

Theoretically, Stiglitz's negative assessment of the mainstream general equilibrium model is formidable, and it does indeed amount to a (non-Austrian) rejection of the celebrated Lange–Lerner 'solution'. But Stiglitz is empirically weak. His interpretation of market socialism in Eastern Europe, such as Hungary (1994, p. 10), is colored, if not blinded, by the Lange–Lerner spectacles: he seems to believe that these experiences were an application or 'adaptation' of the Lange–Lerner *model*. Perhaps it is convenient for an economist, especially with high opportunity costs of his time (1994, p. 167), to interpret the complex historical record in this light, but misplaced concreteness surely carries a *scholarly* cost itself.

Given Stiglitz's negative critique, it comes as no surprise that the standard Arrow–Debreu model also has little if anything to say about current socialist transformation – it offers no model for dynamic transition problems. Stiglitz, accordingly, offers his own policy advice, based upon the new information economics established by the Greenwald–Stiglitz theorems. But, despite all Stiglitz's claims of having established a new 'paradigm' in economic theory (1994, p. 5), Stiglitz's own application of the new information economics to transition issues is incredibly mainstream: state economic policy should minimize barriers to entry, establish general and credible rules of the game (which includes hard budget constraints and meaningful profit–loss measures), keep a check on inflation, change the incentive structures of management (perhaps before encouraging full-blown privatization), and, finally, establish a more equal distribution of wealth from the start, a sort of 'people's capitalism'. Besides one or two Austrian and renegade neoclassicals who call for anarcho-capitalistic shock therapy in Eastern Europe, wouldn't many, if not most neoclassical economists nurtured on Arrow–Debreu theorems, generally agree with Stiglitz's recommendations? I'd say that Stiglitz's theoretical differences with the mainstream do not make much of a policy difference for the post-communist transition problems that plague Eastern Europe today.[2]

Stiglitz's criticism is cast in a post-Arrow–Debreu framework, which gives it a certain air of originality. Perfectly competitive defenses of capitalism are flawed, and so, too, are perfectly competitive defenses of market socialism. Stiglitz wants none of either, and calls for some new thinking about market socialism, torn from the traditional general equilibrium trappings which plagued the Langean vision. I contend, however, that Schumpter had already perceived this problem, and rebutted Lange, 50 years before Stiglitz. Let's take a closer look.

LANGE'S AND SCHUMPETER'S COMPETING VISIONS OF MARKET SOCIALISM

Specifically, I shall briefly discuss Lange and Schumpeter on the following issues: (a) the role of markets in promoting consumer sovereignty; (b) rational economic production; (c) income distribution; (d) the time element and its role in capital accumulation, saving and investment.

Consumer Sovereignty Under Market Socialism

Lange (1964) assumes, for most of his essay, that citizens will enjoy freedom of choice in consumption. He argues that consumer preferences, expressed through consumer demand and corresponding 'prices', ought to be the guiding criteria in planning production (1964, p. 72). Prices are established through the 'trial-and-error' model, which is so well known by now that it does not need repeating here. Suffice it to say that those prices are claimed to play a 'parametric function' – taken as given by agents within the market socialist economy and fully reflecting an equality between marginal opportunity costs and benefits – because they rest upon perfectly competitive equilibrium conditions.

Lange concedes that his trial-and-error procedure could be directed, in principle, by the preference scales of the bureaucrats who compose the central planning board (1964, pp. 96–7), but he wishes to maintain consumer sovereignty on most items while allowing the CPB to deviate from his so-called market prices 'only in exceptional cases in which there is general agreement that such deviation is in the best interest of social welfare' (1964, p. 97). Lange imagines some 'Supreme Economic Court whose function would be to safeguard the use of a nation's productive resources in accordance with the public interest' (1964, p. 98) in order to adjudicate between free consumer choice and those exceptions.

Schumpeter (1976) accepts Lange's trial-and-error procedure, but predicts that a market socialist system, if actually put into practice, would more likely restrict the scope of consumer sovereignty in favor of bureaucrats' preferences. 'Only outright beefsteak socialism', Schumpeter argues, will be content with attempting to maximize the satisfaction of consumers (1976, p. 184). It would simply be more rational for planners to pursue their own preferences (even if developed in the name of some vague 'public good'). Schumpeter recognizes that, by abolishing a market process in favor of trial-and-error planning,

> there would have to be an authority to do the evaluating. . . . Given its system of values, that authority could do this in a perfectly determined manner exactly as a Robinson Crusoe can. . . . The vouchers, prices, and the abstract units would still serve the purposes of control and cost calculation, although they would lose their affinity to disposable income and *its* units. All the concepts that derive from the general logic of economic action would turn up again. (1976, p. 184)

Score one for Schumpeter on this general point – *not on the alleged ability for planners to calculate rationally* – but for his forecast that the planners' preferences would be much more likely to guide production than Lange's dream of upholding the sovereign consumer outside a market process based upon the exchange of private property rights.

Stiglitz, on the other hand, offers no such prediction. He imagines state bureaucrats and planners pursuing the *goal* of nudging the market socialist economy closer toward Pareto optimality. And just what set of rules of the game – what underlying institutions – would provide bureaucrats with both the knowledge and the incentives to do so?

Production: Perfect Competition or Monopoly Capitalism?

Lange, we all know, founded his system of production on the perfectly competitive, general equilibrium model. Stiglitz argues that this was Lange's crucial mistake. Of course, the Austrians had offered that argument long before Stiglitz. But there is an important difference. The Austrians employed the theory of the market process; Stiglitz seeks to replace perfect competition with the theory of imperfect competition and market failure.

Yet, this had been Schumpeter's theme all along. 'Our socialism borrows nothing from capitalism', Schumpeter insisted (1976, p. 182). Schumpeter wants nothing to do with the perfectly competitive model:

> We might almost speak of a school of socialist thought that tends to glorify perfect competition and to advocate socialism on the ground that it offers the only method by which the results of perfect competition can be attained in the modern world. The tactical advantages to be reaped by placing oneself on this standpoint are indeed obvious enough to explain what at first sight looks like surprising broad-mindedness. . . . But the analytic advantages of stressing that family likeness are not equally great.
>
> In all that really matters – in the principles governing the formation of incomes, the selection of industrial leaders, the allocation of initiative and responsibility, the definition of success and failure – in everything that constitutes the physiognomy of competitive capitalism, the blueprint is the very opposite of perfect competition and much further removed from it than from the big-business type of capitalism. (1976, p. 183)

Schumpeter remained all too aware of the models of imperfect competition that were emerging at the time to uphold a fascination with the perfectly competitive ideal. He realized that worldly conditions cannot, either in a capitalist or market socialist economy, attain the perfectly competitive benchmark. Stiglitz has merely filled in some of the technical details of Schumpeter's original position.

Income Distribution

Lange sought to link income with marginal productivity, while striving to maximize the total welfare of the population. Of course this assumes his planners have resort to some hypothetical social welfare function.

Wages would be tied to estimates of a worker's marginal productivity (though again, how would that be measured without market prices of the inputs and other non-human, socially owned factors of production?). As to the distribution of any 'social dividend' that might arise, Lange wishes to distribute the social dividend in a manner that does not influence the workers' apparently 'free' choice of occupation. For example, he suggests the social dividend could be distributed equally per capita (1964, p. 84). Lange assumes that the consumers' marginal utility curves are identical – not an empirically descriptive assumption, but a practical assumption that allows planners to 'strike the right average' in estimating the relative marginal utilities of income. He claims, in this framework, errors would be random, which would be superior to the capitalist system which 'introduces a constant error – a class bias in favor of the rich' (1964, pp. 102–3).

Schumpeter differs. 'The most important logical – or purely theoretical – difference' between capitalism and socialism is that only under socialism can the distribution of income be 'completely severed from production' (1976, p. 173):

> Since *prima facie* there are no market values of the means of production and, what is still more important, since the principles of socialist society would not admit of making them the criterion of distribution even if they did exist, the distributive autonomism of commercial society is lacking in a socialist one. The void has to be filled by a political act, let us say by the constitution of the commonwealth. (1976, p. 173)

So Schumpeter expects that income will not be tied directly to productivity. Instead, he supposes the market-socialist society would be geared toward an equalitarian distribution of income. But he does suggest that income should be distributed through a voucher system, the vouchers themselves being expressed in the form of some arbitrary numeraire good.

Like Schumpeter, Stiglitz hopes for a more equalitarian distribution of income (1994, p. 266), though it is remarkably *unclear* just how the state will accomplish this ideal. Stiglitz does recognize, against Schumpeter, that distribution cannot be fully severed from production; he realizes that 'efficiency and equity considerations cannot be separated' (1994, p. 46), and thus has one up on Schumpeter on this point. At the same time, however, Stiglitz resorts to an information-constrained social welfare function model and assumes planners will harbor *enough* of the right incentives and information to strive consistently towards maximizing the welfare of the population (1994, pp. 45–50). He offers no argument – theoretical or empirical – as to why anybody should expect that to happen in the real, postcommunist world. Again, Stiglitz remains content with his own formalism, and fails to appreciate the institutional and epistemological issues that would harness precisely the right kinds of incentives and information that would allow his bureaucrats successfully to seek Pareto improvements.

The Time Element

Lange's model certainly collapses once he struggles with the issues of time and economic dynamics. He cannot allow household saving to occur, as the rate of saving would be affected by the distribution of income, which he finds 'irrational' (1964, p.108). He also employs Keynes' old 'paradox of thrift' concept to buttress his claim (1964, p.109). But these are only claims. Lange offers no arguments in their support.

Lange proposes, once again, a 'trial-and-error' routine for establishing interest rates, with disequilibrium being discovered through shortages or surpluses of aggregate 'capital', and adjusted accordingly in the short run (1964, p.84). For Lange, the long run process must allow for capital accumulation, but the rate must be established by the central planning board, rather than the time preferences of the citizens:

> If the accumulation of capital is performed 'corporately' before distributing the social dividend to individuals, the rate of accumulation can be determined by the Central Planning Board *arbitrarily.* (1964, pp.84–5; original emphasis)

> The arbitrariness of the rate of capital accumulation 'corporately' performed means simply that the decision regarding the rate of accumulation reflects how the Central Planning Board, and not the consumers, evaluate the optimum time-shape of the income stream. (1964, p.85)

> One may argue, of course, that this involves a diminution of consumers' welfare. This difficulty could be overcome only by leaving all accumulation to the savings of individuals. But this is scarcely compatible with the organization of a social-ist society. (1964, p.85)

Stiglitz correctly recognizes that the Lange model can only work if it assumes a set of Arrow–Debreu futures markets under general equilibrium conditions (1994, pp.90–107). And Stiglitz, acknowledging that the real world is replete with information and incentives problems, rejects the Lange model because he rejects the Arrow–Debreu model.

But consider Schumpeter. His model of market socialism, to this point, is based on imperfect competition *and* on static conditions. Schumpeter argues that, in such a 'stationary state', interest rates play no economic func-tion. The issue of capital accumulation, on the other hand, necessarily intro-duces the time element, and drastically alters the market-socialist paradigm.

Schumpeter approaches the problem of time and dynamics by consider-ing the problem of new investment (1976, pp.178–9). He supposes that a new and more efficient piece of machinery has been introduced into the socialist production process. Because it is more efficient, plant managers must adopt it (adhering to the first production rule of maximizing efficiency in production); but by its very nature they will realize a 'profit', which violates another production rule (because marginal cost is now less than price). If resources are fully employed, citizens in the market-socialist community would have to work beyond the hours which (Schumpeter assumes) are fixed by law, and/or reduce consumption. And Schumpeter recognizes that the rules of plant management, which he shares with Lange in the static model, can no longer be expected to provide the so-called 'automatic solution' to the coordination problem in a dynamic system (1976, p. 179).

So how to grapple with the time dimension and the coordination problems associated with capital accumulation? Schumpeter casts out many of the earlier features of his model discussed above:

> All we have to do if we wish to have such an automatic solution is to repeal the law invalidating all claims to consumers' goods that are not used during the period for which they are issued, to renounce the principle of absolute inequality on incomes and to grant power to the central board to offer premiums for overtime and – what shall we call it? – well, let us call it saving. (1976, p. 179)

Schumpeter *does* allow saving and interest in his dynamic model. And as to leaving it exclusively in the hands of the central planning board, Schumpeter once again anticipates Stiglitz's criticism. Schumpeter concedes,

> we may also leave it to the individual comrades to decide what and how much work they are to do. Rational allocation of the working force would then have to be attempted by a system of inducements – premiums again being offered, in this case not only for overtime but for all work, so as to secure everywhere the 'offer' of labor of all types and grades appropriate to the structure of consumers' demand and to the investment program. (1976, p. 180)

Of course, both Schumpeter and Stiglitz see the state as playing a fundamental role in coordinating the capital structure through time. Their failure lies in their inability to model capital as an integrated structure (cf. Lachmann, 1978; Kirzner, 1996; Lewin, 1999 and Horwitz, 2001); instead, they rely upon traditional aggregate analysis that has yet to appreciate the Austrian knowledge-problem argument regarding coordination through time in a non-Arrow–Debreu setting.

LANGE AND SCHUMPETER IN SUMMARY

Clearly Lange and Schumpeter cannot be viewed as twins in their advocacy of market socialism. Lange's vision remained trapped in the perfectly competitive framework, promoting atomistic production guided, via the planning board, by consumer sovereignty and democratic socialism. Schumpeter's vision stressed equalitarianism and the advantages of large-scale businesses, including advantages of cooperation in terms of knowledge and innovation, and would not consider atomistic competition a goal even if it were achievable. On these points, I contend, the core of Stiglitz's current defense of 'market socialism' is found in Schumpeter.

Stiglitz stresses the crucial problem of a lack of Arrow–Debreu futures markets. But we've also seen that Lange, and especially Schumpeter, begin to strip off some of their socialist ideals when the problem of coordination through time is introduced. Lange reduces the scope of consumer sovereignty by not allowing their time preferences to be demonstrated through private saving and borrowing decisions. Schumpeter reneges on his equalitarianism ideal in light of dynamic issues, and grants the necessity of savings – or at least a proxy thereof – to coordinate the capital structure through time.

Stiglitz is correct in his observation that

> Market socialism is premised on the economy of information/communication afforded by the price system. *All* relevant information, between consumers and producers and among producers, is communicated through the price system. But with technological change, this simply isn't so!
>
> It is here that perhaps Hayek's criticism of central planning becomes most relevant. It is essentially impossible for all the relevant information to be communicated to a central planner. There is really no alternative other than some form of decentralization and a far more fundamental form of decentralization than envisaged by the market socialism model (1994, p. 152; original emphasis).

It seems to me, however, that Schumpeter already recognized the need for socialist decentralization that was not wedded, like Lange, to perfectly competitive general equilibrium. That is not to say that I am satisfied with Schumpeter's attempted solution. I applaud him for recognizing the problem five decades ago, but I find that he, and Stiglitz today, seem to be nodding to Hayek without understanding the power and import of his argument. Neither Walrasian, Arrow–Debreu, nor Greenwald–Stiglitz equilibria capture the heart of Hayek's concerns. They all remain trapped in a non-institutional, non-dynamic, empirically empty neoclassical formalism.

THE ROLE OF STIGLITZ'S STATE

It is precisely here that Stiglitz invites criticism upon himself, not so much because he wants to save some socialist ideals – incredibly, however, through a 'people's capitalism' (1994, p. 265) – but rather because of his unexamined *presuppositions* regarding how to do so, and thereby move towards the Good Society.

In his chapter on 'Asking the Right Questions', which anticipates his tentative policy proposals, Stiglitz insists that we shouldn't ask whether the state has a role to play in the economy, but rather how large a role, and in what specific tasks (1994, p. 231). This might appear to be a corrective to the Rothbard–Cordato approach to welfare economics. For Stiglitz, the problem is posed correctly only when we seek an 'appropriate balance between markets and government' (1994, p. 267), *as suggested by the results of the Greenwald–Stiglitz theorems* mentioned earlier. But Stiglitz himself offers no historical or comparative institutional reasons why the state is here to stay. He doesn't even bother to provide a couple of obligatory citations to the *other* classic analysis of Schumpeter (1918) or the contemporary arguments of Offe (1984) to prop up his claim. No, Stiglitz believes he *formally* demonstrates the potential efficiency-enhancing properties of the state based upon the Greenwald–Stiglitz theorems, and comfortably believes that solutions to our worldly problems (and, apparently, the flourishing of certain utopian ideals) can become illuminated by formulating a new set of mathematical theorems to replace the old set of Arrow–Debreu/Lange–Lerner (1994, pp. 4–6, 231–2). While I criticized the Rothbard–Cordato version of welfare economics for its attempt at a purely formal, praxeological defense of anarcho-capitalism, Stiglitz errs in pursuing a purely formal neoclassical welfare model that – he thinks – can be used to scientifically address institutional change under post-communism.

To his credit he mentions that economics must be recast as something more than a Samuelsonian constrained maximization problem (1994, p. 201) – so, too, did Rothbard and Cordato – but Stiglitz's own alternative – a mathematical theorem that encompasses more complex, non-linear vectors – fails to appreciate the institutional and epistemological issues that plagued Samuelson and the other neoclassical economists he criticizes. This becomes most troubling if Stiglitz hopes to break beyond mere intellectual puzzling about the world and use his models to *change* the world.[3]

Moreover, if Stiglitz's main insight is generally correct – that the state cannot be ruled out (or, in his case, that it should be ruled in) – then he cannot continue to ignore the grand constitutional questions. *How* will the coercive institutions of the state be constrained? What is the relationship between the state and civil society in the Stiglitz model, let alone his utopian-inspired vision? As a project in political economy, and an updated argument in the socialist calculation debate, Stiglitz cannot continue to ignore the crucial questions regarding both the state's power to enforce rights and the rights of the state collectivity itself. The best of the post-communist socialist literature, such as Habermas (1998), must eventually be addressed. Although he may not agree with the details of Buchanan's constitutional economics (Buchanan, 1975), Stiglitz's current effort fails to persuade as a project in contemporary political economy without seriously addressing the broader constitutional concerns that Buchanan and other economists have raised. How can he defend his claims that state planners can deliberately propel the market-capitalist system or the market-socialist system closer towards the Pareto-optimal outcome? How would they come to know, in advance, what any Pareto-optimal outcome of a complex economy would look like? And what incentives would they have to try to find out and act upon it, while keeping within their previously established (*how? using what means?*) constitutional limits?

IGNORING THE RIGHT QUESTIONS

Stiglitz merely assumes that the planners, bureaucrats and citizens can solve these problems. My concern is not only with these real-world problems – as large and significant as they surely are. My concern is also with Stiglitz's understanding of the economic problem that undergirds his theoretical approach. It suffers from what Buchanan had called – some four decades ago – a 'physical-computational' mentality to economic science. Speaking in particular of the older, Arrow–Debreu framework, Buchanan observed:

> The individual responds to a set of externally determined, exogenous variables, and his choice problem again becomes purely mechanical. The basic flaw in this model of perfect competition is not its lack of correspondence with reality; no model of predictive value exhibits this. Its flaw lies in its conversion of individual choice behavior from a social-institutional context to a physical-computational one.
>
> A market is not competitive by assumption or by construction. A market *becomes* competitive, and competitive rules *come to be* established as institutions emerge to place limits on individual behavior patterns. It is this *becoming* process, brought about by the continuous pressure of human behavior in exchange, that is the central part of our discipline, if we have one, not the dry rot of postulated perfection. (1964, p. 29; original emphasis)

Although Buchanan – like Stiglitz today – was criticizing the more traditional models of perfect competition, and its applicability to real welfare economics issues, his criticism also strikes at the core of the Greenwald–Stiglitz variety as well. 'Our whole study becomes one of applied maximization of a relatively simple computational sort', Buchanan laments. 'Once the ends to be maximized are provided by the social welfare function, everything becomes computational . . . If there is really nothing more to economics than this, we had as well turn it over to the applied mathematicians' (1964, p. 24).

Stiglitz himself is trying to join the broader dialogue in political economy, and asks at the end of the book 'whether the insights of modern economic theory and the utopian ideals of the nineteenth century can be brought closer together' (1994, p. 277). Where? In the real world, or only in the halls and journals of the academy? If also in the real, post-communist world, then how? By having more mathematical economists – nurtured on Greenwald–Stiglitz theorems – staff the bureaux of the state? How will Stiglitz's commitment to the new-new welfare economics – one scientific tradition among many competing alternatives – have a liberating effect on the very real people whose lives he hopes to (Pareto) improve?

Stiglitz, I fear, is simply wrapping formal, abstract economics in a cloak of radical political-economic change – a new case for what Schumpeter called beefsteak socialism, if not, simply, the modern welfare state geared toward Pareto-improving interventions. It remains quite mainstream in its core, and in its vision.

NOTES

1. This chapter builds on two previous papers of mine. It draws from my book review of *Whither Socialism?* (Prychitko, 1997c) as well as a previously unpublished paper that I had written several years before, which compared the market socialist blueprints of Oskar Lange and Joseph Schumpeter (Prychitko, 1983).
2. In terms of a debate about technical economics, free market economists will find Stiglitz's book both challenging and frustrating. Neoclassicals, in particular, should be challenged by Stiglitz's thoroughgoing critique of the perfectly competitive model of capitalism. To the extent that they believe the perfectly competitive model describes, or can describe (1994, pp. 22–3), actual or future capitalist economies – although I'm not sure they do – free-market economists invite Stiglitz's criticisms, and they should rise to the challenge by providing both formal and empirical research to the contrary. Frankly, I think Stiglitz has the theoretical edge on them, though again he's as empirically thin as a sliver: of his more than 300 references in the book's bibliography, I count less than a dozen that are fundamentally empirical – this in a book purported to address the central problems of socialist transformation. As an Austrian, on the other hand, I'm irritated if not frustrated by Stiglitz's occasionally questionable interpretations of Hayek (1994, pp. 24, 273) and especially his tendency to lump Austrian efficiency arguments together with that of their free-market neoclassical brethren (1994, p. 43). Austrians will probably maintain that Stiglitz's argument is 'really' against *neoclassical* general equilibrium modeling and its corresponding welfare claims, but, as I've tried to demonstrate elsewhere (Chapter 7 in this book), Austrians often import capitalist efficiency arguments from their neoclassical colleagues, and thus unwittingly invite their own frustration: yesterday Lange, today Stiglitz.
3. I'd suggest here that Stiglitz reacquaint himself with Hayek's (1979b) discussion of scientism, and *also* that he delve into Jürgen Habermas' (1974) discussions of the problems linking feasible practice with abstract theory (especially because he hopes to answer the Big Questions with mathematical models), as well as Claus Offe's (1985) examination of the incoherent logic of state planning in the market complex. As a contribution to the cause of salvaging socialist–utopian ideals, Stiglitz's project has to inform itself with the best of *that* literature.

13. Socialism as Cartesian legacy: the radical element within F.A. Hayek's *The Fatal Conceit**

Virtually all the benefits of civilization, and indeed our very existence, rest, I believe, on our continued willingness to shoulder the burden of tradition. These benefits in no way 'justify' the burden. But the alternative is poverty and famine.

F.A. Hayek (1988, p. 63)

[I]f it were the case that there were no single locus of solidarity remaining among human beings, whatever society or culture or class or race they might belong to, then common interests could be constituted only by social engineers or tyrants, that is, through anonymous or direct force. But have we reached this point? Will we ever? I believe that we would then be at the brink of unavoidable mutual destruction.

Hans-Georg Gadamer, letter to Richard Bernstein (Bernstein, 1983, p. 264)

During the spring of 1989 dozens of internationally recognized Marxist philosophers met for two weeks in Dubrovnik to re-examine the potential of the Marxist critique of capitalism and its corresponding vision of socialism. As with any intellectual conference of this sort, there were sharp differences of opinion over particular details of Marxist and post-Marxist thought.

Nevertheless, most, if not all, were willing to abandon completely the goal of comprehensive planning and concede that the 'anarchy' of market processes delivers both economic rationality and political freedom. Karl-Otto Apel's session was the most telling. Apel argued that the vision of Lenin, Mao, and the others suffered from what he called 'the great pretension'. The market system, he maintained, is a great evolutionary achievement of mankind, much more complex than the utopians and Marxists could ever imagine. Albrecht Wellmer, the chair, smiled, nodded his head in agreement, and symbolized the consensus of the audience.[1]

Socialism is clearly on the run. The experiments, the 'really existing socialisms' of our time, are a collective failure. The intellectuals, such as those who gathered in Dubrovnik, now leap from the crumbling foundation

* Originally published in *Market Process*, 8, 1990, pp. 8–18.

upon which they once steadfastly stood. The Hayekian overtones of many of their arguments – Apel's, for instance – are striking.

Hayek, in fact, deserves partial credit for the intellectual disillusionment within socialism. His writings, which span over 60 years, represent one scholar's indefatigable defense of the market as a system to which advanced society owes its *raison d'être*. In 1988 the University of Chicago Press published Hayek's latest statement, written in his eighties, which summarizes his lifelong argument against socialist planning. Hayek's *The Fatal Conceit: The Errors of Socialism*, the first of a projected 22 volume collection of his works, represents a serious scientific challenge to those intellectuals who believe a deliberately guided society is more rational than a spontaneously evolved one. Moreover, Hayek's summary may also challenge classical liberals as well. Some seem to believe that Hayek has caved in, in the sense that he may now grant too much to the forces of tradition, and too little to the potential of human reason to shape our future.

Hayek's classical liberal critics maintain that his argument may allow for only a very small role for the critical scrutiny of tradition, and little prospect for the ability to use reason to overcome the growing problems of our age.[2] Does Hayek's recognition that it is impossible to emancipate ourselves from tradition necessarily imply a conservative defense of existing society? I wish to show, to the contrary, that Hayek's case against socialism and his corresponding defense of the market derive from a sophisticated epistemological research program, one that points toward a realizable political radicalism.

THE EPISTEMOLOGICAL ERROR OF SOCIALISM

Hayek argues that the problems of socialism go well beyond incentive problems, motivation problems and social choice problems. Certainly those specific problems exist, and much interesting research is being undertaken to explain their origins and persistence. But the whole notion of socialism, Hayek believes, is founded upon a factual error.

That error is based upon a misconception of the way knowledge is distributed and used in society. The knowledge necessary to coordinate the complex activities in advanced society cannot be given in complete and objective form to a single mind or even a committee of minds that occupy a central planning bureau. Certainly data – information pertaining to historical prices and quantities of material goods produced, technical information relating to actual production processes used in the past, the various outlays by consumers on final goods and services, and so forth – can be collected by a vast computer network for the planner's examination. But data only partially corresponds with the type of knowledge that lies at the basis of economic decision-making.

Statistical data is the measurable result of individuals following their own clues and judgments, judgments which, when combined with monetary price signals, allow individuals to integrate their plans into the overall market order. Data does not, however, encompass the entire realm of knowledge. The actual knowledge necessary to coordinate interlocal and intertemporal production and consumption plans is never available in its totality. Rather, it is dispersed among hundreds of thousands of individual minds in the form of local contextual knowledge, knowledge which is largely embodied in the form of individual skills and tacit know-how. The blueprints of socialism, as well as the standard models of capitalism, are questionable because they tend to assume that the relevant knowledge is given and known, or that it can be obtained if one is willing to bear the transaction costs of collection. Both the neoclassical theory of Walrasian *tatonnement*, and the socialist's assumption that the central planning board would be able to gather the relevant information as efficiently as an entrepreneur, is mistaken, at least if either theory is understood to be a description of the real world or a practical possibility.[3]

Whether the formal theorist is a proponent of the market or planned economy, he conceals if not misunderstands the discovery process of the market system: 'the problem is not how to use given knowledge available as a whole', Hayek argues, 'but how to make it possible that knowledge which is not, and cannot be, made available to any one mind, can yet be used, in its fragmentary and dispersed form, by many interacting individuals – a problem not for the actors but for the theoreticians trying to explain those actions' (1988, p. 99).

The epistemological mistake of socialism appears in the long-held socialist hope to abolish the market institutions of property, commodity production, and the general medium of exchange in order to realize social and economic justice through a unified, comprehensive plan. The traditional socialist belief that our advanced society could be 'emancipated' from the ungoverned market process – by transforming principles used to organize relatively simple phenomena for the organization of complex social phenomena as a whole – is the basis of what Hayek calls 'the fatal conceit'. Comprehensive planning sought to replace *ex post* discovery based upon rivalry, or the inevitable clash of millions of often conflicting plans, with *ex ante* coordination based upon scientific reason. Any attempt consciously to engineer society must end in utter failure, because it presupposes that the knowledge required to accomplish that task can be captured outside the extended order established by voluntary competition and cooperation.

Socialist theory has traditionally failed to understand the knowledge-disseminating character of spontaneous social orders:

> The efforts of millions of individuals in different situations, with different possessions and desires, having access to different information about means, knowing little or nothing about one another's particular needs, and aiming at different scales of ends, are coordinated by means of exchange systems. As individuals reciprocally align with one another, an undesigned system of a higher order of complexity comes into being, and a continuous flow of goods and services is created that, for a remarkably high number of participating individuals, fulfills their guiding expectations and values. (Hayek, 1988, p. 95)

Because socialists did not understand that the spontaneous order of the market system is the very basis of advanced society, and that such an ordering process cannot be abolished without destroying the future reproduction of society, they erroneously believed they could choose between a spontaneously ordered system and a comprehensively planned system:

> The demands of socialism are not moral conclusions derived from the traditions that formed the extended order that made civilisation possible. Rather, they endeavour to overthrow these traditions by a rationally designed moral system whose appeal depends on the instinctual appeal of its promised consequences. They assume that, since people had been able to generate some system of rules coordinating their efforts, they must also be able to design an even better and more gratifying system. But if humankind owes its very existence to one particular rule-guided form of conduct of proven effectiveness, it simply does not have the option of choosing another merely for the sake of the apparent pleasantness of its immediately visible effects. The dispute between the market order and socialism is not less than a matter of survival. To follow socialist morality would destroy much of present humankind and impoverish much of the rest. (1988, p. 7)

SOCIALISM AS CARTESIAN LEGACY

Hayek maintains that the error of socialism is an intellectual error whose roots trace well back to Descartes' philosophy of knowledge. Hayek does not make the wild claim that Descartes was a socialist, or that contemporary socialists are self-proclaimed followers of Descartes. There is no need to. Instead, Hayek argues that socialism's assumptions about the nature of knowledge are based upon similar premises and presuppositions as Cartesian rationalism. They have their origins in Cartesian rationalism.

In its attempt to uphold the products of human reason as the highest form of rationality, Hayek maintains that Cartesian rationalism misunderstands the nature of our reason. Logically, it leads to constructivism, which abuses reason. How can that be?

Descartes strove to attain pure reason. In the *Meditations Concerning First Philosophy*, for example, Descartes writes: 'Since reason already convinces me that I should abstain from the belief in things which are not entirely certain and indubitable no less carefully than from the belief in those which appear to me to be manifestly false, it will be enough to make me reject them all if I can find in each some ground for doubt' (1964, p. 75). He explicitly sought the Archimedean point upon which to ground our knowledge claims. Claims to knowledge outside pure reason, those under the influence of opinion, prejudices, authority, or tradition were, to Descartes, mere nonsense. Prejudices, authority and tradition are said to block one's reason. They are considered obstacles which must be overcome in our search for truth. We must emancipate ourselves from these constraints by way of a proven method in order to achieve pure reason, for, if we do not succeed, Descartes feared, we will wallow in the waters of relativism.

This may sound reasonable to many still today, for it characterizes the knowledge claims of modernity. Hayek argues, however, that this epistemology is 'plainly false' (1988, p. 49), a 'product of an exaggerated belief in the powers of individual reason and of a consequent contempt for anything which has not been consciously designed by it or is not fully intelligible to it' (1946, p. 8). Hayek is not alone in that respect. With Hayek, a growing body of literature in hermeneutics argues that the dichotomy between reason and tradition, between objectivism and relativism, is untenable. The dichotomy does not enhance reason and objectivity. It unintentionally destroys it.[4]

The continental philosopher Hans-Georg Gadamer argues that Descartes' attempt to design a methodology that would overcome prejudices, authority and tradition was futile. He sought a method that would 'safeguard us from all error', a goal which erroneously presupposes a 'mutually exclusive antithesis between authority and reason' (1985, p. 246). Richard Bernstein, following Gadamer's observation, remarks that Descartes' *Meditations* exemplifies the modern quest for a 'foundation' upon which to support knowledge claims, and the parallel belief that without an objective foundation, we will succumb to relativism. He has dubbed that belief the 'Cartesian Anxiety', an intellectual fear associated with what is now considered a very misleading and debilitating notion of reason and rationality (1983, pp. 16–20).

Cartesian rationalism, or 'constructivism', as Hayek also puts it, assumed that the institutions which benefit society have been consciously created by the power of human reason. Its goal was to overcome the spontaneous process of historical evolution. This goal was expressed by the utopian socialists such as Saint-Simon and Fourier, and later by Marx and his followers. They all sought to overthrow the 'anarchy' of the market system with a scientifically determined comprehensive plan.[5]

Marx in particular faced a similar anxiety: without a comprehensive plan to ground and guide society, he believed, people will be estranged from their species potential. They will be victimized by alienation. Understandably, the anxiety spread from Descartes's theory of knowledge to Marx's theory of history. More specifically, what originated as a method which tried to ground knowledge and produce epistemological certainty, Hayek shows, led to a method which tried to order society and design institutions for the benefit of humanity. It logically led to the call for the conscious ordering of society.

In sum, just as Descartes argued that man must overcome tradition, authority and prejudices in order to attain pure reason, so, Marx would later argue, must he be emancipated from the alienation and false consciousness of markets in order to 'return' to himself (1964, p. 135). Man cannot 'return' to himself, that is, he cannot become a whole, fully creative being, until he develops a method – a comprehensive plan – by which to overthrow the entire market system. For Marx, 'The life-process of society, which is based on the process of material production, does not strip off its mystical veil until it is treated as production by freely associated men, and is consciously regulated by them in accordance with a settled plan' (1906, p. 92). This is a specific example of what may be called the 'Constructivist Anxiety'.

It makes sense that both the Cartesian quest for pure reason and the socialist search for rational social construction are motivated by the same type of anxiety. Hayek's profound insight that the spirit of Cartesian rationalism logically leads to socialism seems to be an insight, however, that many classical liberals would like to do without. For it may also radically challenge their own intellectual presuppositions.

IF REASON CANNOT OVERCOME TRADITION . . .? THE CLASSICAL LIBERAL ANXIETY

Hayek's stance against socialist pretension, first popularized in *The Road to Serfdom* some 50 years ago, has certainly garnered a respectable following. But to some classical liberals, Hayek's emphatic synopsis in *The Fatal Conceit* may have hit negative returns. That is, Hayek's final summary of his six decades of research may do more harm than good. Specifically, some seem disenchanted with Hayek's final statement because it is now quite clear that his criticism of socialism has really been a criticism of rationalist philosophy. There is a growing anxiety among classical liberals themselves that Hayek's critique may imply that reason and rationality are in fact powerless in the face of authority and tradition.

It is a reasonable apprehension. Consider, for instance, Hayek's following remarks:

> Learnt moral rules, customs, progressively displaced innate responses, not because men recognized by reason that they were better but because they made possible the growth of an extended order exceeding anyone's vision, in which more effective collaboration enabled its members, however blindly, to maintain more people and to displace other groups. (1988, p. 23)

> The idea that reason, itself created in the course of evolution, should now be in a position to determine its own future evolution (not to mention any number of other things which it is also incapable of doing) is inherently contradictory, and can easily be refuted . . . It is less accurate to suppose that thinking man creates and controls his cultural evolution than it is to say that culture, and evolution, created his reason. (1988, p. 22)

Would it not be ironic, indeed, if one of the leading exponents of classical liberal philosophy, a philosophy which sprang forth during the Enlightenment, now maintains that humankind must blindly submit to tradition and prevailing authority? Can we not question the rules and social institutions in society in order to improve the lot of humankind? What, in fact, is Hayek's case for reason and rationality? As James Buchanan puts it, 'Is the implication that we must remain quiescent before the forces of cultural evolution? . . . Despite his earlier denial, is Hayek, after all, a conservative?' (1988–89, pp. 4, 5).

Every reader must interrogate *The Fatal Conceit* with this very question. I believe, however, that the contemporary hermeneutics literature helps overcome the anxiety that the nature of the question elicits. Let's therefore consider Hayek's discussion of the role of cultural evolution and tradition in a bit more detail.

Hayek maintains that morality is not the product of deliberate consideration. People were never so intelligent as to be able consciously to design a system of rules by which to guide society for the better. It may appear 'as if' humankind had the foresight to establish rules of several property, honesty, the social division of labor, monetary exchange, and so on. But this interpretation is very misleading. In fact, nothing of the kind occurred. Rather, those groups that first adopted practices such as the use of several property probably did so accidentally. Nevertheless, they had a better chance to prosper compared to those that did not. These practices enhanced the wealth of the small bands of people, which further allowed them to multiply their numbers. They acquired rules and characteristics, which, even though they were not fully understood, were passed from generation to generation through imitation. Our moral heritage is not the product of rational foresight, but of cultural evolution.

Hayek has extended his discussion of market competition as a discovery procedure to human history in general. Market competition selects particular individuals who are economically efficient, while cultural evolution selects overall groups which follow practices that increase the wealth prospects for the average member. Both selection processes disseminate primarily inarticulate knowledge to individuals through space and time.

While Hayek considers this an extension of his earlier work, others argue that it conflicts with his earlier methodology. For example, John Gray and Viktor Vanberg suggest that Hayek's emphasis on the selection of groups rather than individuals represents a departure from the principle of methodological individualism.[6] But it is not clear what they mean by methodological individualism. If it is understood as a position that studies human action in an isolated context (the Robinson Crusoe approach to economics), then it is true that Hayek's approach differs dramatically. Hayek moves well beyond a naïve, atomistic individualism, and accounts for human action in a social context. For Hayek, society is composed of individuals who are not immune to, nor can they fully transcend, the influence of language, economic institutions, and other rule-guided practices of which they may be only faintly aware. Nor can they fully account for the effect of their actions on others. Hayek's approach to methodological individualism is sophisticated, and suggests that the study of individuals in isolation cannot account for the development of rules through time. It seems successfully to break from atomistic individualism without adopting the opposite extreme of a naïve holism which posits a group mind approach to history and institutions, an approach that has proven to be dangerous.

Socialism failed to understand the historical basis of our extended market order and consequently tried to overthrow the rule-guided practices of several property, monetary calculation, and so forth. In other words, its futile hope to uncouple society from the 'economic base' of capitalism is a direct result of the fallacious notion that reason can criticize the totality of human history. Socialism not only failed to recognize that the market system acts as an indispensable discovery procedure. In addition, it did not understand that crucial knowledge is also communicated from generation to generation through tradition itself.

Perhaps now we may be in a better position to understand Hayek's claim that we must still be willing to 'shoulder the burden of tradition' (1988, p. 63). Hayek argues that we owe our very intelligence to that realm between instinct and reason which is tradition (1988, p. 21). Tradition is the undesigned result of a process of selection from among rival beliefs. By the same reasoning that the market economy gives rise to a level of intelligence far beyond the capability of an individual human mind, so tradition is 'in some respects superior to, or "wiser" than, human reason' (1988, p. 75). 'The whole of tradition is', Hayek argues, 'so incomparably more complex than what any individual mind can command that it can be transmitted at all only if there are many different individuals to absorb different portions of it' (1988, p. 79).

The knowledge problem argument holds in both cases. In the economic sphere, the efficiency and compatibility of certain production plans can be judged only within a concrete market process, as opposed to some abstract theoretical standard. Economic activities comprise, of course, only a portion of a much larger social domain which consists of art, politics, science, family relationships, and so on. If economic plans must be rationally appraised within the context of the market process, then it follows that social interaction in general can be rationally understood and criticized only from within: 'The only standard by which we can judge particular values of our society', Hayek writes, 'is the entire body of other values of that same society' (1970, p. 19).

We cannot transcend all of society, for we exist only within society. That may sound either trivial or redundant. One is reminded, however, of Marx's notion of the economic base and superstructure. Marxism understood itself to pierce through the veil of the superstructure, or social consciousness, by fully explaining the realm of material production, the base. But if ideas were to some extent determined by the base, as Marx argued, then why weren't Marx's own ideas also determined by the base? What gave Marx the remarkable ability to rise outside society itself?

Hayek's words seem right on target: 'The picture of man as a being who, thanks to his reason, can rise above the values of his civilisation, in order to judge it from the outside, or from a higher point of view, is an illusion. It simply must be understood that reason itself is part of civilisation' (1970, p. 20).

If the basic Hayekian insight into the market order is correct, that there is no Archimedean position by which to judge the rationality of economic activities, and that the spontaneous ordering of economic activities is defined only within the process of its emergence, then it sensibly follows that there is no objective framework by which to judge human history itself.

There is no fundamental difference between Hayek's claim and Gadamer's notion that 'we stand always within tradition' (Gadamer, 1985, p. 250, cf. p. 324). In particular, like Hayek, Gadamer argues that tradition is not an object that can be overcome in the name of enhancing knowledge: 'That which has been sanctioned by tradition and custom has an authority that is nameless, and our finite historical being is marked by the fact that always the authority of what has been transmitted – and not only what is clearly grounded – has power over our attitudes and behavior' (1985, p. 249).

In Hayekian fashion, Gadamer concludes: 'The validity of morals, for example, is based on tradition. They are freely taken over, but by no means created by a free insight or justified by themselves. This is precisely what we call tradition: the ground of their validity' (1985, p. 249).

Equally important, Gadamer makes it clear that real authority is based upon reasoned judgment and not blind obedience, something one should keep in mind when reading Hayek:

> It rests on recognition and hence on an act of reason itself which, aware of its own limitations, accepts that others have better understanding. Authority in this sense, properly understood, has nothing to do with blind obedience to a command. Indeed, authority has nothing to do with obedience, but rather with knowledge. (1985, p. 248)[7]

The hermeneutical understanding of knowledge suggests that authority enables rather than debilitates human intelligence. It suggests that the appeal to authority is a fundamentally rational act, and that the prejudice against all authority rightly understood is a misleading and dangerous pretension. If true, then the recognition of authority does not necessarily lead to uncritical conservatism. Hayek understands that authority is based upon knowledge, and now explicitly links the division of knowledge to the division of authority. (1988, p. 77)

OVERCOMING OUR ANXIETIES

The anxiety some of us face has its origins in the belief that reason can and must overcome authority and tradition. But that fear is based upon a misunderstanding of human reason. To believe that we actually can break with the whole of tradition is to believe that we can leap outside time and history. It is utopian in the strict sense of the term. Although it is a burning desire among modern scientists and intellectuals, such an idea remains an utter impossibility in the here and now of human existence.

It may be worthwhile, by way of conclusion, to recall an aspect of the celebrated Habermas–Gadamer debate. It seems that the early Habermas, like Marx before him, wanted to subject all of tradition at once to unrelenting criticism, in order to penetrate what he perceived to be dominating interests and false consciousness. Gadamer argued that Habermas's project was futile, an epistemological impossibility. Gadamer also maintained, however, that although authority and tradition communicate indispensable knowledge among peoples and generations, that by no means precludes the possibility of critique. In particular, Gadamer argued that our human experience of the world, for which we rely on our faculty of judgment, consists precisely in the possibility of our taking a critical stance with regard to every convention. In reality we owe this to the linguistic virtuality of our reason and language does not, therefore, present an obstacle to reason. (1985, p. 496)

We can question everything, Gadamer concluded, but not all at once.

Hayek concurs with Gadamer. We stand within tradition. We cannot escape it. Nor can we fully explain it, because the totality of tradition is at a higher level of complexity than that of the individual human mind. Hayek has, truly, extended his Goedelesque argument that the human mind can never be capable of fully explaining itself (1963, especially pp. 184–90) into the domain of human history itself. Reason is incapable of fully explaining or criticizing human history. And like Gadamer, Hayek also argues that we can question everything, but not all at once. Although traditions are passed down because they tend to enhance human survival, Hayek is quick to point out that recognition 'certainly does not protect those rules from critical scrutiny' (1988, p. 20). '[We] are indeed called upon to improve or revise our moral traditions', Hayek assures us. As opposed to critical scrutiny from some exterior, utopian position, our task must be 'based on immanent criticism' (1988, p. 69).

Hayek's research program develops a profound account of the errors of truly utopian reasoning. It is a criticism of a major element, a tradition, as it were, of modernity. The spirit of Hayek's research suggests that the alternative to utopianism does not have to be conservatism at all:

> I must warn you . . . that the conservatives among you, who up to this point may be rejoicing, will now probably be disappointed. The proper conclusion from the considerations I have advanced is by no means that we may confidently accept all the old and traditional values. Nor even that there are any values or moral principles which science may not occasionally question. The social scientist who endeavors to understand how society functions, and to discover where it can be improved, must claim the right critically to examine, and even to judge, every single value of our society. The consequence of what I have just said is merely that we can never at once and the same time question all its values. Such absolute doubt could lead only to the destruction of our civilisation and – in view of the numbers to which economic progress has allowed the human race to grow – to extreme misery and starvation. (1970, p. 19)

One does not have to be conservative if one jettisons the utopian project, whether that project is associated with Descartes, Marx or Habermas. It seems to me that, beyond a non-human utopia and a reactionary conservativism, there lies a sophisticated radicalism waiting to be explored. Hayek points us in that direction. It's up to his students to continue the quest.

NOTES

1. The conference I refer to is 'Philosophy and Social Science: The End of Utopia?' Inter-University Center for postgraduate studies, Dubrovnik, Yugoslavia, 27 March–7 April 1989. Apel's session was entitled 'Critique of Utopian Reason'. Unfortunately, the paper he prepared for the session was confiscated by the Italian customs police while Apel was en route to Yugoslavia.
2. This is apparent in some of the essays written for the special Hayek symposium issue of the *Humane Studies Review*, **6**(2).
3. To be sure, contemporary neoclassical theorists do not defend the formal equilibrium model as a practical possibility or even an accurate description of real-world markets. While it is true that many in the past had once argued that the market really does solve a system of excess demand equations (cf. Patinkin, 1965, pp. 38–9), most, following Arrow and Hahn (1971), understand that the standard model is only about the imaginary construction of equilibrium as such, and not about the actual operation of real existing markets. Others, following Friedman (1953), justify the assumptions of the model on the grounds that unhampered markets perform 'as if' the relevant information is given and known and market participants behave like price-takers. But this still does not help us to understand the following question: how is society possible in light of the fact that the knowledge necessary to achieve any degree of order is dispersed among many people? With this question in mind, Hayek's discussion of the problem is at once a criticism of the socialist attempt to plan society comprehensively and a criticism of the standard theory of the market system. It is no exaggeration to say that Hayek's earlier articles about the knowledge problem (1937, 1945, 1948b, 1968) are as much a criticism of standard economic theory as they are a criticism of the assumptions of socialism.
4. I specifically have in mind Gadamerian-type hermeneutics. For a good introduction see Weinsheimer (1985) and Bernstein (1983). Rabinow and Sullivan (1979) provide a good representation of original essays on the major themes of hermeneutics in general and its implications for the human sciences.
5. Wrote Hayek: 'Rationalism in this sense is the doctrine which assumes that all institutions which benefit humanity have in the past and ought in the future to be invented in clear awareness of the desirable effects that they produce; that they are to be approved and respected only to the extent that we can show that the particular effects they will produce in any given situation are preferable to the effects another arrangement would produce; that we have it in our power to shape our institutions that of all possible sets of results that which we prefer to all others will be realized; and that our reason should never resort to automatic or mechanical devices when conscious consideration of all factors would make preferable an outcome different from that of the spontaneous process. It is from this kind of social rationalism or constructivism that all modern socialism, planning and total-itarianism derives' (1965, p. 85).
6. Cf. Gray (1984, pp. 45–55, 1988–89) and Vanberg (1986). Also see Hayek's earlier statement about cultural evolution in the epilogue of his *Law, Legislation, and Liberty* (1979b).
7. Also cf. Gadamer (1985, p. 524, n. 187). The insight that authority is based upon a division of knowledge in society rather than command was in fact recognized by one of the earliest critics of Marxism, the anarchist Michael Bakunin, over a century ago. See his brilliant passage in Bakunin (1970, pp. 32–5).

14. The collapse of communism – a decade later*

I'd like to take you back exactly ten years ago.

Little did any of us know, back in January 1989, that the year would become sealed in history as one of the most important revolutionary – or, more precisely, counter-revolutionary – years of the century, at least on par with 1917. Some have gone so far as to claim that 1989 represents the end of modernity.

Communism and state socialism had collapsed. We could hardly imagine that possibility in January 1989. But by April the signs of change became clearer: Solidarity had gained legal status in Poland on 17 April. By 4 June Solidarity candidates defeated the Communists in that country's first free election since the Communists took over. (On that same day, however, we witnessed the Tiananmen Square massacre in China.) Yet, a month later, on 6 July, Gorbachev promised a *laissez-faire* approach to liberalization in Poland and in Hungary. In fact, demolition of the barbed-wire barrier between Hungary and Austria had already begun in May. By 10 September, the Iron Curtain had collapsed, as East Germans were allowed to vote with their feet and exit through Hungary. By October the Communist Party was abolished in Hungary, which then declared itself an independent democratic republic.

Who could have imagined, standing in January 1989, that the Berlin Wall would be opened in November of that same year? Later that month Czechoslovakia's Communist Party lost its monopoly powers, and free elections would be declared in the near future. By early December East Germany and Bulgaria followed the Czech lead. Ceaucescu and the Communist Party soon fell in Romania.

With this unprecedented momentum, the rest was inevitable. Within a year East and West Germany were unified (3 October 1990); Lech Walesa was elected president of Poland (9 December 1990), and the Soviet Union was rapidly disintegrating as the Communist Party's constitutional monopoly of power was repealed (March 1990). By December 1991, Gorbachev resigned and the Soviet Union ceased to exist.

* Delivered at the 2nd Vital Issues Forum – 'Geopolitical Forces: The World as a Nation', Northern Michigan University, 28 January 1999.

Within a matter of months, one state-socialist regime after another crumbled. From the Baltics to the Balkans, from Eastern to Central Europe, classical liberalism seemed to rise triumphantly. Even leftist intellectuals (Robert Heilbroner comes to mind) published eulogies on socialism and claimed capitalism the winner in the battle of economic systems and political ideologies.

In addition, 1989 marked the year of the dissident intellectual in Eastern Europe, espousing liberal principles of economic and political freedom, of the civil or open society and the global market. And people listened.

Now my wife and I spent the first six months of 1989 in Zagreb, Croatia. I was a freshly minted PhD trying to make sense out of Yugoslavia's economic system. I must admit, I hadn't a clue that the Soviet Union and its satellites were about to crumble. I realized Yugoslavia was in deep trouble – with a healthy 2–300 per cent inflation in January 1989, and civil strife in some obscure place called Kosovo in southern Serbia. But heck, I thought it was a big deal when, in the Spring of 1989, I attended a two-week postgraduate seminar on the theory of anarchism – the first above-ground gathering of intellectuals on that topic in Eastern Europe for decades. Little did I myself know.

The years 1989 to 1991 were indeed exhilarating, exciting times. The path, though difficult, seemed clear: the great socialist experiment had come to an end. The Communist Party and central economic planning were dead. A constitutional rule of law and a market economy were to take their place.

But the 1990s are a stubborn and sobering reminder that classical liberalism doesn't necessarily replace socialism by default. Although there have been some success stories – I think of countries like the Czech Republic, Slovenia, and Poland to a lesser extent – the 1990s might likely become notoriously known for the Bosnian War, the crisis in Kosovo, and the return of the camps. Who knew in January 1989 that the Berlin Wall would soon fall? And who knew, after we witnessed its fall, that Ethnic Cleansing would soon follow in its wake?

I see two lessons in this. The first has to do with economics and is something that I was skeptical about from the beginning. The second has to do with ideology, which I must admit I didn't foresee in advance.

LESSON 1: THE TRANSITION PROBLEM: CAN A FULL-BLOWN MARKET SYSTEM BE INTENTIONALLY CREATED?

The transition from state socialism to private ownership, market competition, spontaneous cooperation, and individual responsibility has been terribly difficult. Often chaotic and uncertain, it can generate a massive redistribution in wealth and power, and it raises new questions regarding exactly who was responsible for the oppressive past and who is responsible for the growing economic problems of the present. (As an aside, for example, should past oppressors and communist informants be punished or should they be given the same political and economic rights as everyone else? What procedures will be used to answer these and similar questions? Should liberal post-communists now trust what they read when *they* reopen the hidden police files and archives?)

Throughout much of Eastern Europe, former communists are now entrepreneurs, yet *they* are writing the rules of the game. This is not the kind of market economy that the rest of us had in mind! Crony socialism has been replaced by crony capitalism.

The lesson? As I teach my Economics 101 students, the market is not a thing, nor is the market a place. Things can be designed and produced at will. Places can be planned, engineered and organized. But the market is a process. It's a process of competing bids and offers. It's a process of cooperative inducements and persuasion. It's a multifaceted process of people *working things out* without detailed, central guidance. A market *system* is something that tends to *evolve over time* under appropriate social-political structures, which themselves cannot be engineered at will. A lasting market system requires clearly defined and enforced property rights. But that's not all. It also requires a sense of general social trust and a respect for legitimately acquired property rights. These structures of trust, legitimacy, respected and understood rules, and the overall market process itself cannot be designed or put in place simply because 'we' want them in place. It's not an engineering problem. It seems to me more of an evolutionary problem.

Thus, I have always been suspicious of the so-called 'shock therapy' solution to the transition from socialism to a market economy. This is the claim that the radical and the quick is the only viable road to reform. It's often expressed in one of two metaphors. The first is that of the heroin addict. The best way to quit heroin permanently is to go cold turkey. Therefore the best way to quit socialism permanently is to go cold turkey – 'dismantle' the system as rapidly as possible, suffer through the terrible pain and hardship, and before too long all will enjoy the mass benefits of the market system.

The rules of the road provide the other metaphor. The transition from socialism to capitalism is like, we are told, the transition from having everybody drive on the left side of the road to everybody driving on the right side of the road. If everyone's been driving on the left side, the only sensible approach would be to declare on such-and-such date that all must now drive on the right side of the road. It makes no sense to experiment slowly – say, only to allow cars to drive on the right side but trucks and buses will still drive on the left side. It has to be done all at once or it won't be successful at all.

Again, the transition from a planned economy to an open economy is really not all that much like a physiological problem or a traffic-engineering problem. This is not to say that economic shock therapy cannot work. But it is probably better to expect that the emergence of a stable market economy in Eastern Europe might indeed take quite some time – perhaps decades. In fact, while most of my fellow PhD graduates were espousing shock therapy in the early 1990s, I recall Douglas North, an economic historian, claiming that it might take a good twenty to fifty years before full-blown markets emerge in the post-communist countries. I've tended to side with his argument. Don't expect much from shock therapy. Unfortunately, there's a further corollary: don't expect too much from any other approach either. It's a mess.

LESSON 2: COMMUNISM IS DEAD, BUT COLLECTIVISM LIVES ON

I shall now move on to the second lesson, the one on ideology.

I'm a classical liberal. And I still have hope for the post-communist countries. But what I didn't 'predict' after witnessing the fall of communism was that the power of collectivist ideology would live on.

Communism died in 1989, but collectivism has grown all the stronger. Socialist internationalism (recall, for example, Tito's writings) has now been replaced by populist nationalism – yet both are similar in that they offer some promise of final emancipation from history. Whereas socialism once declared the unification and collective freedom of all workers around the world, the new, post-communist vision is abandoning that myth for a much narrower but perhaps equally deadly one. The new political vision in many former socialist regimes – Romania or Serbia, for example – is not the Western ideal of the freedom of the individual, the emergence of civil society and democratic constitutional political institutions. Class analysis may be dead, but the default hasn't gone to the person as the subject of dignity and rights. Now the 'nation' is becoming the subject of freedom, the subject of emancipation, in many former socialist countries.

And the liberal dissident intellectual is in retreat. In Europe's post-communist era, the dissident's Western ideals have been drained of their immediacy. The harsh reality of reform – getting from there to here, as it were – has pushed people back to an idealized, even pre-communist past, one that champions anti-liberal values, national aggrandizement, and the return of scapegoating of ethnic minorities – Jewish, Turkish, Gypsy, Albanian, and so on. And the people listen.

The ideological problems of post-communism remain because the fight is less about the freedom of individuals, and more about the emancipation of the ethnic enclave, the nation itself, whether Croatian, Serbian, Romanian, Ukrainian or Polish. While Karl Marx's focus on class interests and its emancipatory potential is dead under post-communism, now the focus is much more fragmented, but still collectivist: now throughout Eastern and Central Europe 'the nation' is paraded as the true subject of history, the source of dignity, the subject of sorrow and oppression. Hence the spectre of the Ustashi in Croatia, or the Romanian Cradle movement, or Slobodan Milosevic's push for a Greater Serbia. This emergent populist nationalism seeks to destroy individuality, pluralism and democracy and instead champions unity, stability and authoritarianism, nicely wrapped up in a new myth of historical inevitability, the rights of the nation and the protection of the Fatherland. Forget about uniting the workers of the world. And certainly forget about diversity, or the notion of the 'world as a nation' (the subtitle of the Vital Issues Forum). It's time for the Serbs (or the Croats, or the Bulgarians, or Ukrainians, or what have you) to unite and finally fulfill the mission of their glorious past.

But the promise of civil society cannot be fulfilled, of course, when the rights of the nation supersede its citizens. Other groups – 'outsiders' – are blamed for oppressing the rights of the nation: the ethnic minorities, foreigners and the Jews, for example, are singled out as the source of all the evil and problems within the post-communist nation-states. The logic alone is twisted and bizarre.

In *Fantasies of Salvation: Democracy, Nationalism, and Myth in Post-Communist Europe*, Vladimir Tismaneanu (1998), a Romanian dissident and Professor of Government and Politics at the University of Maryland, explains why collectivism has re-emerged in many post-communist states. It's worth quoting at length. He writes:

> The end of communism has left individuals with a sense of loss: even if they hated their cage, it offered at least the advantage of stability and predictability. Like former prisoners, they now have freedoms but do not know exactly what to do with them. Under these circumstances, they are ready to espouse the rhetoric of the tribe with its emphasis on group identity and community values. The neurosis of the transition period, the collective fear of a general collapse, the closing of the historical horizon and the anger at the new economic barons, the *nouveax riches*, no less brazen and amoral than Balzac's characters in *La comedie humaine*, nourish sentiments of revolt, distress, and intolerance. There is need to find scapegoats, to identify those culpable for the ongoing sorrows. The political myth of lost and reconquered ethnic unity serves precisely this purpose: to

explain defeats and alienation and reassure the individual that he or she has a place within the *volkisch* community. (1998, pp. 30–31)

Under these conditions, the easiest way to find the scapegoat is to look for those who do not belong (ethnically or religiously), the inner enemy, the potential traitors, the intruders, the 'cosmopolitans'. . . . Any rational questionings of the mythological premises of such views are immediately denounced . . . They are obsessed with homogeneity, unity, and purity. (1998, p. 31)

In the face of all this, Tismaneanu remains optimistic about the long-run prospects of the liberal dissidents in the post-communist countries and their continued resistance against this growing collectivist nationalism. I hope he is right. The emergence of liberal institutions – a market economy, a fully flourishing civil society, and constitutional democracy – remains critically dependent upon them.

Getting back to the subtitle of the forum – 'The World as a Nation'. As I see it, the emergence of market systems throughout the post-communist countries helps to propel us in that direction, economically at least, and using the word 'nation' very loosely. But collectivism is, unfortunately, still alive and well. We've witnessed this month in January 1999, the continued bloodshed in Kosovo. I'm afraid that the idea of the 'world as a nation' whatever that means – will not become a reality unless we abandon the utopian, fanatical, and anti-liberal myth of the ethnically pure nation-state.

15. Thoughts on Austrian economics, 'Austro-punkism' and libertarianism

The preceding chapters were written with a peculiar, overarching norma-tive vision of mine. I would be untruthful were I to claim that I wrote them in a manner totally divorced from my normative concerns. My criticisms, for the most part, are immanent – attempting to get within the framework of Marxism or that of my Austrian colleagues, to determine whether their own arguments logically support their grand claims, whether or not those claims favor self-managed socialism, which I have no special fondness for, or anarcho-capitalism, which lies closer to my own sentiments.

As I mentioned in several places throughout the book, against a handful of my left-wing interpreters and critics, my vision is, of course, neither a Marxist nor generally a socialist vision. I have no interest in rehabilitating Marx, nor in envisioning some new system of decentralized socialism. Perhaps misinterpretation is a potential peril with immanent critique: if one takes an opposing argument seriously, others might wrongly interpret that as an effort to *improve* those arguments – in this case, the Marxist and post-Marxist claims regarding the viability and desirability of socialist self-management.

Actually, I'm more fascinated by the responses I've received directly, and also indirectly through the hallowed 'verbal tradition', from my Austrian colleagues. For here is the other side of the perils associated with immanent critique: if one strongly criticizes arguments within one's own school of thought, one's allies might wrongly interpret that as an effort to *destroy* those arguments, if not the entire school – in this case the strictly praxeological claims for the free market process, both in its strong epistemological pretenses and its grand anarchic conclusions. Put the two misinterpretations together and I suppose a case can be erected (only on top of thin and mighty tall stilts!) that we have in our midst a post-modern Marxist and punk Austrian. Or, at least, somebody who's remarkably confused. But questionable deductions abound from ques-tionable premises.

I think it might be a fitting conclusion to indulge briefly, if I may, in the opportunity to clarify my normative vision, and the motivation behind my critical efforts in this book. I shall address the latter issue first.

PUTTING PRAXEOLOGY TO THE TEST

Among some Austrians, a peculiar form of praxeology plays the defining role. As a deductive approach to the study of human action, praxeology makes a great deal of pragmatic sense. But some Austrians have anointed praxeology, and therefore Austrian economics as a whole, with grand and apparently unquestionable epistemological claims. The praxeologist is a self-described deducer of apodictic certainty, of ironclad proofs that display the Truth about empirical economic phenomena. Hard-core praxeology seems to be the unshakable trunk of the great tree of Austrian economics. Mises and Rothbard stand among its champions in their appeal to scientific *certainty* regarding, in Mises's case, the viability of the completely unhampered market/minimal state system, and in Rothbard's case, outright anarcho-capitalism. (Strange how praxeology is employed to deduce two fundamentally different positions on the role of the state.) And it's that unflinching certitude about the equilibrating properties of the unhampered market system that has, shall I say, both fascinated and irked me over the years.

I have become convinced, on a more general methodological level, by Bernstein's (1983) and Kolakowski's (1987) criticisms of Husserl. Particularly in Bernstein's book, one can replace Husserl's name with Mises, and find that Mises shared the same concerns, anxieties, and flaws as Husserl. I myself (1994b) had penned a general criticism of the kind of praxeology defended by Mises and Rothbard. Questioning the epistemologically grand form of praxeology in this way apparently merits the labels 'anti-economist' (Gordon, 1995), or 'Anti-Austrian Austrian' (Block, 1999). But when *they* claim the *only purported test* of praxeology is to examine its chains of logical deductions, what is an Austrian economist bent on testing the theory to do? Chapter 7 and especially Chapters 9 and 10, reported the results of my praxeological tests regarding market processes, anarchy and self-managed firms. Those three subjects form part of my overall normative vision (a market system composed of self-managed firms under limited government if not an anarchic political system); my motivation is to test, and continue to test, the Austrian (and other) views on these matters. I find, contrary to Walter Block's (1999, p. 5) dogmatic claim that the 'rational camp' of Mises and Rothbard 'is totally consistent', some remarkable flaws. Block sees complete theoretical consistency. I see, in the subject areas that have interested me most, some errors and a cartload of dogmatism.

ON BEING A PUNK AUSTRIAN

Apparently that also makes me a punk. Joe Salerno (n.d.) reported, in a sincere and entertaining panel paper on the future of Austrian economics, that the school is rife with younger 'Austro-punks' who are bent on deconstructing the entire tradition and radically reconstructing Austrian economics anew. Austro-punks have no special reverence for the past or present Masters, nor for the Tradition in general. Malcoordinated products of 1970s left-libertarianism (if not intellectually doped by the punk-rock music movement itself), lacking formal graduate work in Austrian economics, and enthralled with Ludwig Lachmann's radically subjectivist and hermeneutic research agenda, Austro-punks – by hook or by crook – might destroy, Salerno believes, the future of Austrian economics.

Salerno was speaking in generalities, and was careful not to point fingers at anyone in particular, but I guess he would lump me in this imaginary punk counter-revolution. Forget that I was a skinny teenager chasing girls and beer and something to smoke in the late 1970s (with mixed success), listening to Crosby, Stills, Nash and Young, the Moody Blues, and Yes (the very music punk rock reacted violently against), and harboring no interest whatsoever in any political movement (my most 'political' activity was attending the great Anti-Disco Demonstration at Chicago's Comiskey Park in July 1979). Forget all of that. It *is* true that nobody in my graduate program led me through Mises's masterpiece, *Human Action*, first by my nose, next by my ear, and finally, 'humbled and scraped', an exhausted third time after which only then was I prepared to appreciate and understand its Wisdom. (Salerno believes that approach represents formal graduate training; I thank God for avoiding academic hazing and indoctrination of that or any other kind.) As for Lachmann: I rank him among the 'masters' of contemporary Austrian economics, alongside Mises, Hayek, Kirzner and Rothbard.

Salerno's concern is that Austro-punks, in the intellectual name of hermeneutics, interpret and deconstruct the great texts of the Austrian School in *any* manner that suits their purposes – a youthful and willy-nilly desire for radical reconstruction. He reports that Mises had not dared criticize Boehm-Bawerk until the mature age of 52, and that Rothbard had not publicly disagreed with Mises until he reached the towering summit of 48 years old, and then only with some understandable fear and trembling. Salerno places a great deal of weight on those facts. The pesky punks, on the other hand, are off criticizing the Masters' texts in graduate school – imagine that. (Now perhaps this affliction could be solved by selecting a kind of Cardinal Ratzinger, appropriately indoctrinated and possessing a comparative advantage in promoting Austrian absolutism, to oversee the propagation of dogmatic faith within contemporary Austrian economics. But it has been tried, and I shudder at the possibility of its next emergence.)

The fact is, there are flaws in the great chains of praxeological reasoning, which 'testing' ought to reveal and address. Rothbard claimed he offered a purely deductive, apodictically true case for the welfare-maximizing properties of anarcho-capitalism. Tracing carefully through his deductions, however, I found his case logically flawed. Cordato attempted to improve upon Rothbard, but preserved the same mistakes, and also failed to live up to his own scientific standards. Rothbard deduced that self-managed firms will find it impossible to calculate rationally. He was wrong again. Most recently, Scott Beaulier and I examined Mises's praxeological case for market processes composed of actors unhampered by moral conscience, and found it, too, to be invalid (Beaulier and Prychitko, 2001). Mises believed he found a praxeological (and therefore necessary) link between moral conscience and interventionism into the otherwise free market process. We demonstrate instead that Mises took an (ideological?) leap of logic to reach that conclusion.

Even Adam Smith knew better. Market processes cannot be maintained without people guided by moral sensibilities. We do not discover this through purely deductive, praxeological exercises alone, for those exercises rely upon thought experiments of market processes, severed from cultural and institutional forces. Working through thought experiments and chains of careful, deductive logic is an important part of the Austrian economists' approach, but it is not enough to address the problems that we find in history – past or contemporary. The problems of post-communism – our contemporary experience – are not merely theoretical. They are all too empirical as well.

HONING OUR CONCLUSIONS WITH EPISTEMOLOGICAL HUMILITY

Nothing attracts those predisposed to dogmatism more than resorting to the rhetoric of apodictic certainty and the like. Austrians do have much to say and contribute, but among some of them their rhetoric is surely a liability, attracting the noses and ears of disciples rather than the critical faculties of scholars. Let's instead provide our profession with more testing, more arguments, more applications, and less dogma and discipleship.

My motivations have been to prune away the questionable and ridiculously strong epistemological pretences of praxeology to promote stronger growth within the school as a whole. Of course, my critics might interpret that effort as an attempt to destroy the whole tree – which I suppose is understandable if they *define* Austrian economics as the practice of some 'pure' form of praxeology.

THE SEARCH FOR LIBERTARIANISM WITH SOLIDARITY

Conceptually, of course, one can imagine a sphere of Austrian economic theory and a separate sphere of libertarian political philosophy. But the more dogmatic elements within Austrian economics also, it seems to me, tend to attract an equally dogmatic kind of libertarianism, claiming to deduce all sorts of radically individualistic rights claims from unshakable axioms. A kind of abstract, natural rights – and purely negative natural rights – reasoning that raises no moral questions over the voluntary use of private property. Coercion – considered the violent intrusion on the private property of another – is declared to be the ultimate source of evil.

But liberty, in my view, is not only a political end. Liberty is also a means toward the full development of the human person. My normative vision of the ideal community (oh, the life we academics lead) would be politically libertarian *and* infused with a solidaristic moral element – a solidarity not embodied in the administrative–instrumental apparatus of the modern welfare state, but through the institutions of civil society. A restricted state and unhampered market processes would provide the basis for the emergence of truly self-managed firms (though their evolutionary potential may still be a way off), a system of more democratic and participatory non-state institutions, and also, more importantly, a re-energized emergence of the mediating structures discussed at length by Berger, Neuhaus and Novak (1996).

Through these types of cooperative arrangements of private or separate property rights, a libertarian society could be normatively appealing not by promoting libertinism (cf. Block, 1994) but rather the personal dignity of its citizens. As Lord Acton found it necessary to remind us, liberty is not simply the right to do whatever we like, but the power and responsibility of doing what we ought to do.

My work up to this point has been a start in considering some of the economic institutional details of the free society that might further promote Acton's sense of liberty, an attempt to fuse some of the classical liberal moral concerns with contemporary libertarianism, and to shave off its merely libertine and anarchic life-style excesses. I can see the possibility of a future Austrian economics that engenders a more humble epistemological stance, and a libertarianism that promotes not only the expansion of 'my' freedom, but participates in promoting the freedom and growth of others who remain less free than ourselves. Call it Austrian economics with humility, libertarianism with solidarity.

References

Abell, Peter (1995), 'Self-Management: Is It Postmodernist?', *Critical Review*, **9**(3), 311–13.

Albert, Michael and Robin Hahnel (1978), *Unorthodox Marxism: An Essay on Capitalism, Socialism, and Revolution*, Boston: South End Press.

Albert, Michael and Robin Hahnel (1981), *Marxism and Socialist Theory*, Boston: South End Press.

Albert, Michael and Robin Hahnel (1987), 'Socialist Economics', *Socialist Review*, **17**(6), 87–104.

Albert, Michael and Robin Hahnel (1991), *The Political Economy of Participatory Economics*, Princeton, NJ: Princeton University Press.

Alchian, Armen A. and Harold Demsetz (1972), 'Production, Information Costs, and Economic Theory', *American Economic Review*, **62**(5).

Aoki, Masahiko (1986), *The Co-Operative Game Theory of the Firm*, Oxford: Clarendon Press.

Armentano, Dominick T. (1982), *Antitrust and Monopoly: Anatomy of a Policy Failure*, New York: John Wiley and Sons.

Armentano, Dominick T. (1992a), 'Anti-Antitrust: Ideology or Economics? Reply to Scherer', *Critical Review*, **6**(1), 29–39.

Armentano, Dominick T. (1992b), 'Forward', in Cordato (1992).

Arrow, Kenneth and F.H. Hahn (1971), *General Competitive Analysis*, San Francisco: Holden-Day.

Avineri, Shlomo (1968), *The Social and Political Thought of Karl Marx*, New York: Cambridge University Press.

Bakunin, Michael (1970), *God and the State*, New York: Dover.

Barnett, Randy E. (1985), 'Pursuing Justice in a Free Society: Part One – Crime Prevention and the Legal Order', *Criminal Justice Ethics*, Winter–Spring, 30–53.

Barnett, Randy E. (1986), 'Pursuing Justice in a Free Society: Part Two – Power vs. Liberty', *Criminal Justice Ethics*, Summer–Fall, 50–72.

Beaulier, Scott and David L. Prychitko (2001), 'Does Morality Hamper the Market Process? A Reconsideration of the Mises Thesis', *Journal of Markets & Morality*, **4**(1), 43–54.

Bell, Daniel (1978), *The Cultural Contradictions of Capitalism*, New York: Basic Books.

Berger, Peter L., Neuhaus, Richard John and Michael Novak (eds) (1996), *To Empower People: From State to Civil Society*, Washington, DC: AEI Press.

Bernstein, Richard J. (1983), *Beyond Objectivism and Relativism: Science, Hermeneutics, and Praxis*, Philadelphia: University of Pennsylvania Press.

Bičanić, Ivo (1989), 'The Scope for Self-management in the Yugoslav Enterprise', delivered at the conference on 'Self-management in Future Socialism and Capitalism', Inter-University Centre of Postgraduate Studies, Dubrovnik, Yugoslavia, 6–17 March.

Bideleux, Robert (1985), *Communism and Development*, New York: Methuen.

Bideleux, Robert (1986), Review of Don Lavoie, *Rivalry and Central Planning*, *Economic Journal*, (June), 564–7.

Block, Walter (1994), 'Libertarianism and Libertinism', *Journal of Libertarian Studies*, **11**(1), 117–28.

Block, Walter (1999), 'Radical Economics: An Interview with Walter Block', *Austrian Economics Newsletter*, Summer, 1–8.

Boehm-Bawerk, Eugen (1949 [1896]), *Zum Abschluss des Marxschen Systems*. Translated as *Karl Marx and the Close of His System*, New York: Augustus Kelley.

Boettke, Peter J. (1988), 'The Soviet Experiment with Pure Communism', *Critical Review*, **2**(4), 149–82.

Boettke, Peter J. (1990), *The Political Economy of Soviet Socialism: The Formative Years, 1918–1928*, Boston: Kluwer Academic.

Boettke, Peter J. (1993), *Why Perestroika Failed: The Politics and Economics of Socialist Transformation*, New York: Routledge.

Boettke, Peter J. (ed.) (1994a), *The Collapse of Development Planning*, New York: New York University Press.

Boettke, Peter J. (ed.) (1994b), *The Elgar Companion to Austrian Economics*, Brookfield, US and Cheltenham, UK: Edward Elgar Publishing.

Boettke, Peter J. (1995), 'Hayek's *Serfdom* Revisited: Government Failure in the Argument Against Socialism', *Eastern Economic Journal*, **21**(1), 7–26.

Boettke, Peter J. (1998a), 'Economic Calculation: *The* Austrian Contribution to Political Economy', *Advances in Austrian Economics*, **5**, 131–58.

Boettke, Peter J. (1998b), 'Rethinking Ourselves: Negotiating Values in the Political Economy of Postcommunism', *Rethinking Marxism*, **10**(2), 85–95.

Boettke, Peter J. and David L. Prychitko (eds) (1994), *The Market Process: Essays on Contemporary Austrian Economics*, Aldershot, UK: Edward Elgar.

Boettke, Peter, Horowitz, Steven and David L. Prychitko (1994), 'Beyond Equilibrium Economics: Reflections on the Uniqueness of the Austrian Tradition', in Boettke and Prychitko (eds) (1994).

Bonin, John P. and Louis Putterman (1987), *The Economics of Cooperation and the Labor-Managed Economy*, New York: Harwood Academic.

Bookchin, Murray (1986a), *The Modern Crisis*, Philadelphia: New Society Publishers.

Bookchin, Murray (1986b), *Post-Scarcity Anarchism*, 2nd edn, Montreal: Black Rose Books.

Bookchin, Murray (1986c), 'Theses on Libertarian Municipalism', in Roussopoulos (ed.) (1986).

Bookchin, Murray (1989), *Remaking Society*, Montreal: Black Rose Books.

Bookchin, Murray (1990), 'Radical Politics in an Era of Advanced Capitalism', *Our Generation*, **21**(2), 1–12.

Bookchin, Murray (1991), 'The Meaning of Confederalism', *Our Generation*, **22**(1–2), 88–101.

Bookchin, Murray (1994), *Which Way for the Ecology Movement? Essays by Murray Bookchin*, Edinburgh: AK Press.

Bornstein, Morris (ed.) (1965), *Comparative Economic Systems: Models and Cases*, Homewood, IL: Richard D. Irwin.

Bornstein, Morris (ed.) (1973), *Plan and Market: Economic Reform in Eastern Europe*, New Haven, CT: Yale University Press.

Bottomore, Tom (ed.) (1983), *A Dictionary of Marxist Thought*, Cambridge, MA: Harvard University Press.

Boulding, Kenneth E. (1981), *Evolutionary Economics*, Beverly Hills, CA: Sage.

Bradley, Keith and Alan Gelb (1981), 'Motivation and Control in the Mondragon Experiment', *British Journal of Industrial Relations*, **19**(2), 211–31.

Buchanan, James M. (1964), 'What Should Economists Do?', in J.M. Buchanan (ed.), *What Should Economists Do?*, Indianapolis: Liberty Press, 1979.

Buchanan, James M. (1969), *Cost and Choice: An Inquiry in Economic Theory*, Chicago: University of Chicago Press.

Buchanan, James M. (1975), *The Limits of Liberty: Between Anarchy and Leviathan*, Chicago: University of Chicago Press.

Buchanan, James M. (1977), 'A Contractarian Perspective on Anarchy', in J.M. Buchanan, *Freedom in Constitutional Contract: Perspectives of a Political Economist*, College Station, TX: Texas A&M University Press.

Buchanan, James M. (1988–89), 'Hayek and the Forces of History', *Humane Studies Review*, **6**(2).

Buchanan, James M. and Viktor Vanberg (1991), 'The Market as a Creative Process', *Economics and Philosophy*, **7**, 167–86.

Burczak, Theodore (1996/1997), 'Socialism After Hayek', *Rethinking Marxism*, **9**(3), 1–18.

Cahill, Tom (1989), 'Co-operatives and Anarchism: A Contemporary Perspective', in Goodway (ed.) (1989).

Comisso, Ellen Turkish (1979), *Workers' Control Under Plan and Market: Implications of Yugoslav Self-Management*, New Haven, CT: Yale University Press.

Cordato, Roy E. (1992), *Welfare Economics and Externalities in an Open Ended Universe: A Modern Austrian Perspective*, Boston: Kluwer Academic.

Cottrell, Alan and W.P. Cockshott (1993), 'Calculation, Complexity, and Planning: The Socialist Calculation Debate Once Again', *Review of Political Economy*, **5**(1), 73–112.

Cowan, Robin and Mario J. Rizzo (eds) (1995), *Profits and Morality*, Chicago: University of Chicago Press.

Cowen, Tyler (1990), 'What a Non-Paretian Welfare Economics Would Have to Look Like', in Lavoie (ed.) (1990b).

Cullenberg, Steven (1992), 'Socialism's Burden: Toward a "Thin" Definition of Socialism', *Rethinking Marxism*, **5**(2), 64–83.

Davidson, Paul (1989), 'The Economics of Ignorance or the Ignorance of Economics', *Critical Review*, **3**(3–4), 467–87.

Defourny, Jacques (1986), 'Une analyse financière comparée des coopératives de travailleurs et des enterprises capitalistes en France', *Annals of Public and Cooperative Economy*, **57**(1).

DeLeon, David (1978), *The American as Anarchist: Reflections on Indigenous Radicalism*, Baltimore, MD: Johns Hopkins University Press.

Descartes, Rene (1964), *Philosophical Essays*, New York: Bobbs-Merrill.

Devine, Pat (1992), 'Market Socialism or Participatory Planning?', *Review of Radical Political Economics*, **24**(3–4), 67–89.

diZerega, Gus (1989), 'Democracy as a Spontaneous Order', *Critical Review*, **3**(2), 206–40.

diZerega, Gus (1997), 'Market Non-Neutrality: Systemic Biases in Spontaneous Orders', *Critical Review*, **11**(1), 121–44.

Djilas, Milovan (1962), *Conversations with Stalin*, New York: Harcourt, Brace, Jovanovich.

Dolan, Edwin G. (ed.) (1976), *The Foundations of Modern Austrian Economics*, Kansas City: Sheed and Ward.

Domajnko, Danilo (ed.) (1980), *Theoretical and Methodological Aspects of Researching the Development of the Socialist Self-Management Society*, Ljubljana: Yugoslav Center for Theory and Practice of Self-Management, Edvard Kardelj.

Domajnko, Danilo (ed.) (1982), *The Path to the Emancipation of Labour*, Ljubljana: Yugoslav Center for Theory and Practice of Self-Management, Edvard Kardelj.

Domar, Evsey D. (1966), 'The Soviet Collective Farm as a Producer Cooperative', *American Economic Review*, **46**(4).

Dowd, Kevin (1989), *The State and the Monetary System*, Oxford: Philip Alan.

Ebeling, Richard M. (ed.) (1991), *Austrian Economics. Perspectives on the Past and Prospects for the Future*, Hillsdale, MI: Hillsdale College Press.

Ellerman, David (1980), 'On Property Theory and Value Theory', *Economic Analysis and Workers' Management*, **14**(1), 105–26.

Ellerman, David (1985), 'On the Labor Theory of Property', *The Philosophical Forum*, **16**(4), 293–326.

Ellerman, David (1988), 'The Kantian Person/Thing Principle in Political Economy', *Journal of Economic Issues*, **22**(4), 1109–22.

Estrin, Saul and David Winter (1989), 'Planning in a Market Socialist Economy', in Le Grand and Estrin (eds) (1989).

Fink, Richard H. (1984–85), 'General and Partial Equilibrium in Bork's Antitrust Analysis', *Contemporary Policy Issues*, **3** (Winter).

Fisher, Franklin M. (1983), *Disequilibrium Foundations of Equilibrium Economics*, New York: Cambridge University Press.

Foster, John Bellamy (1995), 'Market Fetishism and the Attack on Social Reason: A Comment on Hayek, Polanyi, and Wainwright', *Capitalism, Nature, Socialism*, **6**(4).

Friedman, David (1989), *The Machinery of Freedom: Guide to a Radical Capitalism* 2nd edn, LaSalle, IL: Open Court.

Friedman, Jeffrey (1989), 'The New Consensus I: The Fukuyama Thesis', *Critical Review*, **3**(3–4), 373–409.

Friedman, Milton (1953), 'The Methodology of Positive Economics', in *Essays in Positive Economics*, Chicago: University of Chicago Press.

Friedman, Milton (1962), *Capitalism and Freedom*, Chicago: University of Chicago Press.

Fromm, Erich (1961), *Marx's Concept of Man*, New York: Frederick Ungar.

Fromm, Erich (ed.) (1965), *Socialist Humanism: An International Symposium*, Garden City, NJ: Doubleday.

Furubotn, Eirik (1971), 'Toward a Dynamic Model of the Yugoslav Firm', *Canadian Journal of Economics*, **4** (May).

Furubotn, Eirik G. and Svetozar Pejovich (1970), 'Property Rights and the Behavior of the Firm in the Socialist State: The Example of Yugoslavia', *Zeitschrift für Nationalökonomie*, **30**.

Gadamer, Hans-Georg (1985), *Truth and Method*, New York: Crossroad.

Glasner, David (1989), *Free Banking and Monetary Reform*, Cambridge: Cambridge University Press.

Goati, V., Vidojević, Z., Nešković, R., Milić, A., Joksimović, S. and D. Pantić

(1985), *Političko Angazovanje u Jugoslovenskom Društvu* [*Political Involvement in Yugoslav Society*], Beograd: Mladost.

Goodway, David (ed.) (1989), *For Anarchism: History, Theory, and Practice*, New York: Routledge.

Gordon, David (ed.) (1986), *Murray N. Rothbard: A Scholar in Defense of Freedom*, Auburn, AL: Ludwig von Mises Institute.

Gordon, David (1995), 'What Should Anti-Economists Do?', *Mises Review*, Spring.

Gorz, Andre (1985), *Paths to Paradise: On the Liberation from Work*, Boston: South End Press.

Graham, Robert (1989), 'The Role of Contract in Anarchist Ideology', in Goodway (ed.) (1989).

Gray, John (1984), *Hayek on Liberty*, New York: Basil Blackwell.

Gray, John (1988–89), 'Evolutionary Functionalism', *Humane Studies Review*, **6**(2).

Grossman, Gregory (1963), 'Notes for a Theory of the Command Economy', *Soviet Studies*, **15**(2).

Guerin, Daniel (1970), *Anarchism: From Theory to Practice*, New York: Monthly Review Press.

Guerin, Daniel (1989), 'Marxism and Anarchism', in Goodway (ed.) (1989).

Haan, Norma, Bellah, Robert N., Rabinow, Paul and William M. Sullivan (eds) (1983), *Social Science as Moral Inquiry*, New York: Cambridge University Press.

Habermas, Jürgen (1974), *Theory and Practice*, Boston: Beacon Press.

Habermas, Jürgen (1975), *Legitimation Crisis*, Boston: Beacon Press.

Habermas, Jürgen (1979), *Communication and the Evolution of Society*, Boston: Beacon Press.

Habermas, Jürgen (1986), *Autonomy and Solidarity: Interviews*, ed. Peter Dews, London: Verso.

Habermas, Jürgen (1998), *Between Facts and Norms: Contributions to a Discourse Theory of Law and Democracy*, Cambridge, MA: MIT Press.

Hahn, Frank (1981), 'General Equilibrium Theory', in Daniel Bell and Irving Kristol (eds), *The Crisis in Economic Theory*, New York: Basic Books.

Harper, David (1994), 'A New Approach to Modeling Endogenous Learning Processes in Economic Theory', *Advances in Austrian Economics*, **1**.

Harrison, Frank (1986), 'Culture and Coercion', in Roussopoulos (ed.) (1986).

Harrison, Frank (1991), 'Anarchy, Organization and Scale', *Our Generation*, **22**(1–2), 102–11.

Hayek, F.A. (1937), 'Economics and Knowledge', in Hayek (1948a).

Hayek, F.A. (1944), *The Road to Serfdom*, Chicago: University of Chicago Press.

Hayek, F.A. (1945), 'The Use of Knowledge in Society', in Hayek (1948a).

Hayek, F.A. (1946), 'Individualism: True and False', in Hayek (1948a).

Hayek, F.A. (1948a), *Individualism and Economic Order*, Chicago: University of Chicago Press.

Hayek, F.A. (1948b), 'The Meaning of Competition', in Hayek (1948a).

Hayek, F.A. (1963), *The Sensory Order*, Chicago: University of Chicago Press.

Hayek, F.A. (1964), 'Kinds of Order in Society', in *New Individualist Review*, Indianapolis: Liberty Press, 1991, pp.457–660.

Hayek, F.A. (1965), 'Kinds of Rationalism', in Hayek (1967).

Hayek, F.A. (1967), *Studies in Philosophy, Politics, and Economics*, Chicago: University of Chicago Press.

Hayek, F.A. (1968), 'Competition as a Discovery Procedure', in Hayek (1978).

Hayek, F.A. (1970), 'The Errors of Constructivism', in Hayek (1978).

Hayek, F.A. (1973), *Law, Legislation, and Liberty: Volume I: Rules and Order*, Chicago: University of Chicago Press.

Hayek, F.A. (ed.) (1975 [1935]), *Collectivist Economic Planning: Critical Studies on the Possibilities of Socialism*, Clifton, NJ: Augustus M. Kelley.

Hayek, F.A. (1978), *New Studies in Philosophy, Economics, and the History of Ideas*, Chicago: University of Chicago Press.

Hayek, F.A. (1979a [1952]), *The Counter-Revolution of Science*, Indianapolis, IN: Liberty Classics.

Hayek, F.A. (1979b), *Law, Legislation, and Liberty: Volume III: The Political Order of a Free People*, Chicago: University of Chicago Press.

Hayek, F.A. (1988), *The Fatal Conceit*, Chicago: University of Chicago Press.

Heilbroner, Robert (1989), 'The Triumph of Capitalism', *The New Yorker*, 23 January.

Heller, Agnes and Ferenc Feher (1989), 'Does Socialism Have a Future?', *Dissent*, **36**(3), 371–5.

High, Jack (1986), 'Equilibration and Disequilibration in the Market Process', in Kirzner (ed.) (1986).

High, Jack (1990), *Maximizing, Action, and Market Adjustment: An Inquiry into the Theory of Economic Disequilibrium*, Munich: Philosophia Verlag.

Hirsch, Fred (1976), *Social Limits to Growth*, Cambridge, MA: Harvard University Press.

Hoff, T.J.B. (1949), *Economic Calculation in the Socialist Society*, London: William Hodge and Co.

Holterman, Tom, and H. van Maarseveen (eds) (1984), *Law and Anarchism*, Montreal: Black Rose Books.

Hoppe, Hans-Hermann, (1991), 'Austrian Rationalism in the Age of the Decline of Positivism', in Ebeling (ed.) (1991).

Horvat, Branko (1982), *The Political Economy of Socialism: A Marxist Social Theory*, Armonk, NY: M.E. Sharpe.

Horvat, Branko, Marković, Mihailo, and Rudi Supek (eds) (1975), *Self-Governing Socialism: A Reader*, White Plains, NY: International Arts and Sciences Press.

Horwitz, Steven (1989), 'Keynes's Special Theory', *Critical Review*, **3**(3–4), 411–34.

Horwitz, Steven (1992a), 'Monetary Exchange as an Extra-linguistic Social Communication Process', *Review of Social Economy*, **50**(2), 193–214.

Horwitz, Steven (1992b), *Monetary Evolution, Free Banking, and Economic Order*, Boulder: Westview Press.

Horwitz, Steven (1996), 'Money, Money Prices, and the Socialist Calculation Debate', *Advances in Austrian Economics*, **3**.

Horwitz, Steven (2001), *Microfoundations and Macroeconomics. An Austrian Perspective*, New York: Routledge.

Ikeda, Sanford (1996), *Dynamics of the Mixed Economy. Toward a Theory of Interventionism*, London: Routledge.

Johnston, David (1997), 'Hayek's Attack on Social Justice', *Critical Review*, **11**(1), 81–100.

Kardelj, Edvard (1980), *Tito and Socialist Revolution of Yugoslavia*, Belgrade: Socialist Thought and Practice.

Kassiola, Joel Jay (1990), *The Death of Industrial Civilization: The Limits to Economic Growth and the Repoliticization of Advanced Industrial Society*, Albany, NY: State University of New York Press.

Kirzner, Israel M. (1973), *Competition and Entrepreneurship*, Chicago: University of Chicago Press.

Kirzner, Israel M. (1979), *Perception, Opportunity, and Profit: Studies in the Theory of Entrepreneurship*, Chicago: University of Chicago Press.

Kirzner, Israel M. (ed.) (1982), *Method, Process, and Austrian Economics: Essays in Honor of Ludwig von Mises*, Lexington, MA: Arlington Books.

Kirzner, Israel M. (1984), 'Economic Planning and the Knowledge Problem', *Cato Journal*, **4**(2).

Kirzner, Israel M. (ed.) (1986), *Subjectivism, Intelligibility and Economic Understanding: Essays in Honor of Ludwig M. Lachmann on his Eightieth Birthday*, New York: New York University Press.

Kirzner, Israel M. (1990), 'Discovery, Private Property and the Theory of Justice in Capitalist Society', reprinted in Kirzner (1992).

Kirzner, Israel M. (1992), *The Meaning of Market Process: Essays in the Development of Modern Austrian Economics*, New York: Routledge.

Kirzner, Israel M. (1995), 'The Nature of Profits: Some Economic Insights and Their Ethical Implications', in Cowan and Rizzo (eds) (1995).

Kirzner, Israel M. (1996), *Essays on Capital and Interest: An Austrian Perspective*, Cheltenham, UK and Brookfield, US: Edward Elgar.

Kirzner, Israel M (1997), 'Entrepreneurial Discovery and the Competitive Market Process: An Austrian Approach', *Journal of Economic Literature*, **35**(March), 60–85.

Kolakowski, Leszek (1987), *Husserl and the Search for Certainty*, Chicago: University of Chicago Press.

Koppl, Roger (1997), 'Mises and Shackle on Ideal Types', *Cultural Dynamics*, **9**(1), 63–76.

Kornai, Janos (1980), 'The Dilemmas of a Socialist Economy: The Hungarian Experience', *Cambridge Journal of Economics*, **4**.

Kornai, Janos (1990), *The Road to a Free Economy*, New York: W.W. Norton.

Kosik, Karel (1976), *Dialectics of the Concrete: A Study of Problems of Man and World*, Boston: D. Reidel.

Lachmann, Ludwig M. (1976), 'From Mises to Shackle: An Essay on Austrian Economics and the Kaleidic Society', *Journal of Economic Literature*, **14** (March), 54–62.

Lachmann, Ludwig M. (1978), *Capital and Its Structure*, Kansas City: Sheed Andrews and McMeel.

Lange, Oskar (1964 [1938]), *On the Economic Theory of Socialism* (Benjamin E. Lippincott, ed.), New York: McGraw-Hill.

Lavoie, Don (1985a), *National Economic Planning: What is Left?*, Cambridge, MA: Ballinger Publishing Co.

Lavoie, Don (1985b), *Rivalry and Central Planning: The Socialist Calculation Debate Reconsidered*, New York: Cambridge University Press.

Lavoie, Don (1986), 'The Market as a Procedure for Discovery and Conveyance of Inarticulate Knowledge', *Comparative Economic Studies*, **28**(1).

Lavoie, Don (1986–87), 'Political and Economic Illusions of Socialism', *Critical Review*, **1**(1).

Lavoie, Don (1990a), 'Computation, Incentives, and Discovery: The Cognitive Function of Markets in Market Socialism', *The Annals*, **507**(January), 72–9.

Lavoie, Don (ed.) (1990b), *Economics and Hermeneutics*, New York: Routledge.

Lavoie, Don (1992), 'Glasnost and the Knowledge Problem: Rethinking Economic Democracy', *Cato Journal*, **11**(3).

Le Grand, Julian and Saul Estrin (eds) (1989), *Market Socialism*, Oxford: Clarendon Press.

Lewin, Peter (1999), *Capital in Disequilibrium: The Role of Capital in a Changing World*, New York: Routledge.

Lewis, Flora (1988), 'Young Marx and Old Lenin', *The New York Times*, 11 September, sec 4, 31.

Lindenfeld, Frank (1986), 'Routes to Social Change', *Social Anarchism*, **6**(11), 5–14.

Littlechild, Stephen C. (1979), *The Fallacy of the Mixed Economy*, San Francisco: The Cato Institute.

Lukes, Steven (1997), 'Social Justice: The Hayekian Challenge', *Critical Review*, **11**(1), 65–80.

Lydall, Harold (1986), *Yugoslav Socialism: Theory and Practice*, New York: Oxford University Press.

Machovec, Frank M. (1995), *Perfect Competition and the Transformation of Economics*, London: Routledge.

Malinvaud, E. (1972), *Lectures on Microeconomic Theory*, New York: American Elsevier.

Marković, Mihailo (1974), *From Affluence to Praxis: Philosophy and Social Criticism*, Ann Arbor: University of Michigan Press.

Marković, Mihailo (1975), 'Philosophical Foundations of the Idea of Self-Management', in Horvat, Marković, and Supek (eds) (1975).

Marković, Mihailo and Gajo Petrović (eds) (1979), *Praxis: Yugoslav Essays in the Philosophy and Methodology of the Social Sciences*, Boston: D. Reidel.

Marschak, Thomas A. (1968), 'Centralized Versus Decentralized Resource Allocation: The Yugoslav "Laboratory"', *Quarterly Journal of Economics*, **82**(4).

Marshall, Peter (1989), 'Human Nature and Anarchism', in Goodway (ed.) (1989).

Marx, Karl (1906), *Capital*, 3 volumes, Chicago: Charles Kerr & Co.

Marx, Karl (1964), *The Economic and Philosophic Manuscripts of 1844*, New York: International Publishers.

Marx, Karl (1968), *Theories of Surplus Value*, Pt. 2, trans. and ed. S.W. Ryazanskaya, Moscow: Progress Publishers.

Marx, Karl (1970), *Critique of Hegel's 'Philosophy of Right'*, New York: Cambridge University Press.

Marx, Karl (1978), *The Poverty of Philosophy*, Moscow: Progress Publishers.

Marx, Karl and Frederick Engels (1969), *Selected Works* Vol. 2, Moscow: Progress Publishers.

McPherson, Michael S. (1983), 'Want Formation, Morality, and Some "Interpretive" Aspects of Economic Inquiry', in Haan, Bellah, Rabinow, and Sullivan (eds) (1983).

Meade, James (1979), 'The Adjustment Processes of Labour Co-operatives with Constant Returns to Scale and Perfect Competition', *Economic Journal*, **89**(356).

Miller, David (1989), 'Why Markets?', in Le Grand and Estrin (eds) (1989).

Mises, Ludwig von (1920) 'Die Wirtschaftsrechnung im sozialistischen Gemeinwesen', *Archiv für sozialiwissenschaften*, 47. Translated as 'Economic Calculation in the Socialist Commonwealth' in Hayek (ed.) (1975).

Mises, Ludwig von (1962 [1927]), *Liberalism: A Socio-Economic Exposition*, Kansas City: Sheed Andrews and McMeel.

Mises, Ludwig von (1966), *Human Action: A Treatise on Economics*, 2nd revised edn, Chicago: Henry Regnery.

Mises, Ludwig von (1977 [1929]), *A Critique of Interventionism*, New York: Arlington House.

Mises, Ludwig von (1981 [1936]), *Socialism: An Economic and Sociological Analysis*, Indianapolis: Liberty Classics.

Mises, Ludwig von (1983), *Nation, State, and Economy: Contributions to the Politics and History of Our Time*, trans. Leland B. Yeager, New York: New York University Press.

Mises, Ludwig von (1985), *Theory and History: An Interpretation of Social and Economic Evolution*, Washington, DC: The Ludwig von Mises Institute.

Moss, Laurence S. (1974), 'Private Property Anarchism: An American Variant', in Tullock (ed.) (1974).

Moss, Laurence S. (ed.) (1976), *The Economics of Ludwig von Mises: Towards a Critical Reappraisal*, Kansas City: Sheed Andrews and McMeel.

Musgrave, Richard A. (1980), 'Theories of Fiscal Crises: An Essay on Fiscal Sociology', in Henry J. Aaron and Michael J. Boskin (eds), *The Economics of Taxation*, Washington, DC: Brookings Institution.

Myrdal, Gunnar (1991), *The Political Element in Economic Theory*, New Brunswick, NJ: Transaction.

Neuberger, Egon and Estelle James (1973), 'The Yugoslav Self-Managed Enterprise: A Systematic Approach', in Bornstein (ed.) (1973).

Nove, Alec (1969), *An Economic History of the USSR*, New York: Penguin Books.

Nove, Alec (1983), *The Economics of Feasible Socialism*, London: George Allen and Unwin.

Nozick, Robert (1974), *Anarchy, State, and Utopia*, New York: Basic Books.

Obradović, Josip and William N. Dunn (eds) (1978), *Workers' Self-Management and Organizational Power in Yugoslavia*, Pittsburgh: University of Pittsburgh Press.

O'Driscoll, Gerald P. (1982), 'Monopoly in Theory and Practice', in Kirzner (ed.) (1982).

O'Driscoll, Gerald P. and Mario J. Rizzo (1985), *The Economics of Time and Ignorance*, New York: Basil Blackwell.

Offe, Claus (1984), *Contradictions of the Welfare State*, Cambridge, MA: MIT Press.

Offe, Claus (1985), *Disorganized Capitalism*, Cambridge, MA: MIT Press.

Palmer, Tom G. (1987), 'Gadamer's Hermeneutics and Social Theory', *Critical Review*, **1**(3), 91–108.

Patinkin, Don (1965), *Money, Interest, and Prices*, New York: Harper and Row.

Pejovich, Svetozar (1973), 'The Banking System and the Investment Behavior of the Yugoslav Firm', in Bornstein (ed.) (1973).

Pejovich, Svetozar (1991), Review of David L. Prychitko, *Marxism and Workers' Self-Management: The Essential Tension, Cato Journal*, **11**(2), 327–9.

Pejovich, Svetozar (1992), 'Why Has the Labor-Managed Firm Failed?', *Cato Journal*, **12**(2).

Pejovich, Svetozar (1994), 'A Property Rights Analysis of Alternative Methods of Organizing Production', *Communist Economies and Economic Transformation*, **6**(2).

Pennock, J.R. and J.W. Chapman (eds) (1978), *Anarchism: Nomos XIX*, New York: New York University Press.

Petrović, Gajo (1967), *Marx in the Mid-Twentieth Century: A Yugoslav Philosopher Considers Karl Marx's Writings*, Garden City, NY: Doubleday and Co.

Petrović, Gajo (1983), 'Alienation', in Bottomore (ed.) (1983).

Plant, Raymond (1989), 'Socialism, Markets, and End States', in Le Grand and Estrin (eds) (1989).

Polanyi, Michael (1951), *The Logic of Liberty*, Chicago: University of Chicago Press.

Polanyi, Michael (1957), 'The Foolishness of History', *Encounter*, **9**(5).

Prout, Christopher (1985), *Market Socialism in Yugoslavia*, New York: Oxford University Press.

Prybyla, Jan (1980), *Issues in Socialist Economic Modernization*, New York: Praeger.

Prychitko, David L. (1983), 'The Market-Socialist Blueprints of Oskar Lange and Joseph Schumpeter: A Comparison and Evaluation', unpublished manuscript.

Prychitko, David L. (1987), 'Ludwig Lachmann and the Farther Reaches of Austrian Economics', *Critical Review*, **1**(3), 63–76.

Prychitko, David L. (1988), 'Marxism and Decentralized Socialism', *Critical Review*, **2**(4). Reprinted as Chapter 2.

Prychitko, David L. (1989), 'Social Property and Yugoslav Self-Management: Implications for Anarchist Theory', presented on the panel on Yugoslav Federalism, at the conference 'Political Theory and Political Education – Anarchism: Community and Utopia', InterUniversity Centre for Postgraduate Studies, Dubrovnik, Croatia (20–31 March).

Prychitko, David L. (1991), *Marxism and Workers' Self-Management. The Essential Tension*, Westport, CT: Greenwood Press.

Prychitko, David L. (1994a), 'Marxisms and Market Processes', in Boettke (ed.) (1994b). Reprinted as Chapter 5.

Prychitko, David L (1994b), 'Praxeology', in Boettke (ed.) (1994b).

Prychitko, David L. (1996), 'The Critique of Workers' Self-Management: Austrian Perspectives and Economic Theory', *Advances in Austrian Economics*, **3**, pp. 5–25, reprinted as Chapter 7.

Prychitko, David L. (1997a), 'Expanding the Anarchist Range: A Critical Reappraisal of Rothbard's Contribution to the Contemporary Theory of Anarchism', *Review of Political Economy*, **9**(4), 433–55. Reprinted as Chapter 10.

Prychitko, David L. (1997b), 'Marx, Postmodernism, and Self-Management: Reply to Abell', *Critical Review*, **11**(2), 301–12. Reprinted as Chapter 6.

Prychitko, David L. (1997c), Review of Joseph Stiglitz, *Whither Socialism?*, *Cato Journal*, **16**(2), 280–85.

Prychitko, David L. (2000), 'Communicative Action and the Radical Constitution: The Habermasian Challenge', presented at the J.M. Kaplan Workshop on Political Economy, George Mason University, November 2000.

Prychitko, David L. and Jaroslav Vanek (eds) (1996), *Producer Cooperatives and Labor-Managed Systems. Vol. I. Theory and Vol. II: Case Studies*, International Library of Critical Writings in Economics, edited by Mark Blaug, Cheltenham, UK and Brookfield: Edward Elgar.

Putterman, Louis (1984), 'On Some Recent Explanations of Why Capital Hires Labour', *Economic Inquiry*, 22 April.

Quinn, Kevin and Tina R. Green (1998), 'Hermeneutics and Libertarianism: An Odd Couple', *Critical Review*, **12**(3), 207–23.

Rabinow, Paul and William M. Sullivan (eds) (1979), *Interpretive Social Science: A Reader*, Berkeley: University of California Press.

Rakić Vojislav (1964), 'Fundamental Characteristics of the Yugoslav Economic System', in Stojanović (ed.) (1964).

Reder, Melvin (1952), 'Comment', in Bernard F. Haley (ed.) *Survey of Contemporary Economics Vol. 2*, Homewood, IL: Richard D. Irwin, pp. 34–6.

Ritter, Alan (1980), *Anarchism: A Theoretical Analysis*, New York: Cambridge University Press.

Robbins, Lionel (1935), *An Essay on the Nature and Significance of Economic Science*, 2nd edn, London: Macmillan and Co.

Roberts, Paul Craig (1971), *Alienation and the Soviet Economy. Toward a General Theory of Marxian Alienation, Organizational Principles, and the Soviet Economy*, Albuquerque: University of New Mexico Press.

Roberts, Paul Craig and Matthew A. Stephenson (1973), *Marx's Theory of Exchange, Alienation, and Crisis*, Stanford: Hoover Institution Press.

Robinson, Joan (1967), 'The Soviet Collective Farm as a Producer Cooperative', *American Economic Review*, **57**.

Rothbard, Murray N. (1957), 'In Defense of "Extreme Apriorism"', *Southern Economic Journal*, **23**.

Rothbard, Murray N. (1970), *Man, Economy, and State*, 2 volumes, Los Angeles: Nash.

Rothbard, Murray N. (1976a), 'Ludwig von Mises and Economic Calculation Under Socialism', in Moss (ed.) (1976).

Rothbard, Murray N. (1976b), 'Praxeology: The Method of Austrian Economics', in Dolan (ed.) (1976).

Rothbard, Murray N. (1976c), 'Praxeology, Value Judgments, and Public Policy', in Dolan (ed.) (1976).

Rothbard, Murray N. (1977a), *Power and Market*, Kansas City: Sheed, Andrews, and McMeel.

Rothbard, Murray N. (1977b), *Toward a Reconstruction of Utility and Welfare Economics*, New York: Center for Libertarian Studies.

Rothbard, Murray N. (1978a), *For a New Liberty: The Libertarian Manifesto*, revised edn, New York: Macmillan.

Rothbard, Murray N. (1978b), 'Society Without a State', in Pennock and Chapman (eds) (1978).

Rothbard, Murray N. (1979), *Individualism and the Philosophy of the Social Sciences*, San Francisco: Cato Institute.

Rothbard, Murray N. (1985), 'Preface', in Mises (1985).

Rothbard, Murray N. (1991), 'The End of Socialism and the Economic Calculation Debate', *Review of Austrian Economics*, **5**(2).

Rothbard, Murray N. (1992), *The Present State of Austrian Economics*, Auburn, Alabama: Ludwig von Mises Institute.

Roussopoulos, Dimitrios I. (ed.) (1986), *The Anarchist Papers*, Montreal: Black Rose Books.

Rus, Veljko (1978), 'Enterprise Power Structure', in Obradović and Dunn (eds) (1978).

Rus, Veljko (1986), 'Private and Public Ownership in Yugoslavia', *Scandinavian Journal of Management Studies*, May.

Rutland, Peter (1985), *The Myth of the Plan: Lessons of Soviet Planning*, La Salle, IL: Open Court.

Sacks, Stephen R. (1973), *Entry of New Competitors in Yugoslav Market Socialism*, Berkeley: Institute of International Studies.

Salerno, Joseph (no date), 'The Future of the Austrian School', unpublished manuscript.

Salerno, Joseph (1990), 'Ludwig von Mises as a Social Rationalist', *Review of Austrian Economics*, **6**(2), 113–46.

Salerno, Joseph (1994), 'Reply to Leland B. Yeager on "Mises and Hayek on Calculation and Knowledge"', *Review of Austrian Economics*, **7**(2), 111–25.

Samuels, Warren J. (1993), 'In (Limited but Affirmative) Defense of Nihilism', *Review of Political Economy*, **5**(2), 236–44.

Samuelson, Paul (1947), *Foundations of Economic Analysis*, Cambridge, MA: Harvard University Press.

Scherer, F.M. (1991), 'Antitrust: Ideology or Economics?', *Critical Review*, **5**(4), 497–511.

Scherer, F.M. (1992), 'Anti-Antitrust: Ideology or Economics? Rejoinder to Armentano', *Critical Review*, **6**(1), 41–4.

Schrenk, Martin, Ardalan. Cyrus and Nawal A. El Tataway (eds) (1979), *Yugoslavia: Self-Management Socialism and the Challenges of Development*, Baltimore: Johns Hopkins University Press.

Schumpeter, Joseph (1918), 'The Crisis of the Tax State', in Swedberg (ed.) (1991).

Schumpeter, Joseph (1976 [1950]), *Capitalism, Socialism, and Democracy*, New York: George Allen & Unwin.

Sciabarra, Chris (1987), 'The Crisis of Libertarian Dualism', *Critical Review*, **1**(4), 86–99.

Selgin, George (1988), *The Theory of Free Banking: Money Supply Under Competitive Note Issue*, Totowa, NJ: Rowman and Littlefield.

Selucky, Radoslav (1979), *Marxism, Socialism, Freedom: Towards a General Democratic Theory of Labor-Managed Systems*, New York: St. Martin's Press.

Sen, Amartya (1982), *Choice, Welfare and Measurement*, Cambridge, MA: MIT Press.

Sen, Amartya (1987), *On Ethics and Economics*, New York: Basil Blackwell.

Sennholz, Mary (ed.) (1956), *On Freedom and Free Enterprise*, Princeton, NJ: Van Nostrand.

Shackle, G.L.S. (1992), *Epistemics and Economics: A Critique of Economic Doctrines*, New Brunswick, NJ: Transaction.

Steele, David R. (1992), *From Marx to Mises: Post-Capitalist Society and the Challenge of Economic Calculation*, LaSalle, IL: Open Court.

Stiglitz, Joseph E. (1994), *Whither Socialism?*, Cambridge, MA: MIT Press.

Stojanović, Radmila (ed.) (1964), *Yugoslav Economists on the Problems of a Socialist Economy*, New York: International Arts and Sciences Press.

Šuvar, Stipe (1988), 'Let Socialism Start Moving Forward Again to a Better Future', *Socialist Thought and Practice*, **28**(7–10), 3–50.

Swedberg, Richard (ed.) (1991), *Joseph A. Schumpeter: The Economics and Sociology of Capitalism*, Princeton, NJ: Princeton University Press.

Taylor, Michael (1976), *Anarchy and Co-operation*, New York: John Wiley.

Taylor, Michael (1982), *Community, Anarchy and Liberty*, New York: Cambridge University Press.

Thomsen, Esteban F. (1992), *Prices and Knowledge: A Market-Process Perspective*, London: Routledge.

Trifunović, Bogdan (ed.) (1980), *A Handbook of Yugoslav Socialist Self-Management*, Belgrade: Socialist Thought and Practice.

Tismaneanu, Vladimir (1998), *Fantasies of Salvation: Democracy, Nationalism, and Myth in Post-Communist Europe*, Princeton, NJ: Princeton University Press.

Tullock, Gordon (ed.) (1973), *Explorations in the Theory of Anarchy*, Blacksburg, VA: University Publications.

Tullock, Gordon (ed.) (1974), *Further Explorations in the Theory of Anarchy*, Blacksburg, VA: University Publications.

Tyson, Laura (1980), *The Yugoslav Economic System and its Performance in the 1970s*, Berkeley: Institute of International Studies.

Vačić, Aleksandar M. (1982), 'Concrete Historical and Epochal Significance of Pooling Labour and Resources in the Self-Management System', in Domajnko (ed.) (1982).

Vanberg, Viktor (1986), 'Spontaneous Market Order and Social Rules: A Critical Examination of F.A. Hayek's Theory of Cultural Evolution', *Economics and Philosophy*, **2**.

Vanek, Jaroslav (1970), *The General Theory of Labor-Managed Market Economies*, Ithaca, NY: Cornell University Press.

Vanek, Jaroslav (1971), *The Participatory Economy*, Ithaca: Cornell University Press.

Vanek, Jaroslav (1977), *The Labor-Managed Economy. Essays by Jaroslav Vanek*, Ithaca, NY: Cornell University Press.

Vanek, Jaroslav (1996), 'The Austrians and Self-Management: A Positive Essay', *Advances in Austrian Economics*, **3**.

Vanek, Jaroslav, Pienkos, Andrew and Alfred Steinherr (1975), 'Labor-Managed Firms and Imperfect Competition', in Vanek (1977).

Vaughn, Karen I. (1980a), 'Does it Matter that Costs are Subjective?', *Southern Economic Journal*, **46**(3), 702–15.

Vaughn, Karen I. (1980b), 'Economic Calculation under Socialism: The Austrian Contribution', *Economic Inquiry*, **18**(October).

Vaughn, Karen I. (1992), 'The Problem of Order in Austrian Economics: Kirzner vs. Lachmann', *Review of Political Economy*, **4**(3), 251–74.

Vaughn, Karen I. (1994), *Austrian Economics in America: The Migration of a Tradition*, Cambridge: Cambridge University Press.

Vojnić, Dragomir (1980), 'Self-Management and Economics', in Domajnko (ed.) (1980).

Vranicki, Pedrag (1965), 'Socialism and the Problem of Alienation', in Fromm (ed.) (1965).

Wagner, Richard E. (1989), 'Politics, Central Banking, and Economic Order', *Critical Review*, **3**(3–4), 505–17.

Wainwright, Hilary (1994), *Arguments for a New Left: Answering the Free Market Right*, Cambridge, MA: Blackwell Publishers.

Walicki, Andrej (1988), 'Karl Marx as Philosopher of Freedom', *Critical Review*, **2**(4), 10–58.

Walliman, Isidor (1981), *Estrangement: Marx's Conception of Human Nature and the Division of Labor*, Westport, CT: Greenwood Press.

Walzer, Michael (1990), 'A Credo for this Moment', *Dissent*, **37**(2).

Ward, Benjamin N. (1958), 'The Firm in Illyria: Market Syndicalism', *American Economic Review*, **48**(4).

Ward, Colin (1982), *Anarchy in Action*, London: Freedom Press.

Weinsheimer, Joel C. (1985), *Gadamer's Hermeneutics*, New Haven: Yale University Press.

White, Lawrence H. (1984), *Free Banking in Britain*, Cambridge: Cambridge University Press.

White, Lawrence H. (1989), *Competition and Currency: Essays in Free Banking and Money*, New York: New York University Press.

Wieser, Friedrich von (1967 [1927]), *Social Economics*, New York: Augustus Kelley.

Wright, Anthony (1986), *Socialisms: Theories and Practices*, Oxford: Oxford University Press.

Zaleski, Eugene (1980), *Stalinist Planning for Economic Growth*, London: Macmillan.

Zimmermann, Horst (1980), 'Fiscal Pressure on the "Tax State"', in Horst Hanusch (ed.), *Evolutionary Economics: Applications of Schumpeter's Ideas*, New York: Cambridge University Press.

Županov, Josip (1978a), 'Egalitarianism and Industrialism', in Obradović and Dunn (eds) (1978).

Županov, Josip (1978b), 'Enterprise and Association: Real and Illusory Dilemma', in Obradović and Dunn (eds) (1978).

Index

Printed and bound by CPI Group (UK) Ltd, Croydon, CR0 4YY

23/04/2025

14660960-0001